Roman
Architecture

Roman Architecture

Frank Sear

Cornell University Press
Ithaca, New York

For Molly Cotton

First published 1983 by Cornell University Press
First printing, Cornell Paperbacks, 1983
Second printing, Cornell Paperbacks, 1985
Third printing, Cornell Paperbacks, 1987

International Standard Book Number (cloth) 0-8014-1591-8
International Standard Book Number (paper) 0-8014-9245-9
Library of Congress Catalog Card Number 82-48715

Printed in Great Britain

Contents

Foreword 6
Acknowledgments 7
Bibliography 7
List of Illustrations 8

1 Republican Rome 10

2 Roman Building Types 29

3 The Age of Augustus 49

4 Roman Architects, Building Techniques
   and Materials 69

5 The Julio-Claudians 86

6 Two Roman towns: Pompeii and
   Ostia 103

7 The Flavians 134

8 Trajan and Hadrian 154

9 North Africa 185

10 The European Provinces 210

11 The Eastern Provinces 231

12 The Late Empire 255

Glossary 277
Notes 280
Index 283

Foreword

In writing this book I often found myself mentally explaining and discussing difficult points with the students I have taught in London, Oxford and Adelaide, who always find Roman architecture more difficult than Greek; perhaps not surprisingly because it covers such a large time span and is the product of such culturally and ethnically diverse people. The fact that the Romans were also skilful engineers makes it an even more complex subject. Bearing this in mind I have aimed to be clear rather than comprehensive. I have selected what I regard as the most significant buildings of each era or province, and have in each case attempted to put them into their historical or cultural context. Another author may have chosen different buildings; the choice is a subjective one and I will not pretend that I have not included many of my own favourite buildings.

The first eight chapters are mainly concerned with Italy and I have selected the end of Hadrian's reign as the most suitable point to break off to discuss the provinces. The Late Empire, when provincial cities were as important as the capital, draws all the threads together and is a fitting subject for the last chapter. Rather than constantly interrupt the narrative with explanations about materials and techniques I have devoted a separate chapter to these matters. I was also aware that a purely chronological and geographical approach neglects the development of particular buildings, such as theatres, houses and baths. Therefore I have summarized building types in a separate chapter.

My first contact with architectural history was when I was reading Classics at Cambridge under the guidance of Hugh Plommer. I am grateful to him for reading the manuscript of this book and offering much helpful advice. I was fortunate to have as my research supervisor Donald Strong, whose many perceptive articles on Roman architectural ornament have greatly added to our understanding of the subject. John Ward Perkins enlarged my knowledge of Roman buildings when I was a Scholar at the British School at Rome. I was fortunate to accompany him on several of his trips around the Roman Campagna, and once to the top of the Pantheon dome. His recent death has robbed the world of a foremost authority on Roman Architecture. Martin Fredericksen was able to read some of this book when it was in draft and discussed much of it with me when he visited Australia in 1979. Of younger scholars I would like to mention Janet DeLaine of Adelaide University whose grasp of engineering principles has saved me from many a pitfall in my chapter on building methods. She is also responsible for many of the drawings which illustrate the text. The errors, which I fear are many in a work of this kind, are all mine.

FS
ADELAIDE 1982

Acknowledgments

The author and publishers are grateful to the following for their permission to reproduce illustrations in this book: Alinari, Rome (37); Brockhampton Press (181); Chatto and Windus (131, 133, 150, 151, 156); Fototeca Unione, Rome (163, 175, 177); the German Archaeological Institute, Rome (29, 35, 89, 165, 168); Penguin Books (8, 12, 32, 46, 51, 54, 78, 92, 94, 100, 144, 152, 174, 176, 178); Societa editrice internazionale (132); the Society of Antiquaries of London (148, 149).

Figures 6, 22, 23, 30, 34, 38, 40, 44, 52, 60, 63, 67, 73, 74, 75, 76, 82, 88, 98, 109, 113, 116, 117, 118, 135, 143, 164, 182 were drawn by Janet DeLaine. The remaining illustrations are by the author.

Bibliography

These are a few general works, in English. More detailed studies of particular periods and individual buildings are mentioned in the notes at the back, page 280.

BLAKE, M., *Ancient Roman construction in Italy from the prehistoric period to Augustus*, Washington 1947

BLAKE, M., *Roman construction in Italy from Tiberius through the Flavians*, Washington 1959

BLAKE, M., *Roman construction in Italy from Nerva through the Antonines*, Philadelphia 1973

BOETHIUS, A. and WARD PERKINS, J. B., *Etruscan and Roman Architecture*, Harmondsworth 1970

BROWN, F. E., *Roman Architecture*, New York 1961

FYFE, T., *Hellenistic Architecture*, Cambridge 1936

LYTTELTON, M., *Baroque Architecture in Classical Antiquity*, London 1974

MACDONALD, W. L., *The Architecture of the Roman Empire, I: an introductory study*, Yale University Press 1965

NASH, E., *Pictorial Dictionary of Ancient Rome*, London 1968

PLOMMER, H., *Ancient and Classical Architecture* (*Simpson's History of Architectural Development*, I) London 1956

ROBERTSON, D. S., *Greek and Roman Architecture* (2nd ed.), Cambridge 1974

Vitruvius, *The Ten Books on Architecture* (transl. by M. H. Morgan) New York 1960

WARD PERKINS, J. B., *Cities of Ancient Greece and Italy*, London 1974

WHEELER, R. E. M., *Roman Art and Architecture*, London 1976

The Illustrations

1 Rome, Capitoline Temple: plan and restored view
2 (a) Perugia, Tomb of the Volumnii: plan
   (b) Pompeii, House of the Surgeon: plan
3 Rome, Comitium: reconstruction
4 Rome, Servian Wall
5 Arpinum, polygonal walls
6 Cosa, the Forum
7 Perugia, Porta Augusta
8 Rome, Porticus Aemilia: axonometric plan
9 Rome, Temple of Portunus and Temple of Hercules Victor
10 Tivoli, 'Temple of Vesta'
11 Cori, Temple of Hercules
12 Praeneste, Temple of Fortuna Primigenia: axonometric plan
13 Praeneste, Sanctuary of Fortuna Primigenia
14 Tivoli, Sanctuary of Hercules
15 Rome, Tabularium
16 Pompeii, House of the Coloured Capitals: plan
17 Ferentinum, Market hall
18 Lepcis Magna, Circus: plan
19 Pompeii, Stabian Baths: plan
20 Diagram of the heating system of a Roman bath
21 Diagram of the Arch of Constantine
22 Housesteads Roman fort: plan
23 Rome, Imperial fora: plan
24 Rome, Forum of Julius Caesar
25 Rome, Theatre of Marcellus
26 Rome, Forum Romanum
27 Rome, Forum Romanum: plan
28 Rome, Forum Romanum: view looking north
29 Rome, Basilica Aemilia: drawing
30 Rome, Arch of Augustus: restored elevation
31 Rome, Forum of Augustus
32 Rome, Temple of Mars Ultor and part of the Forum Augustum: restored view
33 Modillions on Augustan buildings in Rome
34 Architectural details
35 Rome, Forum of Augustus: Caryatids
36 Temple of Castor according to Palladio
37 Rome, Temple of Concord
38 Mosaic plan of a bath building
39 Painting from the Tomb of Trebius Justus
40 Diagram to illustrate Roman concrete facings
41 Roman vaults and domes
42 Diagram to illustrate tile-clad vaulting
43 Diagram to illustrate a cross-vault with brick ribs
44 Rome, part of the 'Temple of Minerva Medica'
45 Sperlonga, Grotto of Tiberius: plan
46 Capri, Villa Jovis: plan
47 Capri, Villa Jovis
48 Capri, Villa Jovis
49 Rome, Porta Maggiore
50 Rome, Temple of deified Claudius
51 Rome, fountain court of Nero's Domus Transitoria: axonometric view
52 Rome, Domus Transitoria: restored drawing
53 Rome, Nero's Golden House: plan
54 Rome, Nero's Golden House: axonometric view of the octagonal hall
55 Rome, Nero's Golden House: octagonal hall
56 Pompeii, general plan
57 Pompeii, House of Menander
58 Pompeii, House of the Gilded Cupids
59 Pompeii, House of the Faun: plan
60 Pompeii, Villa of the Mysteries
61 Pompeii, the Forum
62 Pompeii, basilica
63 Pompeii, basilica: restored elevation and section
64 Pompeii, Stabian Baths
65 Pompeii, Forum Baths
66 Pompeii, the amphitheatre
67 Ostia, general plan
68 Ostia, plan of the Claudian and Trajanic harbours
69 Sketch of the lighthouse at Ostia
70 Ostia, the Capitolium
71 Ostia, Forum Baths
72 Ostia, insula
73 Ostia, the Garden Houses and the Insula of Diana
74 Ostia, Horrea of Hortensius, Horrea Epagathiana, Antonine Horrea: plans
75 Ostia, Forum Baths: plan
76 Ostia, House of Amor and Psyche: plan
77 Rome, Colosseum
78 Rome, Colosseum: plans, sections and sectional view
79 Rome, Colosseum: diagram of the staircase system
80 Rome, Colosseum: view of the seating, arena and animal cages
81 Rome, Colosseum: drawing of the concealed springings in the piers and the brick arches supporting a barrel-vault
82 Rome, Colosseum: reconstruction of the system of animal cages
83 Rome, Colosseum: drawing to illustrate the working of the velarium
84 Rome, Colosseum: bollards
85 Rome, Arch of Titus
86 Rome, Flavian Palace
87 Rome, Flavian Palace: plan of the upper level

88　Rome, Flavian Palace: plan of the lower level
89　Rome, Forum of Nerva
90　Rome, plan showing the Esquiline wing of Nero's Golden House incorporated into Trajan's Baths
91　Rome, Trajan's Column
92　Rome, Trajan's Market: axonometric view
93　Rome, Trajan's Market
94　Rome, Trajan's Market: axonometric view
95　Beneventum, Arch of Trajan
96　Rome, Pantheon: plan and section
97　Rome, Pantheon: the porch
98　Rome, Pantheon: the structure of the drum
99　Rome, Pantheon: interior
100　Tivoli, Hadrian's Villa: plan
101　Tivoli, Hadrian's Villa: the Island Villa
102　Tivoli, Hadrian's Villa: plan of the Island Villa
103　Tivoli, Hadrian's Villa: plan of the Piazza d'Oro
104　Tivoli, Hadrian's Villa: plan of the small baths
105　Tivoli, Hadrian's Villa: the large baths
106　Tivoli, Hadrian's Villa: plan of the Serapeum
107　Tivoli, Hadrian's Villa: columns around the Canopus
108　Tivoli, Hadrian's Villa: Temple of Venus
109　Rome, Temple of Venus and Rome: plan
110　Rome, Temple of Venus and Rome: entablature according to Canina
111　Rome, Temple of Deified Hadrian
112　Rome, Mausoleum of Hadrian
113　Alexandria, Tomb I of the Necropolis of Moustapha Pasha: plan
114　Cyrene, general plan
115　Cyrene, the basilica
116　Cyrenaican modillions found at Ptolemais
117　Ptolemais, Palazzo delle colonne: plan
118　Ptolemais, Palazzo delle colonne: reconstruction
119　Berenice, reconstruction of doorways
120　Lepcis Magna, general plan
121　Lepcis Magna, Severan Forum and basilica
122　Lepcis Magna, Severan Forum: part of the arcade
123　Lepcis Magna, Severan basilica
124　Lepcis Magna, the Hunting Baths
125　Sabratha, the theatre
126　Oea, the Arch of Marcus Aurelius
127　Thysdrus, the amphitheatre
128　Thugga, Capitolium
129　Bulla Regia, House of the Hunt
130　Thamugadi, general view
131　Thamugadi, general plan
132　Lambaesis, Camp of the Third Legion, Augusta: plan
133　Cuicul, general plan

134　Cuicul, the Severan Forum
135　Italica, general plan
136　Alcantara, bridge over the Tagus
137　Segovia, aqueduct
138　Nîmes, Pont du Gard
139　Nîmes, Maison Carrée
140　Nîmes, amphitheatre
141　Nîmes, amphitheatre: holes for the masts for the velarium
142　Orange, the theatre
143　Vaison, House of the Silver Bust: plan
144　Augusta Raurica, restored view of the centre of the town
145　Verulamium, plan
146　Silchester, general plan
147　Aquae Sulis, Temple of Minerva and Roman baths: plan
148　Bath, Temple of Minera: reconstructed façade
149　Fishbourne, Roman palace: plan
150　Vetera, plan of the two-legion fortress
151　Salona, general plan
152　Athens, Odeon of Agrippa: elevation and axonometric view
153　Athens, Temple of Zeus
154　Athens, Arch of Hadrian
155　Athens, library of Hadrian
156　Corinth, plan of the central area
157　Pergamon, general plan
158　Miletus, plan of the city centre
159　Ephesus, colonnaded street
160　Ephesus, library of Celsus: reconstruction
161　Ephesus, Temple of Hadrian
162　Baalbek, sanctuary: plan
163　Baalbek, Temple of Jupiter
164　Palmyra, general plan
165　Palmyra, Temple of Bel
166　Gerasa, general plan
167　Gerasa, Temple of Artemis: plan
168　Petra, the Deir
169　Rome, Forum Romanum
170　Rome, Baths of Caracalla: plan
171　Rome, Baths of Caracalla
172　Rome, Baths of Diocletian: plan
173　Spalato, Palace of Diocletian: plan
174　Trier, the basilica: reconstructed view
175　Trier, the basilica
176　Trier, Imperial Baths: restored view
177　Trier, Porta Nigra
178　Thessalonike, Mausoleum of Galerius
179　Piazza Armerina: plan
180　Rome, Basilica of Maxentius
181　Rome, Basilica of Maxentius: reconstruction
182　Rome, 'Temple of Minerva Medica': plan
183　Rome, Mausoleum of St Constantia: section and plan

1 Republican Rome

Cicero praises the natural advantages of the site of Rome (*de Rep.*, 11). It is only 25 kilometres from the coast, and because of its river combines the advantages of a safe inland position with easy access to the sea. The river, rising in northern Etruria, also provided easy communications with the centre of Italy. An island in the middle of the Tiber facilitated the crossing, and the hills of Rome, especially the Palatine and Capitoline, offered good natural defence.

Tradition makes Romulus the first king of Rome and places the date of its foundation in 753 BC although there may have been settlements there before then. Archaeological discoveries of Iron Age huts on the Palatine hill confirm the statement of Dionysius of Halicarnassus (*Ant. Rom.*, 1. 79. 11) who records that one of them still survived in his day and was constantly kept repaired (he wrote at the time of Augustus). According to tradition, during the reign of the seventh-century king Ancus Marcius, a wooden bridge, the Pons Sublicius, was built over the Tiber. The bridge had great significance in the early community and its maker was given the title of Pontifex (bridge-maker). The town was laid out according to religious rites within a sacred boundary, the *postmoenium* or *pomerium* (Varro, *De Ling. Lat.*, V. 143). The earliest pomerium of Rome seems to have taken in only the Palatine and a generous space around so that the sacred area was almost a square (Tacitus, *Annals*, XII. 24). The original walls followed the line of the hill, but were soon extended to include the Capitoline. Under the later kings the city included the Caelian, the Velia, the Oppian, the Viminal, the Quirinal and the Esquiline hills, and, according to tradition, these areas were enclosed in a large circuit of walls by Servius Tullius in the sixth century BC. Fragments of a very old wall built of cappellaccio or local tufa have been found on the Viminal and Aventine hills and these may belong to this old circuit.

In the middle of the seventh century BC Rome was conquered by the Etruscans and was ruled by them for the next one and a half centuries. The Etruscans were responsible for the first truly monumental buildings in Rome, and carried out several important engineering projects such as the draining of the Forum, which at that time was still a swampy valley. The Romans profited greatly from

1 Rome, Capitoline Temple (above), late sixth century BC, plan; (below) restored view of a typical Etruscan temple

10

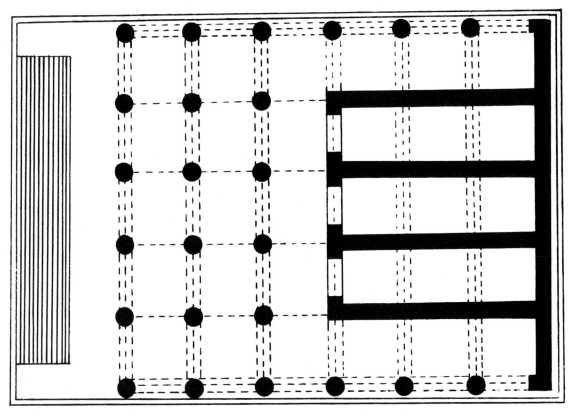

0   20 M

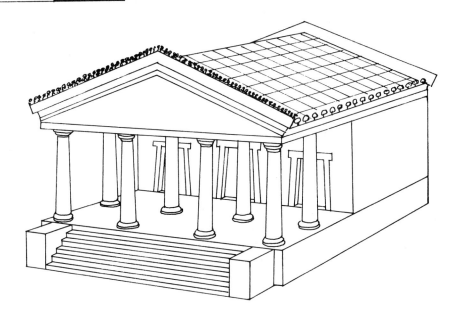

their example, and the Etruscan contribution to later Roman developments in the field of architecture and engineering cannot be overestimated. The Etruscans too had developed a robust and individual style in art, although in their turn they were great admirers of Greek art and architecture. Thus, despite its individuality, Etruscan art bears the unmistakable stamp of Greek influence. This Greek background to Etruscan art is important as it helps to explain Rome's ready acceptance of Greek artistic and architectural taste later on.

Roman temples and houses were closely based upon Etruscan models, and it is worth a closer examination of both of these. Etruscan temples usually rest on a podium, unlike Greek temples, and the emphasis is frontal. Simpler temples have a single cella with or without columns. The columns are normally only in front. More elaborate temples can have up to three cellas, side by side, and as much as half the ground area of the temple can be devoted to an elaborate columnar porch or *pronaos*. The huge Temple of Jupiter on the Capitoline hill at Rome, which was being built by the last Etruscan king before he was expelled in 509 BC, is even more elaborate, with its three cellas and colonnaded wings (fig. 1). Parts of the substructure of the temple came to light in 1919 when the Palazzo Caffarelli was demolished. The surviving remains are a rectangular podium of tufa blocks measuring 62×53 metres. We know that Sulla brought columns from the temple of Olympian Zeus in Athens (see p. 237) to use in the rebuilding of the temple following a fire which totally destroyed it in 83 BC. The height of the columns is 17.3 metres. This means that the columns are exactly one-third of the width of the temple, a ratio prescribed by Vitruvius (*De Arch.*, 4. 7. 2).

Like other Etruscan temples its roof would have been decorated with rich terracotta ornaments. Architrave, frieze, cornice and sima were commonly sheathed in terracotta revetments with relief palmette and leaf ornament, sometimes pierced. Antefixes, often decorated with superbly imaginative heads or whole groups of figures, ran along the eaves. Sometimes full-size terracotta figures stood on the ridge of the temple, like the famous Apollo which formed part of a group on the roof of the Portonaccio temple at Veii.

As for domestic architecture, most of our evidence for large Etruscan houses comes from tombs, which were modelled on the layout of a house. From this evidence we may infer that a large Etruscan house had a number of rooms grouped around a central hall. The tomb of the Volumnii at Perugia has a layout very reminiscent of atrium houses such as the House of the Surgeon at Pompeii (fig. 2). Instead of the doorway and *fauces* (entrance passage) there is a staircase leading down into the tomb. The main rooms are grouped around a hall or *atrium* with a beamed ridged roof. Opposite the doorway is the *tablinum*, or main room of the

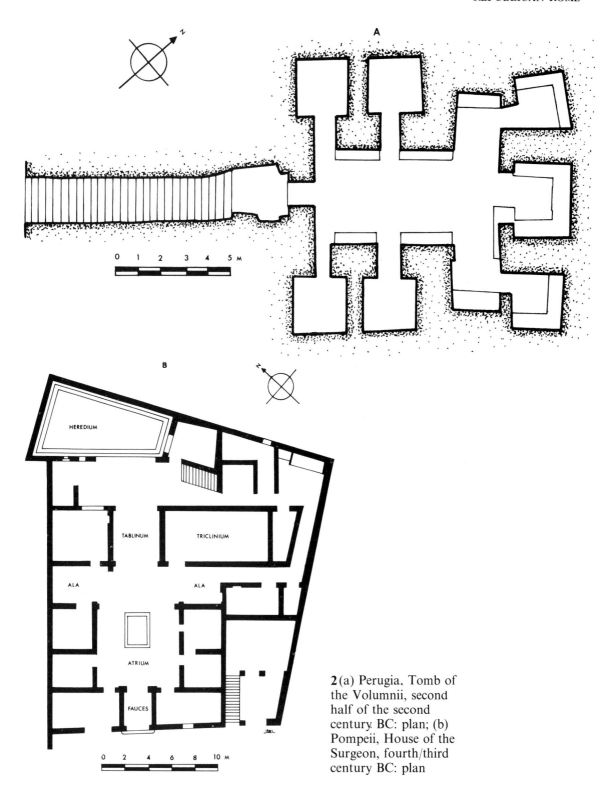

2(a) Perugia, Tomb of
the Volumnii, second
half of the second
century BC: plan; (b)
Pompeii, House of the
Surgeon, fourth/third
century BC: plan

13

3 Rome, Comitium. A possible reconstruction showing the position of the Curia Hostilia

house, with a richly coffered ceiling. Note that the layout of rooms, as in many Roman houses, is symmetrical.

With the expulsion of the Etruscan kings Rome was free to shape her own destinies. The new Roman Republic was governed by elected magistrates and a Senate. There was also a popular assembly or *Comitia* with limited powers. The civic life of the new state was centred on the Forum (fig. 28). The earliest Republican temples included the Temple of Saturn (498 BC) and the Temple of Concord (366 BC). Other early buildings were the House and Temple of the Vestals and the Regia, the official residence of the Pontifex Maximus. The Forum was also full of small shops (*tabernae*). To the north-west was the old Senate House, the Curia Hostilia, which was the council-chamber of the Senate from a very

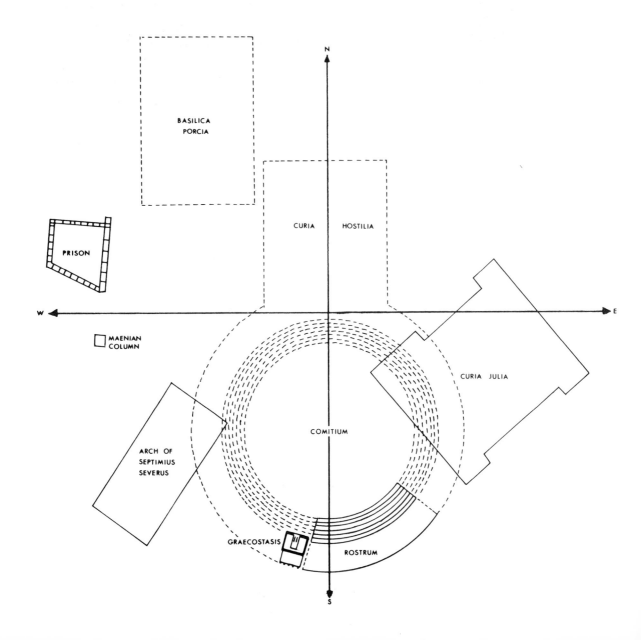

BASILICA
PORCIA

CURIA   HOSTILIA

PRISON

N

W   E

MAENIAN
COLUMN

CURIA JULIA

COMITIUM

ARCH OF
SEPTIMIUS
SEVERUS

GRAECOSTASIS

ROSTRUM

S

4 Rome, so-called 'Servian wall', *c.* 378 BC

early date. In the space in front of it was the meeting place of the people, the *Comitium*, and the speakers' platform, the *Rostra*, called after the ships' prows that were hung there after the Battle of Antium in 338 BC.

The exact shape of the Comitium and its relationship to the Curia Hostilia have long been matters of dispute. Pliny (*Natural History* VII. 212) tells us that midday was announced by an official standing in front of the Senate House when he could see the sun between the Rostra and the Graecostasis (a platform from which foreign ambassadors, mainly Greek, addressed the Senate). The final hour of the day was announced when the sun sloped from the Maenian column to the prison. As the position of the Rostra and the prison is known, the location of the Curia Hostilia can be worked out (fig. 3). Other evidence suggests that the Comitium was circular with steps all round, and that the steps of the Comitium gave access to the Curia.

The new Republic soon became the dominant power of the region and even turned its arms against Veii, its Etruscan neighbour to the north, which fell in 396 BC. However, the Gallic invasion of 390 BC in which Rome was overrun and devastated was a setback. To protect the city against future disasters of this kind the Romans built a massive defensive wall, known as the 'Servian wall'. The attribution is certainly erroneous as it is built of Grotta Oscura Tufa and must date to the period after the Roman conquest of Veii. The wall, laid in uniform blocks of 177 cm × 59 cm × 59 cm, has a total circuit of 11 kilometres. For most of this distance it followed the edges of the hills, but along the flat section of ground on the Esquiline, near the modern railway station, an *agger* or sloping

5 Arpinum, polygonal walls, *c.* 305 BC

mound 42 metres wide had to be built for a distance of 1,350 metres (fig. 4). The mound was contained between two walls, the inner being only 2.60 metres high and the outer about nine or ten metres high. Beyond the outer wall was dug an elaborate ditch, 36 metres wide at the top and about 12 metres deep. This impressive piece of fortification reminds us of the great engineering skill the Romans had already acquired at this early stage.

During the fourth and third centuries BC, as Rome's power spread over Italy she consolidated her conquests by a network of colonies and garrisons with vast and imposing fortifications. In the hills the walls took advantage of natural defensive features and were constructed of massive polygonal blocks of local limestone, for example at Circeii, Norba, Arpinum (fig. 5), Alatrium and Ferentinum. Where tufa was available, for example at Ardea and Falerii Novi, the blocks were well-cut and looked more like the 'Servian Wall' at Rome. Colonies on the plain, like Pyrgi, Ostia and Minturnae, were laid out within rectangular wall circuits, while towns like Cosa had a regular grid plan within an irregular wall circuit. Ostia will be more fully discussed later on (see Chapter 6), but Cosa is such a complete example of an early Roman colony that it is worth looking at more closely.

The town, laid out in 273 BC, is roughly trapezoidal in shape. It is enclosed by two kilometres of polygonal walls. The two highest points, one to the north and one to the south, are the sites of the most important temples. On the higher point stood the Capitolium (built

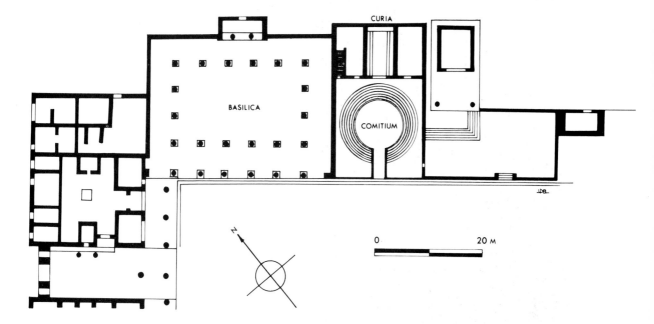

175–150 BC). In style it must have been similar to the old Etruscan temples, with its high podium, three cellas and a deep tetrastyle pronaos which takes up approximately half the ground area of the stylobate. The roofline particularly must have been reminiscent of Etruscan temples with its rich terracotta revetments and overhanging eaves (fig. 1). The long, rectangular Forum seems to have been completely surrounded by buildings in the later second century BC (fig. 6). On the north-east side stood a most important group of public buildings. The circular Comitium surrounded by steps seems to date from the earliest building period (270–250 BC). Behind the Comitium is a rectangular building which has been identified as the Curia. Access to the Curia was by way of the steps of the Comitium, an arrangement which may imitate that in Rome.

At Paestum, which became a Roman colony in 273 BC, a similar circular building surrounded on all sides by steps has been found, facing a rectangular forum like that of Cosa. It has been suggested that this too may have been a Comitium modelled on that at Rome. Next to the Comitium is a temple with an Italo-Etruscan ground plan. It has a high podium, steps at the front and a deep columnar porch. The columns also run along the sides of the temple, but not around the back. It has a single cella. It is thought to have been built shortly after the foundation of the colony, but remodelled about 100 BC with unorthodox Corinthian capitals supporting a Doric entablature.

During the fourth century BC the Romans still built lintelled or corbelled gateways, as at Arpinum (fig. 5), but by the third century BC they began to use the arch. It was not a Roman

6 Cosa, buildings on the north side of the Forum, showing the basilica and Comitium. Plan as it appeared in the late second century BC

17

7 Perugia, Porta Augusta, second century BC

invention. Probably of eastern origin, it was making a tentative appearance in Hellenistic and Etruscan architecture by the fourth century. A fine early example of a voussoir arch (or arch made of separate stones) can be seen in a late fourth-century gateway at Velia. The first voussoir arches in Etruria are found in a gate at Volterra, at Cosa and in two Etruscan tombs at Vulci. An arched bridge on the Via Amerina dates from 240 BC and the gate at Falerii Novi (240–200 BC) has an arch of well-cut voussoirs with a hood moulding running around the top. Another technical advance is seen in an arch from the Ariccia valley. The voussoirs are alternately 'headers' and 'stretchers' so as to bind the arch together. Another fine arch with double voussoirs is the so-called 'Arch of Augustus' at Perugia which dates from the late second century BC (fig. 7). By the beginning of the first century BC arches have double or triple (as in the Cloaca Maxima) rows of voussoirs. Arches with voussoirs cut to bind into the wall surface became common by the time of Augustus. The barrel vault also seems to have been in use in the third century BC to judge by the barrel-vaulted drains on the east slope of the Capitoline hill.

During the third century BC the Romans also learnt the art of making concrete. They did not invent concrete; the transition from rubble to cement walling seems to have taken place in Campania during the fourth and third centuries BC (see p. 73). In Rome we find *opus incertum* or concrete faced with irregular stones used in the Temple of Magna Mater on the Palatine, which dates from 204–191

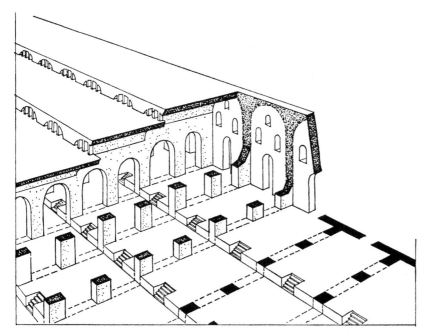

8 Rome, Porticus Aemilia, 193 BC, restored in 174 BC: axonometric plan (from A. Boethius and J. B. Ward Perkins, *Etruscan and Roman Architecture*, Harmondsworth 1970)

BC. The Porticus Aemilia in Rome (built in 193 BC and restored in 174 BC) is an early example of large-scale use of concrete (fig. 8). It is a hall 487 metres long and 60 wide, consisting of rows of barrel-vaults with their long sides pierced with rows of arched openings to produce a continuous open space. There is considerable dispute over its date and its identification, but the theory that it may have been a later rebuilding is disproved by the fact that no trace of an earlier building was found underneath.

By the end of the second Punic war (218–202 BC) Rome was the greatest power in the Mediterranean. The fall of Syracuse in 212 BC had brought a flood of Greek art works to the capital, and the flow was to continue throughout the second century BC as Rome became involved in the affairs of Asia Minor and Greece. The sack of Corinth in 146 BC brought Greece under Roman control and Rome was inundated by a further flood of works of art. Greek craftsmen too migrated to Rome and were in great demand.

This new luxury raised much criticism among the more conservative elements in Rome who were used to austere simplicity. The Rome they were brought up in was a city of irregular winding streets, and buildings of distinctly Etruscan appearance. The temples would have had the wide-spreading eaves of their Etruscan counterparts and perhaps the heavy terracotta statues over the roofline (fig. 1). Houses would still have been of the dark, but grand, Etruscan type with large atria crammed with smoke-blackened busts of ancestors (fig. 57). The first white marble temples, built according to the precise canons of the Classical Orders, must have been as sensational in second-century Rome as were the Italianate buildings of Inigo Jones in seventeenth-century London.

9 Rome, Temple of Portunus, late second century BC (right) and Temple of Hercules Victor, *c.* 120 BC (left)

There must have been many Greek architects active in Italy during the later second century BC. Victorious generals often employed their own architects to build temples *ex manubiis* (from the campaign booty). These generals must have done much to shape architectural taste in late Republican Rome. The first temple in Rome to be built entirely of marble was the Temple of Jupiter Stator (146 BC), the work of a Greek architect Hermodorus of Salamis. It was commissioned by Q. Caecilius Metellus who conquered the Macedonians. Also completely of marble is the circular Corinthian temple built about 120 BC in the Forum Boarium (fig. 9). The building used to be called the Temple of Vesta, but has recently been identified as the Temple of Hercules Victor. The temple seems to have been built by a Greek architect and the material used is Pentelic marble. The columns rest upon a stylobate consisting of three steps, and the marble masonry of the cella wall is drafted. Both of these features come straight from Hellenistic building practice. The capitals with their pointed acanthus leaves and rounded fleshy leaf ribs bear close analogy to Hellenistic capitals in Greece and Asia Minor. Some elements of the entablature and some coffering survive in fragments and these too can be connected with the late Hellenistic architectural tradition.

However, the old Etruscan type of temple with its high podium and frontal emphasis did not entirely disappear. A new type of temple emerged with the groundplan of the old Italo-Etruscan type combined with a purely Hellenistic superstructure. For example the Temple of Hercules at Cori (*c.* 100 BC) (fig. 11), is raised on a high podium, largely built of concrete, although the columns are underpinned with cylindrical stone drums. Its porch of 4 × 3 columns is actually deeper than the cella behind. Working from the ground-plan alone one might conclude that the temple was purely Italic and perhaps had a superstructure with Tuscan columns and a widely-spreading roof like that of an Etruscan temple. However, the entire columnar order is Hellenistic Doric in style, and the proportions of the columns are extremely slender (their height is over eight lower diameters), in keeping with the fashion of the great Hellenistic centres of the time, such as Delos and Pergamon. The lowest third of the shaft is faceted rather than fluted, a device also common to the Hellenistic world. The entablature is so slight that there are three triglyphs to each intercolumniation as well as one over each column. The corner triglyphs are flush with the edge of the frieze, although Vitruvius recommends that they should be set centrally over the corner columns, leaving a small gap at the corner (*De Arch.*, IV. 3. 4).

The Temple of Portunus (formerly known as the Temple of Fortuna Virilis) in the Forum Boarium at Rome (fig. 9) had a similar layout to the Temple at Cori although the order used is Ionic. It was built in its present form in the second half of the second century BC with some rebuilding in the first century BC. The temple is raised on a high podium and a flight of steps leads up to the cella. The porch in this case takes up less than half the area of the temple and has only 4 × 2 columns. However, a row of half columns runs around the outside of the temple engaged into the sides and back of the cella wall. Thus the temple has more of the appearance of a fully

10 Tivoli, 'Temple of Vesta', early first century BC

11 Cori, Temple of Hercules, *c.* 100 BC

peripteral Greek temple than that at Cori. Also, the Ionic order used has two-sided Ionic capitals more in keeping with Hellenistic practice than the four-sided capitals commonly used at Pompeii.

The 'Temple of Vesta' (fig. 10), sited on the edge of a gorge at Tivoli, is a circular Corinthian temple of the early first century BC. Its 18 fluted columns rest on a high podium and the cella walls are in *opus incertum*. The capitals support an Ionic entablature with bucrania and heavy garlands in the frieze. Once again the temple is a fusion of Italic layout and Hellenistic detail, albeit with an Italian flavour.

The earliest known basilicas were built in the second century BC. They have a high, roofed nave lit by clerestory windows and surrounded by aisles, and as such were well suited to the needs of businessmen and the law-courts. The word 'basilica' is a Greek adjective meaning 'kingly', and the noun it originally qualified is likely to have been 'stoa' (Strabo, *Geography*, 5. 3. 8). Although several early basilicas, such as the Basilica Aemilia in the Roman Forum, must have outwardly resembled stoas, with their long two-storey columnar façades, they were quite different internally. A basilica has the advantage of being a covered hall where magistrates could conduct their cases uninterrupted, unlike a stoa, which is a portico open to the noise of the street. Despite the Greek name, the oldest known basilicas are found in Rome: the Basilica Porcia (184 BC), the Basilica Aemilia (179 BC) and the Basilica

Sempronia (170 BC). The assumption of many scholars is that the Romans encountered the basilica in a Greek context and adopted it because they had no other building so well suited to their legislative and commercial needs. Consequently its later development was almost entirely Roman. There may even have been a prototype Stoa Basilica somewhere in the Greek world which had little success because the conventional stoa was preferred. There is no reason why the Greeks should not have developed an aisled building with clerestory lighting and a high roofed nave. Buildings of the same general type were known in Alexandria, and Vitruvius' Egyptian oecus has a similar layout to a basilica (*De Arch.*, 6. 3. 9). The first surviving basilica was found at Pompeii and belongs to the second half of the second century BC. However, it must be borne in mind that basilicas are known to have been built in Rome before that date and therefore there is no *a priori* reason to suppose that south Italy was the home of the basilica.

The earliest baths to have heated rooms and running water, the Stabian Baths at Pompeii, also belong to the second century BC in their present form (fig. 19). However, recent excavations under them have revealed a series of small rooms lined with hip-baths, dating from the fourth century BC. Baths of this type were common in the Greek world at that date, and it may be that Campania was the place where the transition from the Greek to the Roman style of baths took place. The second-century complex consists of an irregular colonnaded *palaestra* flanked by the bathing block. The arrangement of rooms was simple. They are small and rather dimly lit, but offered substantially the same facilities as the great Imperial baths: an undressing room, cold, warm and hot rooms. The heating was provided by braziers until the introduction of the hypocaust system at the end of the second century BC. The Forum Baths at Pompeii, which were begun about 80 BC, were arranged on roughly the same lines.

Another new type of building to appear towards the end of the Republic was the amphitheatre which was used for gladiatorial shows. In form it is clearly related to the theatre, except that it is a total ellipse and there are seats all round the oval arena. Gladiatorial games originated in Etruria and had been held in the Roman Forum as early as the third century BC. Indeed, as Vitruvius points out (*De Arch.*, 5. 1. 1), the cities of Italy had oblong fora so that gladiatorial shows could be held there. Although the first permanent amphitheatre was built in Pompeii about 80 BC, Rome's powerful and vocal conservative lobby prevented a permanent amphitheatre being built there until the Colosseum was started in AD 75. The same elements prevented a permanent theatre being built in Rome until the Theatre of Pompey, which was finished in 55 BC.

Until the second century BC Roman houses had followed the old Etruscan plan with rooms grouped around the tall, rather

12 Praeneste (Palestrina), Temple of Fortuna Primigenia, late second century BC: axonometric plan. (From A. Boethius, *op. cit.*)

dark *atrium* (fig. 2). A passage (*fauces*) led from the street to the atrium and no rooms of any significance faced on to the street. There were bedrooms either side of the atrium and at the end farthest from the street two wings (*alae*) gave added prominence to the three rooms opposite the doorway of the house. The central one was the *tablinum* and the two flanking rooms were usually for dining. Beyond was a small garden or orchard (*heredium*). During the second century BC the peristyle or colonnaded garden became a fashionable addition to a Roman house (fig. 58). Whereas in the Hellenistic east the peristyle was the nucleus of the house and all the rooms were grouped around it, in Pompeii it was usually added to the rear of an atrium house. If possible it was laid out on the same axis as the atrium and the tablinum, so as to produce a vista from the fauces through the tablinum to the peristyle beyond.

The introduction of the peristyle gave a new flexibility to domestic architecture. Summer houses, exedras and even libraries were added around it; fountains, summer dining rooms and even small private baths became common (22 private baths have been found at Pompeii). During this period Romans began to dine upstairs and *cenacula* or dining rooms were built looking down on the street or the atrium (Varro, *de Ling. Lat.*, 5. 162). During the later second century BC houses of enormous size were built, such as the House of the Faun at Pompeii, which covers a larger area than some Hellenistic palaces. The House of the Faun (fig. 59) has two large peristyles and it is clear that this was becoming the most favoured part of the house; while the atrium remained the more formal and official area. The traditional atrium lingered for some time, but towards the end of the Republic most houses were designed with an eye to beauty and nature. Windows became bigger and the wall areas were expanded by the new illusionistic style of wall painting. At Pompeii and Herculaneum we find houses terraced out over the lines of the old city walls, so as to enjoy a fine panorama over the sea or the mountains.

Villas grew to an enormous scale in the later Republic. On the road up to Tivoli can be seen the vast concrete terraces of the Republican villas which once lined the hillsides and faced towards the city of Rome. Villas of a similar type, like the so-called 'Villa of Cicero' at Formiae, lined the coasts between Rome and Naples. A suburban villa, like the Villa of the Mysteries at Pompeii, had over 60 rooms (fig. 60), but was dwarfed by the mid-first-century BC villa at Oplontis. The latter is still being excavated, but the uncovered portion has a façade measuring little less than 100 metres, and the whole may well prove to be double that length.

During the second century BC the influx of great wealth from overseas conquests, combined with the ready availability of cheap concrete, made possible building complexes on a scale hitherto unimagined. The result was a series of huge sanctuaries built on

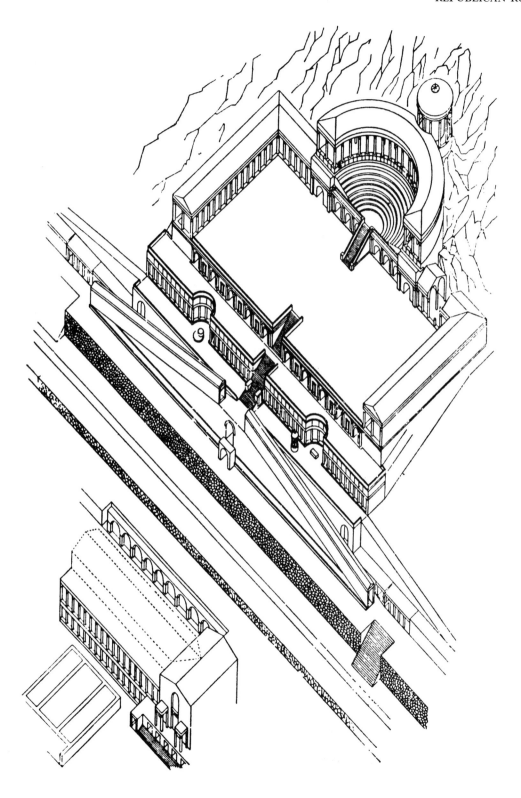

13 Praeneste (Palestrina), Sanctuary of Fortuna Primigenia, late second century BC: one of the two hemicycles with Ionic columns supporting a coffered concrete barrel-vault

stepped terraces in the Hellenistic manner. Perhaps the most remarkable and monumental example of these is the sanctuary of Fortuna Primigenia at Palestrina (fig. 12). There are two groups of monumental buildings. In the lower sanctuary is an older temple with three cellas, a basilica and a curia, and in the hillside behind are two caves, in one of which was found the famous Nile mosaic.

The upper sanctuary was quite independent of the lower. The hillside is terraced on a monumental scale, and a series of ramps and staircases lead from terrace to terrace up to the sanctuary on the top. Connecting the two lowest terraces is a pair of ramps whose roofs are supported by Doric columns with unusual sloping capitals. The upper of the two terraces linked by the ramps contains a row of tabernae interrupted by two hemicycles (fig. 13) with annular barrel-vaults supported on Ionic columns. A staircase leads, via the next terrace, to a big rectangular square, flanked to east and west by double Corinthian colonnades, and on the northern side by arched openings flanked by engaged columns. Above is a huge semicircular exedra with a double annular barrel-vault (of a type similar to the smaller exedras below) supported on two rows of Corinthian columns. A great semicircle of steps leads up to the exedra from the square below. Behind the exedra, on the central axis of the whole complex stands a small round temple.

The whole of the upper sanctuary is built of limestone-faced *opus incertum* with tufa quoins and voussoirs. The projecting bands of tufa in the walls were to take a stuccoed frieze or cornice, and it

seems that the entire concrete facing was covered with white stucco to give the appearance of marble veneer. The dating of the complex has given rise to much controversy, some dating it to the mid-second century BC and others preferring a Sullan date.

There were other large sanctuaries built at this time which also made large-scale use of concrete, for example the Temple of Jupiter Anxur at Terracina. Here the massive substructures, which provide a flat platform for the temple, are all of concrete. As in the Porticus Aemilia, the rows of barrel vaults are pierced by rows of arches producing a comparatively airy space. Another large sanctuary, built in the mid-first century BC, is the Sanctuary of Hercules at Tivoli which again employed concrete substructures and porticoes (fig. 14).

Perhaps the most conspicuous concrete monument of the period is the Tabularium (*c.* 78 BC) which overlooks the Forum from the Capitoline hill (fig. 15). Most of the building is of concrete, apart from the façade which has a series of round-headed openings flanked by half columns. These support a continuous entablature which runs above the arches. An arch combined with half columns in this manner is termed a *fornix* and becomes a stock feature of later architecture. It is used to great effect on the façade of the Theatre of Marcellus and of the Colosseum.

By the third quarter of the first century BC the Republic was tottering after a century of civil war. Too much had happened too quickly for the government to adapt itself to new needs. In architecture also much had happened. There were new techniques,

14 Tivoli, Sanctuary of Hercules: detail of the arcade flanking the temple *c.* 50 BC

outside influences, changing tastes, and complex institutions to be housed. Architects had responded with dynamism and originality to the demands made upon them, but what they achieved during the Republic was only a prelude to the achievements of the Empire.

Even by the end of the Republic the Romans had proved themselves to be among the greatest builders in history. Their major achievements up to then had been in engineering, but they had also learnt a great deal from the Hellenistic world about the use of the Classical Orders. Yet their buildings still lacked a clearly defined style. Roman architecture of the Republic was essentially a response to particular local needs, and the influences came from everywhere. Architects could have received their training in any one of a number of centres, and have been brought up in one of many artistic climates. In short, by the end of the Republic we are not yet in a position to speak of 'Roman architecture'. Roman buildings were still too much of a compromise between late Hellenistic and Italic tradition to be more than hybrid in style. When, then, did a definable architectural style emerge? It was when all of the outside influences had been forged together and assimilated, when techniques and ornaments were so fully understood that they could be used with confidence to create something fresh and original. This process of forging a new style began under Augustus. Only at the end of his reign one can talk about 'Roman architecture'. Yet the seeds of all these developments were already present in the architecture of the late Republic.

15 Rome, Tabularium, 78 BC

2 Roman Building Types

The diversity of Roman institutions required a wide range of specialised buildings, some religious, others secular. There were commercial, domestic and recreational buildings; some were for entertainment and others purely utilitarian; there were honorific buildings such as triumphal arches, and of course a wide range of military and defensive buildings. Many of these buildings had already achieved what might be termed their orthodox form by the time of Augustus. Others, notably baths, still had a good deal of development ahead of them. Some buildings, such as temples and basilicas, remained relatively unchanged in their layout after the time of Augustus, although in the late Empire they occasionally appeared in a striking new form. For example, Hadrian's Pantheon was a breathtakingly original version of a Roman temple, and at the beginning of the fourth century Maxentius built a daringly novel basilica in terms of its layout and structure. Some buildings were affected by fashion or the economic climate. For example, houses were radically modified because of changing economic conditions in Roman towns, and high-rise apartment blocks began to take the place of the old *domus* during the early Empire. Buildings such as amphitheatres and circuses were steadily improved as time went on. For example the *spina* of the circus was angled to allow more space for the chariots at the crucial beginning of the race, and amphitheatres began to be equipped with a complex underground system of cells which allowed a large number of animals to appear in the arena simultaneously, thus increasing the tempo of the spectacle.

While all these changes were going on, the Emperors themselves were planning their own great building programmes. It is easy to look at Roman architecture simply as a series of great imperial projects, but we must remember that the whole fabric of Roman architecture was at the same time undergoing a constant process of modification and change. All these factors combine to make Roman architecture the complex and intriguing subject it is. Therefore it is as well to pause here and take stock of what we know of Roman building types.

Religious buildings

Both Etruscan and Greek architecture played a part in shaping the typical Roman temple. Etruscan temples, with their high podia, deep columnar front porches and strongly emphatic frontality, influenced the layout of Roman temples. Temple superstructure also followed the Etruscan tradition until the second century BC, when the three Greek orders began to be employed in more or less pure form. Marble was used occasionally in the later Republic as in the Temple of Jupiter Stator in the Campus Martius (after 146 BC) and on a large scale from the time of Augustus onwards.

A typical Roman temple was raised on a high podium and dominated the space immediately in front of it. Much emphasis was given to the façade, which was usually approached by a lofty staircase. Preceding the cella was a deep columnar porch. The Temple of Saturn in the Roman Forum (fig. 26) is a fairly representative Roman temple of the prostyle type, that is to say with columns only at the front and not along the sides and back. Fully peripteral temples were more of a rarity in Rome, although the Temple of Castor in the Roman Forum had columns all round, and several Augustan temples had free-standing columns around three sides of the cella. However, of all types of temple one can say that prostyle temples were the most common in the Roman Empire.

Sometimes a prostyle temple had a row of half columns engaged in the sides and back of the cella wall, an arrangement known as pseudo-peripteral. An example of this can be seen in the Temple of Portunus (fig. 9) and the Maison Carrée at Nîmes (fig. 139). The most popular Roman order during the Empire was the Corinthian, with its ornate foliate capitals and cornice supported by the scrolled brackets or modillions, the latter evolved by the architects of Augustus (see p. 62ff). Roman temples were often set either singly or in groups inside colonnaded enclosures. In the Imperial fora the temple was usually set axially at the end of the enclosure dominating the space in front of it. Under Hadrian there was a brief return to the peripteral style of temple, examples being the Temple of Venus and Rome (fig. 109) and the Temple of Deified Hadrian (fig. 111). In both of these Hadrian was influenced by Hellenistic planning as well as architectural detail.

Circular temples had a long history both in Greece and Italy. The Temple of Vesta in the Roman Forum, which housed the sacred flame, maintained its circular form throughout many rebuildings, and is representative of the type. It is raised on a high podium and has a ring of Corinthian columns surrounding a circular cella. It is instructive to compare it to the circular temple of Hercules Victor built in the late second century BC in the Forum Boarium (fig. 9) whose columns rest upon three steps instead of the usual podium. This and the fact that it is of Pentelic marble suggest that a Greek architect was employed in designing it (see p. 20). The most famous of all circular temples is the Pantheon (fig. 97) with its combination of traditional rectangular porch and circular domed rotunda. Its emphasis upon the interior is a development of the Roman tradition of an ample cella at the expense of the external colonnade.

The pagan temples were not the only religious buildings required by the Romans. There was also the large category of congregational religions whose shrines were built on entirely different principles from the pagan temples. The underground basilica found near Porta Maggiore in Rome exemplifies this category of religious building. Built for a neo-Pythagorean sect in the first century AD it has a nave flanked by two aisles with an apse at the end, an arrangement reminiscent of Christian churches. *Mithraea* followed a similar pattern. A long nave flanked by banqueting couches terminated in a recess containing a sculpture or painting of Mithras slaying the bull in the cave. Indeed the whole mithraeum was often made to look like a cave by means of incrustations of volcanic pumice and glass mosaic. The earliest places of Christian worship were rooms in private houses, and only the altar and decorations identified them as Christian. They are in many ways similar to the Synagogues that have been found at Dura Europos and Ostia. With the advent of official Christianity the Roman basilica was adopted as the model for the Christian church, rather than the pagan temple which was unsuited to holding large gatherings.

Public buildings

As Rome grew from a small town into the capital of a great empire her institutions became correspondingly complex. Law courts, money exchanges, treasuries, record offices and assembly places had to be built, in provincial towns as well as the capital. These and other public buildings were grouped around the *forum* or market place.

The forum was an open area usually rectangular in shape and often surrounded by colonnades on one or two storeys as at Pompeii (fig. 61) or Timgad. Important temples often faced onto it and there were in addition the various public offices and meeting places of the *Curia* or town council. There was often an assembly place for the *Comitium* or popular assembly, and sometimes shops or *macella* (provisions markets) were built nearby.

Another building closely associated with the forum was the basilica, which doubled as a money exchange and a law court. It normally had a long high nave supported on arcades and lit by clerestory windows, surrounded, usually on all four sides, by aisles. In the middle of one end opened a tribunal for the magistrate's court. The tribunal faced the entrance to the basilica and its position depended upon whether a long or a short side faced on to the forum area. Examples of both types of basilica are common, the Pompeii basilica (fig. 62) presenting its short side to the Forum; and the two basilicas in the Roman Forum (p. 27) their long sides. Trajan's Basilica Ulpia with its twin apses (fig. 23) and positioned across the main axis of the Forum represents a striking variation on the normal basilican plan, and one which was followed by Septimius Severus in his forum at Lepcis Magna (fig. 123). The Basilica of Maxentius in the Roman Forum (fig. 180) is the most novel in its construction, following the layout of the *frigidarium* of a Roman bath.

Domestic buildings

The main rooms of a Republican Roman house were grouped around an atrium or a large hall usually with an opening (*compluvium*) in the centre of its roof and a water tank (*impluvium*) set in the floor directly underneath the opening (fig. 57). Vitruvius describes five types of Roman atrium house: Tuscan, Corinthian, tetrastyle, displuviate and testudinate. The Tuscan has a compluviate roof supported on wooden beams. In the Tuscan type the roof slopes inwards and in the displuviate it slopes outwards. In the testudinate there is no opening. The other two types, to judge by their names, are Greek in origin. The tetrastyle has four columns supporting the beams around the opening, and the Corinthian a row of columns. Other features of the atrium house are the *alae* or wings which ran across the atrium for the full width of the house (fig. 2). The atrium is entered from a passage from the street (*fauces*). In some cases the rooms which open directly on to the street are used as shops (*tabernae*) and are independent of the house. The main room of the house, the *tablinum*, was usually at the far end of the atrium opposite the front door. The tablinum was the principal room of the master of the house and his wife, and was probably originally a bedchamber and an eating area. Also family archives were stored there.

The origins of the atrium house are still obscure despite much recent excavation of Etruscan and early Roman sites, notably Marzabotto, Rosella, Vetulonia, San Giovenale and Cosa. The available evidence points to two possibilities. Tombs like the chamber-tomb at San Giovenale (*c.* 600 BC) suggest that the earliest Etruscan houses consisted of one large room with a smaller room (tablinum) opposite the entrance. One imagines that this simple arrangement, reminiscent of the Mycenaean *megaron* or the baronial hall of the Middle Ages, was a development from the rudimentary huts which are copied in so many terracotta models. As happened in almost every subsequent form of domestic architecture, the simple plan was elaborated and further rooms were added, bedrooms to either side of the hall and two further rooms, one either side of the tablinum. The developed Etruscan house plan is reflected in the Tomb of the Volumnii (fig. 2) at Perugia (second century BC).

Opening off the totally enclosed testudinate atrium are bedrooms to the sides and three rooms at the end. As the three end rooms were the main public rooms it was sensible to leave passageways (alae) in front so as to provide a dignified entrance to them. The alae may have had windows providing extra light for the somewhat gloomy atrium. The hole in the ceiling may also have been a practical step to add more light since now the atrium was surrounded by rooms on almost all sides and thus cut off from direct sunlight (fig. 57). This step may have had a further advantage in allowing the smoke from the hearth to escape, which, incidentally, is an argument for connecting the word 'atrium' with the Latin *ater* or black. Indeed Seneca (*Epist*. 44. 5) remarked that it was a sign of the old nobility to have one's atrium 'crammed with smoke-blackened images'. Also, excavations in the atria of a number of Pompeian houses show that the impluvium was a secondary feature. Below the impluvium were older floors of beaten earth. From this evidence it is admissible to draw the conclusion that atria were originally completely covered or testudinate.

However, there is a second, totally different theory as to the origin of the atrium house. Maiuri concluded from the absence of an impluvium in the earliest phases of the houses he excavated that 'the space of the atrium was uncovered like the courtyard of a rural house, and the roof coverings were limited to the living rooms'. Patroni, as early as 1902, had already postulated the existence of such a house with one or more main roofs facing on to a rustic courtyard with two or three bedrooms at each side. Excavations in fifth-century Marzabotto may bear out Patroni's theory. There houses have been found with inner courtyards paved with pebbles and three rooms at the end of the court. Graham sees the evolution of the compluviate atrium as a development of such a courtyard house. Surrounded as it was with rooms roofed with deeply overhanging eaves, 'their eventual further extension would result in the court becoming, in effect, a high *room* – the atrium – with a rectangular opening of considerable size in its roof'.

In the course of the second century BC it became common in Pompeii to add to the rear of the house a peristyle of columns, a fashion common in the Greek world (fig. 16). With the introduction of the peristyle other rooms were added: *diaetae* (outdoor rooms for relaxation), *oeci* (reception rooms), *triclinia* (dining rooms). In large houses there could also be a library and a bath.

By no means all Roman houses were so luxurious. Packer in his analysis of Ostian apartment houses gives a heterogeneous list of Pompeian and Ostian domestic buildings which do not conform to the atrium or peristyle layout or indeed any layout at all. They are simply buildings containing a few shops, a few back rooms and small apartments consisting of a group of smaller rooms arranged around a bigger one (see p. 118).

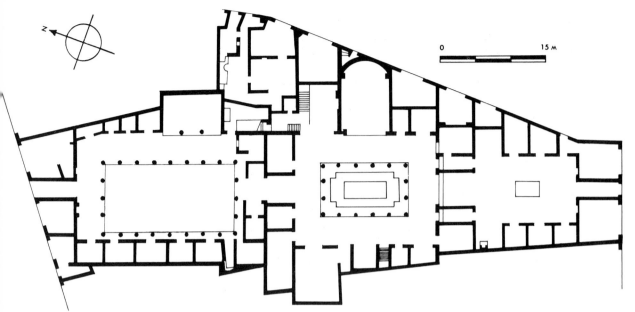

16 Pompeii, House of the Coloured Capitals, second century BC: plan

In the countryside there were many types of villa ranging from the large luxury villa, used by the wealthy as an occasional retreat, to the working farm. Usually even the most opulent villas had some agricultural component if only to occupy the resident staff and contribute to the running of the estate. Luxury villas are found both in the hills and by the coast. Seaside villas lined the coast between Rome and Naples. They mostly feature a *porticus* or long colonnaded gallery flanking the sea-shore, and were sometimes built out to sea. Horace must have had villas of this type in mind when he speaks of builders casting concrete structures into the deep (*Odes* 3. 1. 33–7). In the hills a number of large villas built on terraced platforms can still be seen in the area around Tivoli.

Close to major towns one finds suburban villas whose layout is very like that of a town house except that there is often a small working section. For example, the Villa of the Mysteries at Pompeii has a press as well as some storage jars for wine (fig. 60).

A more practical type of farming establishment is the *villa rustica* which was the centre of an agricultural estate. This type of villa varied a great deal. Sometimes it was primarily residential with farm buildings attached, but quite often it was a working villa with a small residential section. It is often difficult to know whether the owner himself lived in the residential part or his bailiff. In the recently excavated Villa of San Rocco in Campania over half the villa is devoted to comfortable living quarters grouped around a spacious peristyle, while the working section, which was mainly devoted to oil production, is divided off by a roadway. At Boscoreale on the other hand only one-fifth of the villa rustica is devoted to residential rooms, although they do include a three-room bathing suite. The rest of the area is devoted to wine and oil presses, slaves' quarters, a threshing floor and a large open-air wine cellar which contains 84 large storage jars buried up to their necks in the ground. At the other extreme are the *latifundia* or large estates which in Sicily and North Africa swallowed up small farms and were worked by slaves as agricultural factories.

The traditional house underwent much modification in the late Republic. The somewhat gloomy, traditional atrium became less important as most rooms tended to be grouped around the light and airy peristyle (fig. 58). The House of the Mosaic Atrium at Herculaneum shows that by the Flavian period the atrium had shrunk to an entrance hall and was only retained as a concession to tradition. Most rooms were grouped around the spacious peristyle garden and the dining room has views across the sea through an airy portico flanked by two summerhouses. The House of the Stags next door has a similar arrangement and there the atrium is even more perfunctory.

The *domus* or single-family house began to give way to the *insula* or apartment block by the end of the first century AD. As the population grew a new prosperous middle class emerged and the pressure on land became acute. Ostia gives us a picture of a densely populated second-century city with most people living in concrete apartment blocks whose ground-floor rooms usually served as shops — an arrangement still common in the centre of many Italian towns (fig. 72). By the fourth century AD the regional catalogues show that there were 46,000 insulae in Rome and as few as 1,790 domus. Only at the end of the Empire does the pattern begin to reverse itself. With the rundown of trade the gulf between rich and poor began to open once more and at Ostia we find the patrician classes beginning to re-assert themselves and laying out spacious peristyle houses reminiscent of an earlier age (p. 132).

Commercial buildings

The single-unit shop was a common feature in Roman towns and often occupied a portion of a house block facing the street. Sometimes a mezzanine floor provided a storeroom or living quarters for the owner. A wide variety of shops survive at Pompeii and Ostia. A bakery would have counters near the street on which the bread was sold, and at the back of the shop there would be storage space for the grain, the flour mills and the baking ovens. Other shops sold fish, oil, wine, meat and other commodities; some provided cleaning and dyeing services; others were for the sale of wine and snacks. A shop in Ostia has a picture of its wares behind the counter: olives, grapes and pomegranates. Such shops had solid masonry counters with big *dolia* or jars sunk into them where wine and other foodstuffs were kept.

Shops began to be grouped together into shopping centres at an

17 Ferentinum, market hall, *c.* 100 BC

early date, as is shown by the Republican insula at Terracina (*c.* 100 BC) with a row of shops at street level and living quarters above. At Ferentinum another early shopping complex was found with a row of shops opening off a barrel-vaulted arcade (fig. 17). The combination of shops and houses is a common one, as is shown at Pompeii and Herculaneum. As the forum area became more of a civic centre and a focus of civic pride there was pressure to remove shops. This is clearly seen in Rome and Pompeii where *macella* or meat and provisions markets were moved away from the Forum area. Such markets were no doubt designed to segregate the unsightly processes of butchery to an enclosed and hygienic environment. Meat markets have been found at Pompeii, Pozzuoli and in several provincial cities such as Lepcis Magna and Timgad. They usually contain a kiosk or pair of kiosks inside a colonnaded square or rectangular enclosure. The kiosk was perhaps for officials and also housed fountains for washing. The greatest of these meat markets was that built by Nero in Rome (p. 135). Because the great imperial fora had squeezed small traders out of the centre of Rome, Trajan built a dense shopping complex close to his own forum which provided upwards of 150 single-unit shops. This complex (fig. 92) must rank as one of the most astonishing pieces of ancient commercial planning and one which is strikingly reminiscent of shopping centres in our own day.

Entertainment

The three most important buildings designed for mass entertainment in the Roman world were the theatre, the amphitheatre and the circus. Roman theatres derive from the Greek. However, whereas the latter were usually built into a hillside, had a circular orchestra and a low stage building, Roman theatres were normally built from the ground up on masonry or concrete vaults, which served the dual purpose of supporting the auditorium and allowing easy access to the seats. There was often a colonnaded gallery running around the top row of seats and the orchestra was semi-circular. The stage was raised and generally had a row of ornamental niches in front, as seen at Sabratha (fig. 125). The *scaenae frons* or back of the stage was as high as the auditorium, so that the audience could not see outside as they could in a Greek theatre. This back wall was pierced by three doorways, each elaborately emphasized by a pair of projecting columns. A continuous columnar screen ran the whole width of the scaenae frons, sometimes with two, and sometimes three tiers of columns depending upon the overall height of the building. In the late Empire many theatres were modified so that their orchestras could be used for beast hunts or aquatic sports. Externally a Roman theatre had arched entrances all around its curved exterior, and these were repeated on the upper tiers. The arches were flanked by half columns, a system used in the Theatre of Marcellus at Rome, and widely copied thereafter (fig. 25). A *velarium* or awning was usually rigged up to shade the audience from the sun (see p. 143).

The amphitheatre differs from the theatre in that it is a total ellipse, with an oval arena in the centre used either for gladiatorial games or *venationes*. Venationes were fights between men and beasts, which became popular during the First Punic war when 242 Carthaginian elephants were captured at Palermo and were taken to Rome to provide a public spectacle in the Circus Maximus. The other type of event, gladiatorial games, had a long history. There was a very old tradition of prisoners being forced to fight each other to the death on the tomb of a dead hero to placate the gods of the underworld. Such a spectacle is known to have taken place in the Forum Boarium at the funeral of Brutus Pera in 264 BC (Val. Max. 2. 4. 7), and they commonly occurred in the Roman Forum until fire damage caused them to be transferred to the Saepta Julia in 7 BC. Augustus built an amphitheatre in the Campus Martius in 29 BC (Suetonius, *Aug*. 29), but it was burnt down in the fire of AD 64. Caligula also started one near the Saepta Julia, but the Colosseum was the first permanent amphitheatre in Rome. Amphitheatres often had provision for storage of props and animals under the arena floor, and a complex series of mechanisms provided for the appearance of large numbers of animals simultaneously from trapdoors. The Colosseum and the amphitheatres at Pozzuoli and Capua best illustrate these mechanisms (fig. 80). As in theatres a velarium protected spectators from the sun. The ropes which supported this awning were attached to masts which projected above the cornice of the outer wall of the building. The ropes were attached at ground level to winches fixed to a row of bollards encircling the building. The Colosseum has the best-preserved

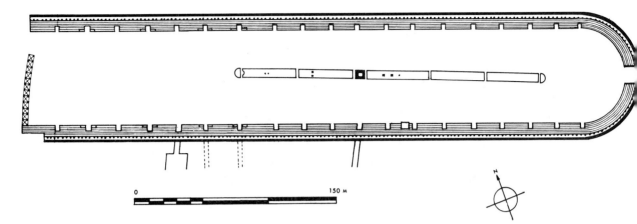

18 Lepcis Magna, Circus, second century AD: restored plan

remains of the system for securing the velarium (fig. 84). Ground-level bollards also survive at Capua, and the mast holes can be seen at the amphitheatre at Nîmes (fig. 141) and the theatre at Orange (fig. 142).

The circus was used for chariot racing and on occasion for venationes. It was the largest of all buildings used for entertainment in the Roman world, the length of full-sized circuses ranging between 400 and 650 metres (fig. 18). Banks of seats lined the two long sides and the curved end, and at the other end were the *carceres* or starting bays. Up to 12 teams of four-horse chariots competed by running seven laps around the arena in an anti-clockwise direction. The carceres were usually set out on a curve to allow each of the teams an equal chance to get through the narrow gap between the end of the median *spina* and the arena wall at the start. In more sophisticated circuses the spina was set at an oblique angle to allow the teams more space at the crucial beginning of the race. A further refinement was to angle the seats nearest the carceres to bring spectators even closer to the action (as at the Circus of Maxentius). The most lavish ornaments were ranged along the spina, perhaps because it was most in view. It had water basins and fountains along its entire length, and at each end were three lofty cones which often stood as high as five metres on top of the already tall spina wall. These were no doubt designed to give the charioteer good warning of when he had to make his turn. Other monuments included statues of victory, imperial statues, honorific columns and sometimes an obelisk in the middle, opposite the finishing line. Towards each end of the spina were set the seven fishes or eggs which marked the number of laps completed.

Recreational buildings

The palaestra, the gymnasium and the baths were all buildings for recreation. Often they were combined in the same complex. The transition from the Greek type of bathing establishment with rows of hip baths filled and emptied by hand to the larger complex of cold, warm and hot rooms equipped with running water and heating systems can be seen in the Stabian baths at Pompeii.

Although the second century BC Stabian Baths had the basic ingredients of the developed Roman bath building they left great scope for improvement in terms of construction and planning. Seneca (*Ep.* 86, 3), who wrote at the time of Nero, compares the small, dark bath in the villa of Scipio Africanus with the light luxurious ones of his day. Scipio's baths would probably have looked rather like the Stabian Baths, which do seem rather small and dark compared with Imperial baths. The complex (fig. 19) consists of a palaestra, although Vitruvius points out that it was not in the Italian tradition (*De Arch.* 5. 11. 1), an *apodyterion* (changing-room), a *frigidarium* (cold-room), a *tepidarium* (warm-room), and a *caldarium* (hot-room). In the caldarium is an apse with a stone basin for cold water (*schola labri*). Vitruvius says (*De Arch.* 5. 10. 5) that a *laconicum* (sweating-room) should adjoin the tepidarium. It should be circular with a hole in its dome in which should be hung a bronze disc suspended on chains. This can be raised or lowered to regulate the temperature of the room. Such circular rooms are found in the Stabian and Forum baths at Pompeii, but are thought to have been cold rooms because there is no trace of under-floor heating in them. However, we know from Pliny (*Natural History*, 9. 168) that underfloor heating (hypocausts) was introduced by Sergius Orata at the end of the second century BC and that the early Pompeian baths must have been heated by braziers, some of which have been found. Therefore these circular rooms could originally have been built as laconica.

The layout of baths was perfected in the Imperial period. The Baths of Titus were the first symmetrically planned, double-circulation baths (fig. 90). It has been suggested that they are in fact no more than a remodelling of the baths of Nero's Golden House as they are aligned to the Esquiline wing of the house. It would be appropriate that the first great imperial baths should have been built at the time of Nero when so much else that was novel was happening in architecture. The Baths of Titus were shortly to be dwarfed by the huge Baths of Trajan, the first of the full-sized Imperial bathing establishments in Rome. The important feature in the Baths of Trajan which is lacking in the Baths of Titus is the open-air swimming pool or *natatio*. Its introduction pushes the frigidarium into the centre of the main block, and as it is now surrounded on all sides by rooms the frigidarium has to rise above the surrounding rooms and be lit by clerestory lighting. This means that it becomes the biggest and most imposing room of the complex as well as a kind of cross-roads through which run the two main axes of the block as a whole.

The Baths of Caracalla, built between AD 212 and 216, have a greater degree of flair and assurance in terms of planning than any of

19 Pompeii, Stabian
Baths, second century
BC: plan

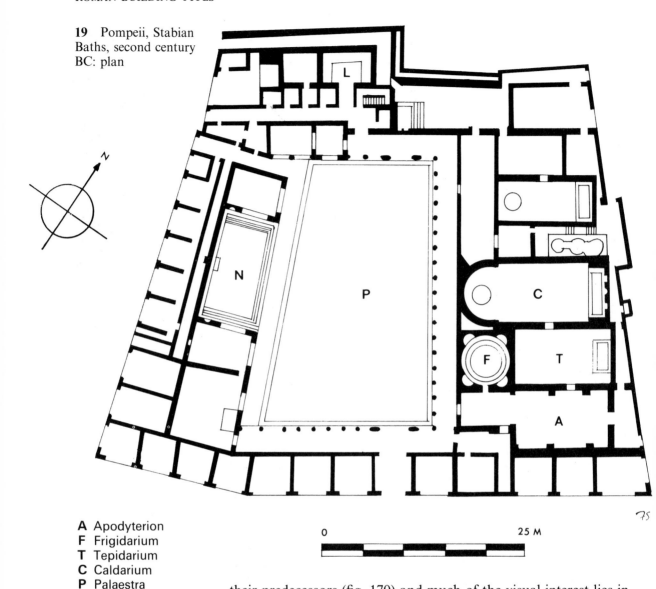

A Apodyterion
F Frigidarium
T Tepidarium
C Caldarium
P Palaestra
N Natatio
L Latrine

0   25 M

their predecessors (fig. 170) and much of the visual interest lies in
the clarity of their layout. The Baths of Diocletian (AD 298–306)
are built on similar lines, but the room shapes have become somewhat stereotyped (fig. 172) and many of the curves and re-entrants
have disappeared.

The Imperial type of bath developed in Rome was much copied
throughout the Empire, for example in the Hadrianic Baths at
Lepcis Magna and the third-century North Baths at Timgad. Some
smaller bath buildings, such as the Small Baths of Hadrian's villa at
Tivoli and the Hunting Baths at Lepcis Magna have a particularly
interesting layout, but neither seem to be in the same tradition as the
great Imperial baths.

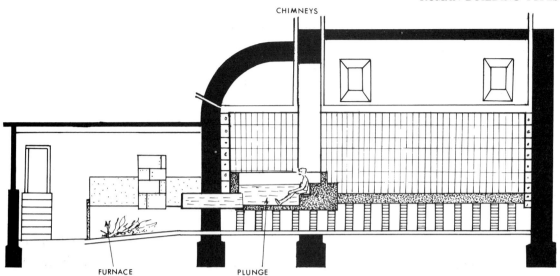

CHIMNEYS

FURNACE   PLUNGE

While discussing baths it is pertinent to mention a little-studied aspect of them, the heating system (fig. 20). All bath buildings had a service corridor, usually partly below ground and running around the south or sunny side of the baths. Along this corridor were located at intervals the furnaces for the heating system. The furnaces were generally behind the hot plunge baths, which were raised up, like the floors, on rows of brick or stone colonnettes. Both plunges and floors were constructed of thick concrete which warmed up slowly but retained heat. When the fire was lit the hot air passed under the plunge baths and then under the hollow floor (fig. 20). Vitruvius (*De Arch*. 5. 10. 2) explains how the floors should be laid so that the heat spreads evenly under them. When the hot air reached the walls it then passed up hollow tubes lining them. Finally, it was ducted out of the roof by means of chimneys. Once the furnace was properly alight the draught rapidly drew the hot air through the complex of wall tubes and heated both the floor and walls of the room. In warm rooms the tubes were generally omitted and the floor only was heated. Sometimes there is evidence that the through draught was too efficient and all the hot air rushed under the floor to overheat the wall opposite the furnace. In these cases one can see that modifications were made to the hypocaust in the form of masonry obstacles to deflect the air current to the other sides of the room.

The fire not only provided hot air for the hypocaust, but also heated a metal water tank which was placed immediately behind the furnace. This tank was fitted into the outer wall of the plunge bath, so that part of it was heated by the furnace and part of it projected into the water. Thus the hot water could flow directly into the bath. Vitruvius also mentions that bronze cauldrons of hot, tepid and cold water were kept in the furnace room. The hot cauldron was heated from the same furnace as the hot water tank for the plunge.

20 Diagram to illustrate the heating system of a Roman bath

Utilitarian buildings

These include bridges, viaducts, sewers, aqueducts and other structures which supplied essential services. To modern eyes buildings in this category include the most impressive Roman achievements. It would probably have surprised a Roman that we should show such interest in the Pont du Gard at Nîmes (fig. 138) or the bridge at Alcantara in Spain (fig. 136), but this type of building should be included in any survey of the Roman architectural achievement.

Some of the most conspicuous Roman monuments, such as the bridge at Alcantara (fig. 136) and the Segovia aqueduct (fig. 137) could never have been built unless the Romans had mastered the arch principle, and developed the use of concrete (p. 73). A road could be carried across a shallow valley by means of a viaduct, which could be a completely solid platform provided there was no stream, but to carry a road across a waterway required a bridge, which in turn used the arch principle. The Romans avoided placing bridge abutments in a fast-running stream whenever possible. This was because of the water activity known as 'scour', which tends to undermine a bridge's abutments. An obstruction anywhere in the stream increases the stream velocity. As turbulence begins at high velocities, and increases with greater velocity, depth or density, the worst place for an obstruction is mid-stream, where depth and velocity are greatest. Turbulence around an object is caused by the stalling of the fluid particles through friction drag, and their breaking away from the smooth flowpath of the stream in whirls and eddies, the activity known as 'scour'. The danger to the bridge abutments is both from the turbulence itself and from the particles of all sizes that the turbulent flow carries with it, even sand in such circumstances being highly abrasive. It is interesting to note that the shape of the abutments used by the Romans, with the narrow face perpendicular to the flow and the long face parallel, and with the blunt end upstream and a tapering end downstream, is approaching the optimum streamlined shape for minimum turbulence.

If possible, the Romans bridged a fast-running stream in one span. This means that the central span of a Roman bridge is often wider than those to the sides. Using the round-headed arch, the central span is therefore higher than the side ones. Unless a rising bridge was required the springing heights of the arches had to be carefully adjusted to maintain a horizontal road over a river. The Alcantara bridge shows how expertly the Romans coped with these problems (fig. 136).

In an aqueduct system there was the additional difficulty of building a water channel on a steady enough incline to achieve an even flow from the source of the water to its destination. For example the water for the Roman town of Nîmes was brought 50 kilometres from the hills outside Uzès. Over this entire distance the incline is maintained at 1 in 3,000. Thus the water falls a height of only 17 metres over the entire distance. Where the channel crossed a river it had to be carried across by means of a bridge, such as the famous Pont du Gard near Nîmes (fig. 138). When the system crossed an important road its passage was sometimes marked by a single or double archway reminiscent of a triumphal arch. The Porta Maggiore (fig. 49), the 'Arch of Drusus' and the Porta Tiburtina at Rome are examples of such aqueduct arches. Not all the water eventually reached its destination in the town. Greedy landowners often piped off considerable amounts for their private use if the aqueduct passed through their land (Frontinus, *de Aquis*, 7, 72 and 75). The water which did get through was fed into a *castellum aquae* or tank from which it was piped off to the various areas of the town. The finest survivals of such castella are found at Pompeii and Nîmes. Regularly spaced water towers such as those in the streets of Pompeii distributed water to a particular neighbourhood. Three pipes brought the water down from these towers: the top pipe fed private houses; the middle public baths and circuses; the lowest public drinking fountains. This ensured that in the event of a shortage the public fountains would run out of water last.

Honorific monuments

There were so many monuments in Rome that in the year 158 BC the Censors ordered a space in the Forum to be cleared of them in order that the people could move about more easily. Every Roman town had its share of busts, inscriptions and equestrian statues. In the middle of the Roman Forum is a row of honorific columns; other famous columns in Rome, those of Trajan and Marcus Aurelius, recount the victories of their dedicators. But perhaps the best-known Roman honorific monuments are triumphal arches.

Fornices, or honorific arches bearing statues, were erected in Rome as early as the second century BC. None of these early arches survive although we know that the Fornix Fabianus (erected 121 BC) was rebuilt in 57 BC. Early dated arches which still survive include the Augustan arch at Rimini (27 BC) and the Arch of Augustus in the Forum (rebuilt in 19 BC, possibly with fragments from an earlier arch of 29 BC).

Triumphal arches were usually dedicated to the Emperor or members of the Imperial family, but sometimes to towns, municipalities or to divinities. The essential characteristics of a triumphal arch are a vaulted passageway supported on pilasters and an attic which carried statues and trophies, etc. Early arches have only one vaulted passageway; later ones sometimes have three, the central one being wider and higher than the flanking ones (e.g. the Arch of Constantine, fig. 21). The double arch is rare, and is normally used in city gates and on bridges. Four-sided arches were sometimes placed at crossroads, mainly in Africa and the east. Internally they have

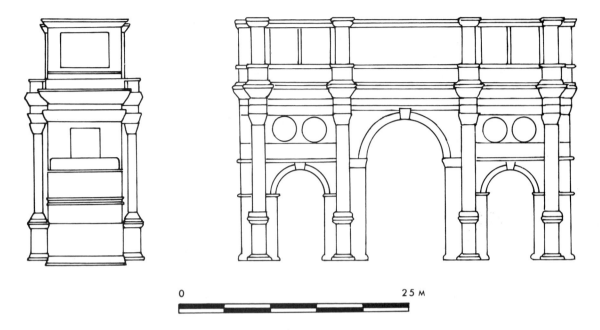

0   25 M

21 Diagram of the
Arch of Constantine

cross-vaults, for example the 'Arch of Janus', Rome, or a cupola, as in the arch of Marcus Aurelius at Tripoli, Libya.

The most elaborate triumphal arches had column plinths adorned with victories, soldiers and prisoners, keystones containing divinities; and spandrels with flying victories (fig. 21). The frieze usually contained a triumphal procession, and in the attic was the dedicatory inscription. In the most richly decorated arches the soffits of the vaulted passages were coffered and sometimes there was a carved panel in the centre, for example the apotheosis of Titus in his arch. The sides of the piers flanking the arched openings, the sides of the arch, parts of the attic, and the walls of the passageways sometimes contained sculpted panels with scenes of triumph, imperial providence, sacrifice, apotheosis, etc.; often bronze figures of horsemen, four-horsed chariots, divinities, trophies, barbarians, etc. stood on the attic.

The Arch of Titus at Rome has a single opening flanked by half columns and columns at the corners (fig. 85), and is an early example of the use of the Composite Order. The Arch of Trajan at Beneventum (c. AD 114), which has a lot more sculpted panels surviving, is so similar to the Arch of Titus that some have thought the latter Trajanic (fig. 95). The Arch of Trajan at Ancona (c. AD 115) is of the same type but of somewhat taller proportions. The Arch of Septimius Severus at Rome (fig. 169) is a classic example of the triple arch, with four detached columns resting on tall plinths on each side. They support a projecting entablature. There are sculpted panels on the façade of the arch and the vaults of the passageways are coffered (AD 203). The Arch of Constantine (AD 312), Rome, is similar, but has more sculpture in the attic. It also has sculpted panels on the sides and in the passageway. The Arch of Janus, Rome (AD 315), is a four-sided arch originally with three tiers of niches flanked by columns. The Arch of the Argentarii (AD 204), Rome, is well preserved and covered in sculpture, but it is unusual in that the passageway is covered by a lintel.

Military and defensive architecture

Imposing fortifications are as old as monumental architecture itself. The Etruscans built fine defensive walls and the Romans followed in this tradition during their period of early expansion in Italy. The so-called Servian wall (fig. 4) shows how advanced their defensive techniques were at an early date (*c.* 378 BC). Soon mighty walls were built to fortify a whole chain of defensive sites along the coast and in the Apennines. The techniques varied to suit the materials available. At Ardea, where there was a ready supply of tufa, the walls were similar to the Servian wall at Rome. In the hills enormous polygonal stones were used. At first the stones were unsmoothed or only partly smoothed as at Circeii or Anagni, but later they were fitted together with admirable precision, as at Segni and Alatrium.

As well as building walled towns the Romans learnt the art of fort construction at an early date. Ostia was originally a Roman fort, built about 349–338 BC to protect the river mouth from pirates (p. 120). In plan it was a rectangle covering about 2.2 hectares ($5\frac{1}{2}$ acres) surrounded by strong walls and pierced by four gateways for the two streets which traversed it (fig. 67). It was designed for a garrison of about 300. Until the late first century AD most camps and forts consisted of earthworks with timber palisades, but by the second century AD forts were often built with stone walls, although earthworks were still common. They could vary between one and 2.2 hectares ($2\frac{1}{2}$–$5\frac{1}{2}$ acres), depending upon the strength of the garrison. The Borcovicium fort (Housesteads) on Hadrian's Wall is a good example of a second-century fort (fig. 22). It has the customary playing-card shape, with straight sides and curved angles, and it is pierced by four gateways. The east and west gates were on the route of the military road which ran close to the wall itself. In the centre of the fort is the *principia* or headquarters-building. It consisted of a courtyard with colonnades on three sides. On the fourth side was a cross-hall which could hold the whole contingent. At the end of the cross-hall stood a *tribunal* from which the commanding officer could address troops on official occasions. Five rooms opened off the cross-hall; the central one was a chapel and contained a statue of the Emperor and the unit's standards; two others were occupied by the battalion adjutant (*cornicularius*) and his clerks, and the other two by the standard-bearers (*signiferi*) whose duties included company book-keeping and payment of the troops. To the south of the principia was the *praetorium*, or the

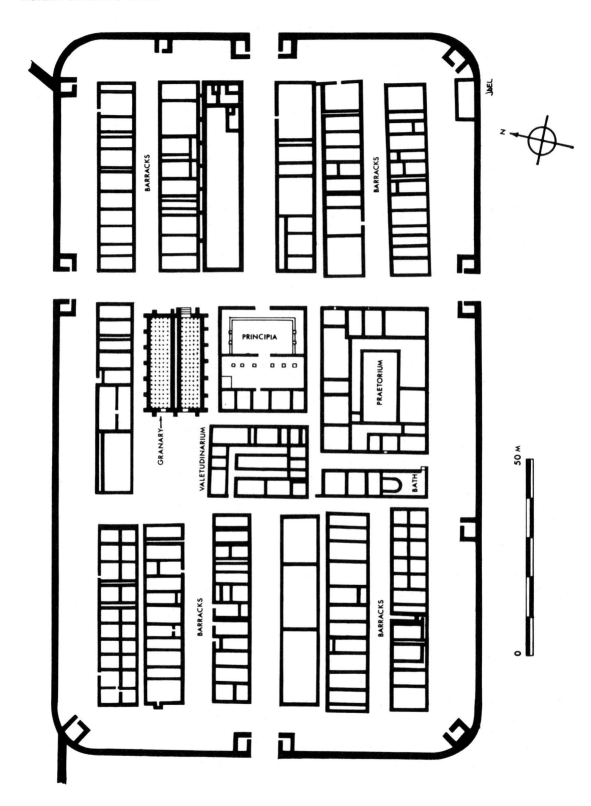

commandant's private residence, with rooms grouped around a peristyle courtyard on the standard Roman house plan. Other buildings in the centre of the fort were the *valitudinarium*, or hospital, and the granaries. A 2.2 hectare fort accommodated 800 men or ten centuriae of 80 men each. They were housed in long barrack-blocks each divided into about ten parts. These quarters were further subdivided into two rooms, one for eating and sleeping and the other for storing equipment. A centurion and his junior officers had quarters at the end of each barrack-block. Other buildings in the fort included stables, workshops and sometimes a bath building for the use of the commander.

On Hadrian's Wall the Romans developed a fully integrated defence system of walls, watchtowers and a chain of forts, all served by a military road and protected by ramparts. In addition to the forts there are castles measuring 20×25 metres every Roman mile. Each mile was further divided into three lengths by two turrets, each of which would have been manned by four soldiers, two on duty on top of the wall and two resting in the turret.

During the Empire the Romans never concerned themselves with defence of the capital itself until the invasions of the third century AD. As a result of that threat Aurelian built the magnificent circuit of walls around the city which has largely survived to this day. The circuit is roughly star-shaped, with the principal roads entering the circuit in the angles so that the approaches to the gates would be visible from the walls. The climax of Roman skill in fortification is the walls of Constantinople built by Theodosius II in AD 413–440 after the sack of Rome. The total width of the defences is 70 metres and there are 300 towers. There are two parallel walls as well as an outer moat and other defences. The vertical distance from the bottom of the outer moat to the top of the highest part of the wall is 35 metres. Its remarkable success is attested by the fact that it defended the city for over 1,000 years.

Funerary

The Romans regarded it as essential to bury their dead, only certain criminals being denied this right. Etruscan tombs were rock-cut and either partially or completely subterranean. At Cerveteri (Caere) the tombs are of the tumulus type, covered with conical mounds of earth. A class of Roman tombs is derived from these Etruscan tumuli and takes the form of a circular masonry drum with a conical mound of earth on top. The Tomb of Caecilia Metella at Rome (*c.* 20 BC), the Mausoleum of Augustus (*c.* 25 BC) and the Mausoleum of Hadrian (*c.* AD 135) are examples of this class of tomb. A second class of tomb, probably derived from Syria, is composed of a number of superimposed columnar structures capped by a conical or pyramidal roof. Examples of this type are 'La Connochia' at Capua and the monument of the Julii at S. Rémy. In the later

22 Housesteads Roman fort, second–fourth century AD: plan

Republic and the first two centuries of the Empire cremation was common and ash-chests or urns were placed in the niches of *columbaria* or sepulchral chambers, so-called because of their similarity to dovecotes. Chamber-tombs are also commonly found, and can be seen lining the roads out of Rome, Pompeii and Ostia. Many are elaborately decorated outside, like the Tomb of Annia Regilla at Rome, and inside, like the Tombs of the Valerii and Pancratii on the Via Latina. When inhumation became more common in the third century AD the tradition of elaborately carved sarcophagi began. Christians rejected cremation and buried their dead in the maze of subterranean burial-grounds known as catacombs. There were four main burial methods: *formae*, burials in the ground covered with a stone slab; *loculi*, a burial slot in the wall of a catacomb; *arcosolia*, an arched recess with the body either immured or in a sarcophagus underneath; and the chamber-tomb, for the richer Christians.

3 The Age of Augustus

The age of Augustus represents the coming of age of Roman architecture. Until then Roman building had been a somewhat rough and ready mix of Roman engineering techniques and Hellenistic veneer. During the 40 years of his reign Augustus practically rebuilt the entire city of Rome, and his ambitious building programme almost certainly resulted in a major influx of foreign craftsmen and architects. Outside influences, particularly eastern and Greek, are a constant factor in Augustan art and architecture. It seems that after an initial experimental period at the beginning of his principate he had determined that Classical and Hellenistic Greek art was to be his model. The Prima Porta statue of Augustus in full armour is closely modelled upon the fifth-century Doryphorus of Polycleitus. The walls of the Farnesina house are decorated with copies of mid-fifth-century Classical Greek paintings, with delicate outline figures on a white ground. A series of terracotta plaques found on the Palatine in the vicinity of the Temple of Apollo contain figures in an eclectic style which combines features of late Archaic and Classical Greek art. The Ara Pacis (13–9 BC) draws its inspiration from both the Classical and the Hellenistic period. A more obvious example of Augustan classicism is the Forum he built in Rome and dedicated in his own name. The deeply carved Corinthian capitals are almost certainly the work of Greek craftsmen, as, one might imagine, were the Caryatid figures which adorned the surrounding colonnades (fig. 35). Unfortunately, one of them bears the signature, Caius Vibius Maximus, an un-Greek name to say the least. However, in the ferment of building which took place under Augustus it is perhaps not surprising to find that Roman sculptors were being trained in Greek workshops. Indeed the Caryatid in question has a certain Italian peasant quality about her.

Another reason for the powerful influence Augustan architecture exerted upon later periods is that Augustus only used the best materials for his building programme. Rome was rapidly transformed as gleaming white marble buildings took the place of the old tufa ones. Once the technique of marble carving was mastered it was never forgotten. Tufa and peperino were in future only used for the

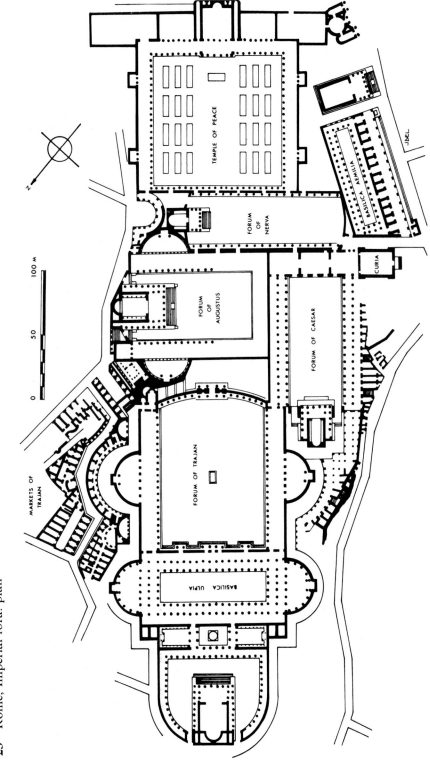

23 Rome, Imperial fora: plan

subsidiary parts of public buildings. A flourishing marble trade was established and soon extended itself throughout the Empire. This highly developed trade, not only in marble but also in ready-made statues and architectural elements, accounts for the later rapid diffusion of sculptural and architectural styles throughout the empire. In essence it meant that henceforth Roman art had no fixed geographical centre, but was the product of the entire Roman world. It is under Augustus that we see the foundations laid for an art and architecture which crossed ethnic and geographical boundaries.

Suetonius in his biographical work *The Twelve Caesars*, devotes book I to Julius Caesar, because although he was not the first emperor, many of Julius Caesar's actions and projects foreshadow the principate that was to follow. In a letter written to Atticus in 54 BC (*Ad Att.*, IV. 16) Cicero mentions that Caesar had recently spent 60,000,000 sesterces acquiring land in order to enlarge the Forum. The land he acquired was north of the old Forum, bounded to the west by the Capitoline hill and to the north by a spur of land linking the Capitoline and Quirinal hills (this spur was later cut away to make room for the Forum of Trajan, see p. 147). The plan was for an enclosed, rectangular forum dominated by a temple to Venus, mother of Aeneas and grandmother of Iulus, founder of the gens Julia. The rectangular enclosure is surrounded on three sides by double colonnades (fig. 23), and behind the western colonnade is a row of shops in tufa and travertine. The temple itself has a high podium covered in white marble, probably from the Carrara quarries which were first beginning to be exploited at this time (fig. 24). The building has columns on three sides only, eight on the façade and nine on each of the flanks. Most of the superstructure of the temple was restored by Trajan, who also extended the Forum northwards and added the Basilica Argentaria behind the temple. The complex was again rebuilt by Diocletian following the fire under Carinus in AD 283. The Forum was to be an influential one and set the model for later Imperial fora. The idea of a temple within a colonnaded enclosure is a Hellenistic one and no doubt Julius Caesar would have been familiar with similar complexes, like the sanctuary of Athena at Pergamon, when he stayed with the King of Bithynia earlier in his life.

His new forum encroached upon the old Comitium which he moved further south; this also necessitated moving the Rostra to a new position at the west end of the Forum. The Senate House too had to be rebuilt after the old one was burnt down in the riots of 52 BC (fig. 28). Like many other of Caesar's schemes this was left uncompleted at the time of his assassination and only finished by Augustus. But even before his death the Forum was being drastically reshaped at its western end by the displacement of Rostra, Comitium and Curia, and beginning to assume the familiar layout that it was to retain until the end of Roman Imperial history.

24 Rome, Forum of Julius Caesar, showing the columns of the flanking porticoes, and three columns of the Temple of Venus Genetrix. Planned *c.* 54 BC and completed by Augustus. Rebuilt by Trajan

25 Rome, Theatre of Marcellus, dedicated in 13 or 11 BC. To the right is the Temple of Apollo in Circo (Sosianus) begun 34 BC and finished before 20 BC

Another project was the building of a new theatre in the Campus Martius (fig. 25). It was built over the curve of the Circus Flaminius, which henceforth became an open square. The façade was in travertine and had 41 bays flanked by 42 half columns. The lowest storey was Doric, the middle Ionic and the upper (now destroyed) was probably a blank wall adorned by Corinthian pilasters. The arrangement was to be used again in the façade of the Colosseum (see p. 136). The first ten metres of the radial passageways are in tufa and thereafter in brick. The theatre was not finished until 17 BC and was dedicated by Augustus to the memory of his grandson, Marcellus. However, the brick probably dates to the building as completed by Augustus and is one of the earliest examples of its use in the capital. After the building of the new theatre, the Circus Flaminius fell into disuse and a passage in Pliny (*Natural History* 36. 101–102), in which Julius Caesar is said to have rebuilt the Circus Maximus, may suggest that this was to compensate for the loss of the other Circus.

Julius Caesar was full of other schemes, including a plan to drain the Pomptine marshes and to dig a canal through the Peloponnesian isthmus, when he met his death at the hands of the conspirators in 44 BC. Ironically, he died not in his new Curia Julia which at that time was still unfinished, but in a hall in the theatre complex built by his rival, Pompey.

After Julius Caesar's death the conspirators, Brutus and Cassius, were hunted down by Octavian and Mark Antony and killed in the Battle of Philippi (42 BC). Antony's involvement with Cleopatra brought about a split between the two victors and the defeat of Anthony at Actium in 31 BC assured Octavian unchallenged control over Rome's destinies. After his triumphant return to Rome in 29 BC he set about establishing that control on a more permanent footing and yet avoiding the overt dictatorship which had cost Julius Caesar his life. His solution was a subtle concentration of power in the hands of one man whose chosen title was 'princeps' or first citizen. As 'princeps' Octavian, who in 27 BC took the honorific title, 'Augustus', dominated the Roman state until his death in 14 AD, and established a political system that was to give Rome a more or less stable government for at least 300 years and was to endure, in one form or another, for one and a half millennia.

Never had Rome been so comprehensively rebuilt as it was at the hands of Augustus and his son-in-law, Agrippa. The Augustan building programme is well documented, not least by Augustus himself who was never reticent in drawing attention to his own achievement. His *Res gestae* inscribed on two bronze pillars set up in front of his mausoleum, and elsewhere, gives a valuable account of his principate and, more relevantly, his building programme. The document is an impressive one. In it he records:

I built the Curia [Julia, 29 BC] . . . the Temple of Divine Julius [29

26 Rome, Forum Romanum, showing in the foreground the Temple of Saturn, (left) the Arch of Septimius Severus and (extreme left) the Temple of deified Vespasian (see also fig. 27)

BC]... I completed the Forum Julium and the Basilica [Julia]... I rebuilt eighty-two temples of the gods in the city during my sixth Consulship [28 BC] in accordance with a decree of the Senate... On [my] private land I built the Temple of Mars Ultor and the Forum of Augustus from the spoils of war... I built the theatre which was to bear the name of my son-in-law M. Marcellus.

(*Monumentum Ancyranum*, IV. 19–21)

Looking at Rome quarter by quarter his achievement was indeed a notable one. He entirely remodelled the Roman Forum as well as laying out his own Forum Augustum to the north of it. In the Forum Boarium area he rebuilt a series of Republican temples, including the old-fifth century temple of Apollo which he finished about 20 BC (fig. 25). A whole new building complex was laid out in the Campus Martius area by Agrippa, including the Saepta, the Pantheon, the Basilica of Neptune and the Baths of Agrippa. Agrippa also superintended the execution of more severely practical projects such as the two new aqueducts, the Aqua Julia (33 BC) and the Aqua Virgo (19 BC). Agrippa's practical turn of mind is illustrated by the fact that he took a personal tour of Rome's sewers in a boat, and as a result of his trip made the necessary repairs.

Augustus' most spectacular achievement was in the city centre. It was here that, in Suetonius' words 'he found Rome of brick and left it in marble' (*Aug.*, 28. 3). The old Roman Forum had been transformed over the centuries from being a market-place of a moderate-sized town to the hub of a great empire (fig. 26). In this small area were concentrated all of the main institutions of the city.

During the principate of Augustus this highly significant part of Rome was to receive its most radical transformation.

Early in his reign, he completed the Basilica Julia which had been begun by Julius Caesar in 54 BC (fig. 27). The basilica occupied the site of the Basilica Sempronia, which had been built by Tiberius Sempronius Gracchus, the father of Tiberius and Gaius Gracchus, in 170 BC. The basilica served as the court of the *Centumviri*, the Chancery court, whose 180 members sat in four panels and dealt with matters of wills and inheritance. The building is 101 metres long and 49 metres wide and its long side opened on to the Forum. Internally it was divided into five naves by three rows of piers and the big central area could be divided off by partitions into the four separate courts. These could be removed when a more important

27 Rome, Forum Romanum: plan

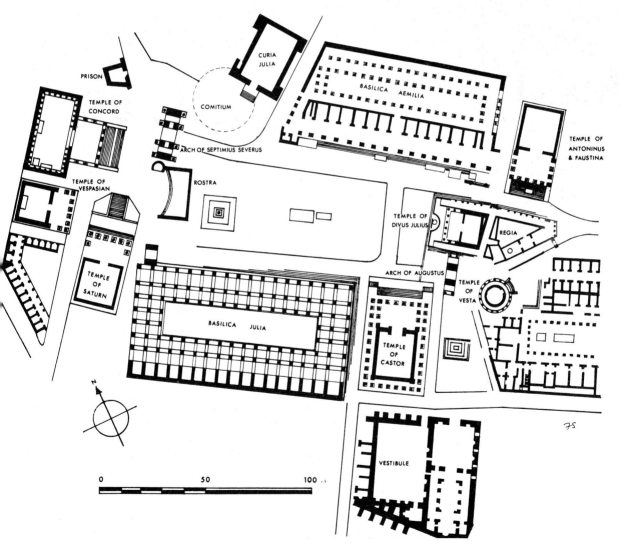

28 Rome, Forum Romanum, view looking north. In the foreground are (left) the three columns of the Temple of Castor, and (right) some re-erected columns of the Temple of Vesta. Behind the Temple of Vesta is the platform of the Temple of deified Julius Caesar, and to the right, under the tin roof, is the Regia. Behind the Regia (on the extreme right) is part of the Temple of Antoninus and Faustina. To the left of the Temple of Castor is the Basilica Julia. In the middle ground from left to right are the Arch of Septimius Severus, the Curia and the Basilica Aemilia. In the background (left) is the Capitoline hill, and (right) the columns of the Temple of Mars Ultor in the Forum of Augustus. Between the two domes in the middle of the background can be seen the Column of Trajan. (See also fig. 27)

case required the whole area, as described by Pliny the Younger (*Letters*, 6. 33). The building was damaged by fire in 12 BC and had to be rebuilt once again. This time Augustus rededicated it in the name of his two grandsons, Gaius and Lucius, whom he hoped to be heirs to the Empire (*Monumentum Ancyranum*, IV. 20). The old name, Basilica Julia, however persisted. The building was once again burnt by fire in AD 283 and the present brick arcading dates to a reconstruction by Diocletian.

On the northern side of the Forum, opposite the Basilica Julia, was the other great basilica, the Basilica Aemilia (fig. 27). This too had been restored at the time of Julius Caesar, but was rebuilt by Augustus in 14 BC. Like the Basilica Julia it was damaged in the fire of 12 BC, and not rebuilt again until AD 22 by Tiberius. The façade it presented to the Forum was a very sumptuous one with its 16-bay two storey arcade. It is known from a drawing by Sangallo (fig. 29) to have had Doric half columns supporting a triglyph frieze on the lower storey. The interior was paved in marble and the nave columns were of africano; the lower order, Ionic, belongs to the restoration of 14 BC and the upper, Corinthian, dates to the restoration of AD 22. The building must have been an extremely rich one and this may be the reason that Pliny (*Natural History*, 36. 101–2) places it among the three most beautiful buildings of his day.

Augustus also completed the Curia Julia, begun by Julius Caesar to replace the Curia Hostilia which had been burnt down in the riot of 52 BC. In its present form it dates to a restoration by Diocletian who rebuilt it in brick-faced concrete (fig. 28). The lower part of the

Inscription on the drawing:

Q. IN BOVARIO
P·P·S·P·Q·R·
PRO·PAGATVM
IMP·COS·XII

DAFVSO AFVSO BVſ

façade with its great bronze door in the middle was covered with marble and the upper part with the three great windows was covered in stucco moulded to imitate marble ashlar masonry. The original Curia Julia appears to have had a similar ground plan and recent excavations have shown that the theory that the Curia formed part of a larger complex of buildings has no existence in fact. The Curia is a very tall building in proportion to its width, 21 metres high × 18 metres wide × 27 metres long. However these are almost exactly the proportions Vitruvius (*De Arch.*, 5. 3. 1) recommends for such buildings, i.e. width plus length divided by two, equals height. Inside the building there are three rows of broad shallow steps to left and

29 Rome, Basilica Aemilia, after 14 BC. Drawing by Giuliano da Sangallo. (*By courtesy of the German Archaeological Institute, Rome*)

30 Rome, Arch of
Augustus, 19 BC:
restored elevation

right. On these steps were placed the seats for about 300 senators. At
the far end is a podium for the speaker and a statue-base presumably
for the statue of Victory which Augustus brought from Tarentum
and placed in the Curia.

The Curia Julia was built against the side of the Forum Julium.
The building of the latter greatly constricted the area of the old
Comitium and necessitated the removal of the old Rostra to a new
site to the west. In its new position it dominated the new rectangular
Forum whose long sides were dictated by the Basilicas Aemilia and
Julia.

Augustus was actively building at the eastern end of the Forum
too (fig. 27). On the spot where Julius Caesar's body was cremated
he erected a temple to Deified Julius, and it was dedicated in 29 BC.
In the front of the podium is a semicircular recess in which is a
circular altar, which corresponds to the cremation place. The
podium rises sheer from the ground leaving a rostra or speaker's
platform in front of the colonnade. On this rostra were hung the
prows of the ships captured from Antony and Cleopatra at the
Battle of Actium. The rostra in front of the Temple of Divus Julius
would have been the family rostra of the Julian family from which
private funerary orations would have been given. At the far end of
the Forum was the public rostra hung with the prows of the ships

58

captured in the Battle of Antium (338 BC). Thus the two rostra faced each other across the Forum and reminded Romans of the glories of the old Republic, and the more recent triumphs of the restored Republic and its new leader, Augustus. Next to the Temple stood the Arch of Augustus. Augustus built an arch on this spot in 29 BC to celebrate his victory at Actium. In 19 BC he replaced the arch (fig. 30) with a larger one, with three openings, to celebrate his Parthian victory in which he recovered the legionary standards lost by M. Crassus in the Battle of Carrhae (53 BC). However, he re-used the earlier inscription in the attic of the new arch. The later arch is a curious one when compared to the mature triumphal arch of a century later. Only the central opening is arched and the flanking ones are in effect aedicules with flat entablatures and pediments. Over these were two statues of Parthians, and over the central opening was a statue of Augustus in a *quadriga*. Near the arch were found the *Fasti Consulares* or lists of Roman consuls dating back to the beginning of the Republic. They are engraved on marble panels which originally fitted into the sides of the minor openings of the Arch. These lists emphasized Augustus' claim that the Republic was being perpetuated under his rule.

31 Rome, Forum of Augustus showing the Temple of Mars Ultor

On the northern side of the Temple of Deified Julius was another arch which fitted into the angle between the Temple and the Basilica Aemilia (fig. 27). Its inscription shows that it was dedicated to Augustus' sons, Gaius and Lucius. The arrangement of the two arches, either side of the Temple dominating the east end of the Forum, cannot be accidental. In the centre is the Temple of Divine Julius to whom Augustus owed his claim to power. Next to the Temple on the south is the Arch of Augustus, the present ruler. The arch shows his victory at Actium, his defeat of the Parthians and through the Fasti Consolares his position as defender of the Republic. Finally abutting on to the north side of the temple is the arch of Gaius and Lucius, the heirs presumptive.

The last Augustan buildings in the Roman Forum were the richly detailed Temple of Castor and Pollux (fig. 28) dedicated in AD 6, and the Temple of Concord, dedicated in AD 10. The latter occupied a cramped site at the foot of the Capitoline hill and had a transverse cella with a porch of six columns facing towards the Forum.

Augustus did not confine his building activities to the old Forum, but following the precedent of Julius Caesar, laid out a new forum of his own to the north of the Forum Julium (fig. 31). The Forum Augustum owes much to its predecessor in terms of layout (fig. 23). Like the latter it consisted of a rectangular space surrounded on three sides by colonnaded porticoes. On the fourth side an axially-planned temple faced down the long axis of the enclosure. Fully in the Italic tradition, the Forum was planned to be entirely symmetrical. However, although the enclosure appears to be symmetrical a glance at its groundplan shows that it is not (fig. 23). The irregularity in the east corner of the complex is carefully concealed on the ground by the neatly contrived pair of porticoes which flank the temple. The irregularity is explained by Suetonius (*Aug.* 56), who states that Augustus was unable to purchase all the land he wanted in order to lay out his Forum, a striking proof of the democratic lines on which the Rome of the first emperor was run. But although fair to this nameless owner of derelict tenements of the Subura, Augustus was none the less anxious that the din and squalor of that crowded area should be fenced off from his lavishly marbled Forum by means of the high peperino wall which is still today such a feature of his Forum. It also served as a fire break.

The temple which dominates the enclosure is dedicated to Mars Ultor (Mars, the Avenger) in accordance with a vow made before the Battle of Philippi (42 BC) in which Brutus and Cassius, the assassins of Julius Caesar, were killed. The Forum was not completed until 2 BC. According to Macrobius (*Saturnalia*, 2. 4. 9), Augustus himself joked about the slowness of the architect. The temple is similar in plan to that of Venus Genetrix in the Forum Julium although its scale is larger. It has a façade of eight tall Corinthian columns and eight on each flank. These rest on a high

32 Rome, restored view of the Temple of Mars Ultor, dedicated in 2 BC, and part of the Forum Augustum (from A. Boethius, *op. cit.*)

podium approached by a frontal staircase. A relief of Claudian date shows the façade of the temple and its pedimental statuary. In the centre was Mars, leaning on his lance and looking curiously like Augustus himself, and to the left and right were Venus and Fortune. The left corner of the pediment was occupied by a seated Romulus and a reclining personification of the Palatine; and the right by the goddess Rome and the Tiber god. Inside the temple, under the apse, were statues of Mars, Venus and Deified Julius Caesar. Also in the temple were kept the legionary standards lost to the Parthians and restored by Augustus. At the end of the north portico, at the side of the temple, is a square room in which stood the famous 14-metre-high colossus of Augustus mentioned by Martial. Behind the two flanking porticoes are a pair of deep exedras which create a discreet cross-accent, a feature that was to be developed more fully in Trajan's Forum. The porticoes consisted of rows of cipollino columns which supported a high attic. In the attic were copies of the caryatids of the Erechtheum at Athens, and between each pair were shields with heads of Jupiter Ammon and other divinities (fig. 35). In the back wall of the porticoes and around the two exedras were a series of cipollino half columns flanking a row of niches. In the niches of the north exedra stood large statues of Aeneas, Anchises and Ascanius, and in the opposite exedra was a statue of Romulus. In the portico niches on Aeneas' side were statues of members of the Julian gens and the kings of Alba Longa, while on Romulus' side were the great men of the Republic. Augustan propaganda was, as ever, stressing the duality of Rome's foundation by Aeneas and later by Romulus, and their divine links with Mars and Venus, foundress of the Julian gens. Thus the Empire under Augustus was the logical conclusion to the Republic. Augustus himself presided over this portrait gallery in the form of a bronze statue on a pedestal in the middle of the Forum.

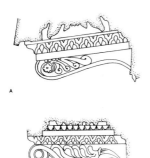

The whole Augustan period was one of great architectural ferment and new ideas were continually being tried and sometimes rejected. Perhaps because of Augustus' own policy, which laid stress on traditional values and styles, most of this effort was directed towards reshaping and developing the Classical Orders. Augustus' own mausoleum in the Campus Martius is the only major monument to be built largely of concrete, with the exception of the Theatre of Marcellus which Julius Caesar began and Augustus completed. However, even in the Mausoleum the concrete is only used for the concentric rings of walling which support the structure; there is no Augustan parallel to vaulting of the kind seen at Palestrina and Tivoli.

Temples are perhaps the most significant monuments of Augustus' reign because it was in the course of building them that Augustus' architects invented the Composite Order (see p. 146) and developed the orthodox Roman Corinthian Order. It will perhaps be useful firstly to describe the Corinthian order as it was in the late Republic. The 'Temple of Vesta' at Tivoli is a good example of a Corinthian temple of this period. Its capitals have lush, shaggy leaves with a large flower on the upper part of the bell. This type of capital seems common in Pompeii and central Italy. The outer and inner spirals are very thick and the outer ones terminate in a volute which projects in a corkscrew profile reminiscent of the volutes of four-sided Ionic capitals. It is important to remember that the Corinthian Order at this time had no distinctive entablature of its own. For example the 'Temple of Vesta' has an Ionic entablature, and the Corinthian Order at Palestrina has a Doric triglyph frieze.

Vitruvius, who published his famous treatise on architecture about 25 BC, probably reflected late Republican building practice with regard to the Corinthian Order when he wrote:

> The other members which are placed above the columns, are composed either of Doric proportions or according to Ionic usages in the case of Corinthian columns, because the Corinthian order never had any scheme peculiar to itself for its cornices or other ornaments. It may have mutules in the coronae and guttae on the architraves according to the triglyph system of the Doric style, or, according to Ionic practices, a frieze may be used adorned with sculptures and accompanied with dentils and coronae. (*De Arch.*, 4. 1. 2)

33 Modillions on Augustan buildings in Rome: (a) the lower order of the Basilica Aemilia; (b) the Temple of Mars Ultor; (c) the Temple of Concord. A scroll from the north doorway of the Erechtheum at Athens is shown in (d)

It was doubtless buildings like the 'Temple of Vesta' that Vitruvius had in mind rather than the more *avant garde* creations of his contemporaries. In fact the Corinthian order had been undergoing a radical transformation for at least 20 years before Vitruvius published his book and one feature of the transformed Corinthian order was the bracket or modillion placed under the cornice. The modillion became a feature of Hellenistic buildings

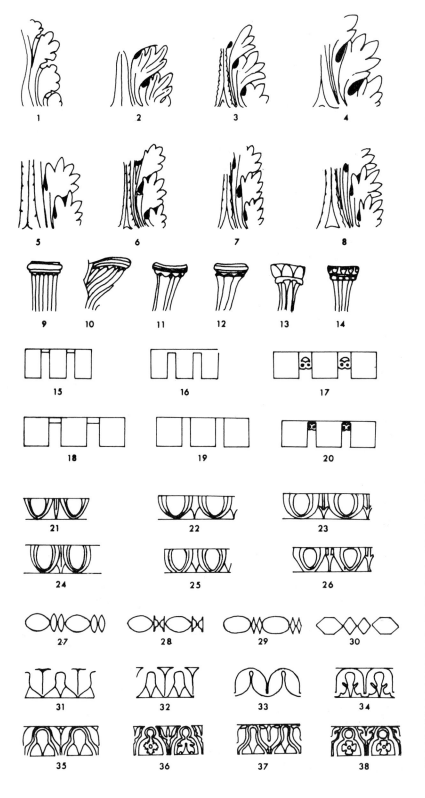

34 Architectural details. *Acanthus capitals*: 1. Temple of Apollo in Circo. 2. Temple of Castor. 3. Forum of Augustus. 4. Ostia, Temple of Rome and Augustus. 5. Palace of Domitian. 6. Forum of Trajan. 7. Pantheon. 8. Temple of Antoninus and Faustina. *Cauliculi*: 9. Rimini, Arch of Augustus. 10. Temple of Apollo in Circo. 11. Temple of Castor. 12. Temple of Mars Ultor. 13. Palace of Domitian. 14. Pantheon. *Dentils*: 15. Forum of Augustus. 16. Temple of Concord. 17. Palace of Domitian. 18. Forum of Trajan. 19. Arch of Septimius Severus. 20. Arch of the Silversmiths. *Egg and tongue*: 21. Forum of Augustus. 22. Temple of Concord. 23. Palace of Domitian. 24. Forum of Trajan. 25. Arch of Septimius Severus. 26. Arch of the Silversmiths. *Bead and reel*: 27. Temple of Mars Ultor. 28. Palace of Domitian. 29. Forum of Trajan. 30. Arch of the Silversmiths. *Cyma reversa*: 31. Temple of Apollo in Circo. 32. Building of Eumachia, Pompeii. 33. Arch of Titus. 34. Forum of Nerva. 35. Forum of Augustus. 36. Brescia Capitolium. 37. Forum of Trajan. 38. Arch of Septimius Severus

from about 150 BC onwards, and appeared in Roman stucco of the early first century BC. When the form first made its appearance in large-scale architecture is unknown, but as D. E. Strong says: 'The general form of the entablature which was to become the orthodox Corinthian of the Roman Empire was thus created, like so much more in Roman art and architecture, between the death of Julius Caesar and the Battle of Actium.'

Although the general form of the Corinthian entablature had been created by 31 BC it still had to undergo a process of refinement. Strong has distinguished three phases of Augustan architecture, firstly an 'early decorated period' in which there was a series of bold and unorthodox buildings with very rich decoration; then came a classicizing period during the last two decades BC, as seen in the Temple of Mars Ultor and the Forum of Augustus, many features of which were copied from Classical Athens, especially the Erechtheum; finally there was a return to rich detail combined with a purer handling of the Orders, as seen in the Temple of Castor (AD 6) and the Temple of Concord (AD 10). Figure 34 shows how Augustan mouldings developed, and how they changed even further in subsequent periods.

Typical of the 'early decorated' buildings are the Temple of Apollo (the so-called 'Temple of Apollo Sosianus'), the arch erected by Augustus in the Forum in 19 BC and the lower order of the Basilica Aemilia which dates to the rebuilding of 14 BC.

The Temple of Apollo has a number of outlandish features which justify Strong's designation 'early decorated' (fig. 25). For example, both tori of the column bases are richly decorated with an oblique cable pattern; the scotia is double and the column flutings are alternately broad and narrow; between the top of the shaft and the base of the Corinthian capital runs a gigantic bead-and-reel pattern; the highly enriched architrave has four steps instead of the normal three; the cornice is supported by S-shaped modillions and between each pair the soffit panel is divided into nine small coffers surrounded by an egg-and-tongue moulding. The nearest parallels to these details come from Side in Asia Minor, a part of the world where Sosius spent much of his military career. The cornice of the Arch of Augustus received similar treatment, while the flanking openings had an elaborate Doric Order with highly enriched capitals (fig. 30). In general appearance they resemble the equally rich Doric Order employed in the Basilica Aemilia a few years later (fig. 29).

The mood of exuberance and richness changed to a much more sober one over the next few years as a result of influence from Athens. One of the first products of this new influence was the Ara Pacis, vowed in 13 BC and dedicated in 9 BC. The procession breathes the spirit of the Parthenon frieze, and the figures, especially the allegorical ones on the short ends, are those of Periclean Athens. The acanthus scrolls could be Polycleitan, and the very form of the

altar is inspired by the Altar of the Twelve Gods in the Athenian Agora.

Augustus' greatest monument in Rome, the Forum Augustum, is a product of the same influence. Finished in 2 BC, it is doubtful whether any of the actual architecture was begun before about 10 BC. The sculpture and architectural detail is strongly Classical in feeling and the caryatids which adorn the attic of the surrounding colonnades are close copies of those in the Erechtheum (fig. 35). Indeed, we know that the Erechtheum underwent drastic repairs in 27 BC and that the circular Temple of Rome and Augustus on the Acropolis, built a few years later, was heavily based upon the Erechtheum in its capitals and other architectural details. It would be no surprise if some of these same craftsmen were at work on the Forum of Augustus.

35 Rome, Forum of Augustus, *c.* 10–2 BC: caryatids from the flanking colonnades. (*By courtesy of the German Archaeological Institute, Rome*)

Even in the Temple of Mars Ultor the Corinthian Order had not yet achieved full orthodoxy. The modillions still had a Hellenistic S-shaped profile (fig. 33b). The Temple of Castor, dedicated in AD 6, was the first to have the full scrolled modillions typical of Roman Corinthian, with an acanthus leaf on the underside. In other respects the temple is similar to Mars Ultor, except that the detail shows a return to the richness which marked early Augustan architecture. The capitals of the Temple of Castor are worth studying because they represent some of the finest Augustan carving (fig. 36). The capitals are cut from two blocks of Carrara marble. (Corinthian capitals composed of two blocks are common in the Republic, but by the end of the Augustan period they are usually carved from one block.) The lower half of the bell is decorated with a row of acanthus leaves alternately high and low. The overlapping lobes of the leaves form pear-shaped cavities while in later Corinthian capitals the cavities become wedge-shaped and near vertical. From the leaves spring the cauliculi to support the volutes which run up to the corners of the abacus. From the same cauliculi spring the helices which join together under the middle of the abacus to support a flower. Unusually the two helices of the Castor capitals interlock. The abacus is decorated, a fairly uncommon feature later on, but used more often in this early period.

It is worthwhile to examine the entablature too, as the Temple of Castor may be regarded as the first fully orthodox Corinthian Roman temple. The architrave is divided into three horizontal fascias divided by elaborate mouldings. The frieze is plain. Above are the dentils, framed by an egg and tongue below and a cyma reversa above. Full scrolled modillions support the corona. The sima is unadorned save for the lion's-head spouts which are set at intervals along its length.

The last great Augustan temple, the Temple of Concord, finished in AD 10, had extremely rich mouldings (fig. 33c). Like the Temple of Castor it has full scroll modillions, probably inspired by those on the north doorway of the Erechtheum (fig. 33d). Part of the cornice, now housed in the Tabularium (fig. 37) shows how rich the mouldings were, so rich in fact that they were thought to belong to a later rebuilding of the temple. Above the architrave and frieze (not shown in the illustration) is a row of dentils capped with an egg and tongue moulding. The corona is supported by richly decorated modillions with coffered panels on the soffit between. Here the sima too is decorated, with a rich acanthus leaf pattern.

Thus, by the end of Augustus' reign the Corinthian Order was fully developed. How many temples using this same basic Order were to be built throughout the Roman world over the next three centuries is almost beyond counting. Even when the western Empire had fallen the Corinthian Order continued to be used with modifications in Byzantine and Romanesque architecture. From the

36 The Corinthian Order of the Temple of Castor according to Palladio

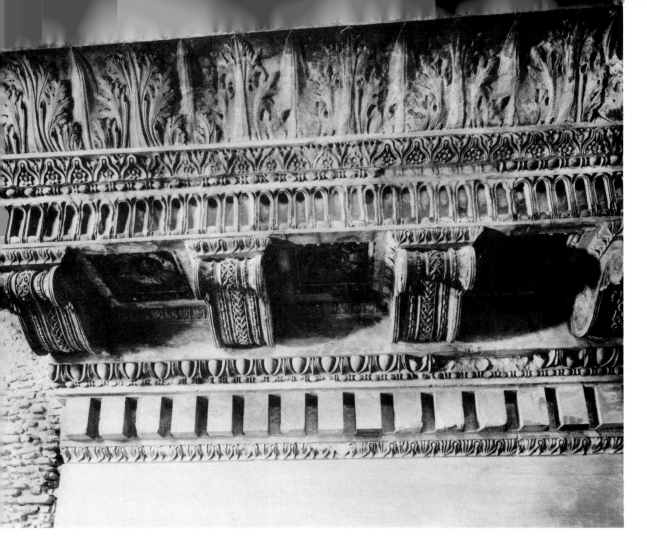

37 Rome, Temple of Concord dedicated AD 10: fragment of the cornice, now in the Tabularium. (*By courtesy of Alinari*)

earliest Renaissance to the Baroque period the Corinthian Order remained the most commonly used of the Classical Orders. The Corinthian Order according to Palladio shows a typical Corinthian elevation of the Roman type. It could almost be Augustan except for some minor details, and with some toning down of exuberant detail.

To recount all of the influences of the Augustan period is beyond the scope of this book. Suffice it to say that in this highly formative period of Roman architecture much more was achieved than the simple evolution of a new architectural order. The sound proportions, good materials and the high level of workmanship in Augustan buildings established a tradition of fine building which was to endure until the end of the Roman Empire and beyond.

4 Roman Architects, Building Techniques and Materials

Roman architects worked for the army, the civil service or were in private practice. Many were former slaves or Greeks, as Pliny the Younger notes (*Letters*, 10. 40). We possess a good deal of background evidence about them as well as an entire treatise on the subject, written by Vitruvius in about 27 BC. Amongst other things he explains how a Roman architect drew up plans, elevations and shaded perspective drawings of his buildings. A skilled draughtsman, he says, ought to be able to produce coloured drawings 'to convey an impression of the work which he proposes'. He goes on:

> Geometry, also, is a great help in architecture. It teaches us the use of the rule and compasses, and facilitates the layout and planning of buildings by the use of the set-squares, the level and the plumbline. Moreover by means of optics the light in buildings can be correctly drawn from fixed quarters of the sky. Also it is by arithmetic that the total cost of buildings is calculated and measurements are computed, and difficult questions of symmetry are solved by means of geometrical theories and methods.
>
> (*De Arch.*, I. I. 4.)

The architect's training appears to have been a rigorous one and included not only a training in draughtsmanship and surveying, but also in sciagraphy and costing. Unfortunately, the only actual plans to survive are those made on marble or in mosaic, for example a mosaic plan of a bath building in the Capitoline Museum (fig. 38). This plan is of some interest because it shows a number of conventions still used by draughtsmen today. Walls are shown enclosed between two solid lines. Unbonded walls are shown as such. For example, the triangular re-entrant between the room marked XI and X and the adjacent room to the left was built independently of the outer wall. Windows are shown as a pair of solid lines in the uninterrupted wall area, while doorways are shown as breaks in the wall. Plunge baths are shown in blue to represent water. The angle of the lettering in each case indicates the dimension meant. Thus, in the room marked VII and XII, the VII indicates the width of the apse and the XII the overall length of the room along

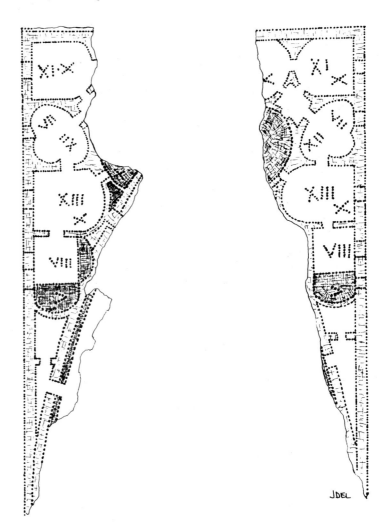

38 Mosaic plan of a bath building (Capitoline Museum, Rome): drawing

the other axis. Architects' drawings must have included a whole range of standard conventions such as the triangles which indicate staircases on the marble plan of Rome. The Romans were of course well used to abbreviations and conventions, as a study of their inscriptions reveals.

To draught his plans the architect used dividers, folding foot-rules, calipers and plumb-bobs, tools similar to those employed today. A set of such architect's tools was found at Pompeii and is now in the Naples Archaeological Museum.

The architect's assistants must have drawn details of mouldings and delivered them to the site. Profiles of mouldings are sometimes found drawn on the marble of a building. For example on the platform of the temple of Dionysus at Pergamon, built in the second century BC and renovated by Caracalla, there are some full-scale profiles of the apophygee and upper torus of a column base. Perhaps the columns were finished on the spot and the mouldings checked against the plan on the floor.

An architect undertaking a big Imperial project would have had a large staff working under him. Frontinus records (*de aquis*, 25, 96, 99, 100, 117) that as *curator aquarum* he had about two dozen specialist administrators working under him in the *statio aquarum*. These included engineers, architects, assistants, secretaries and clerks. There were also measurers, levellers, pipe makers, keepers of reservoirs, inspectors and men to relay the streets which had been torn up to replace water mains. Thus, one can imagine that the architect in charge of an important imperial building project would have had at his disposal a similar staff to carry out his orders.

A mosaic in Le Bardo Museum at Tunis shows an architect and his assistants at work. The mosaic is in three registers. At the top left is the architect holding his five foot measuring stick and to the right is an assistant shaping a small column with a hammer and chisel. Between them is a column capital, a set square, a plumb-bob and a stake for setting out lines. Below is a man bringing mortar and another mixing it. At the bottom a horse-drawn cart is bringing another column to the site.

When the plans had been drawn up and the site selected some clearing work was often needed. The Romans did not necessarily demolish and remove all buildings on the site. Often, earlier foundations were encased or vaulted over, or an older building was filled with rubble and incorporated into the foundations. For example, the Esquiline wing of Nero's Golden House was used in the foundations of the Bath of Trajan. In Ostia the galley which brought Caligula's obelisk to Rome was filled with concrete and used as the foundation for Claudius' lighthouse.

Sometimes, when the ground level had to be lowered, immense excavations were undertaken. To build Domitian's palace on the Palatine, large amounts of earth were excavated to produce a flat platform for the lower part of the palace. The same earth was then piled behind concrete retaining walls to level the upper part of the site. Domitian's engineers must have been skilled in the art of excavation because they later went on to cut away the spur of land which linked the Capitoline and Quirinal hills, the site of the later Forum and Markets of Trajan. The sheer scale of the enterprise can be judged by the fact that the top of Trajan's Column marks the original height of the hill cut away.

When the ground was ready foundation trenches were dug, either to bedrock or to an adequate depth, five or six metres in the case of a temple. Foundation walls were mainly of concrete, but stone was used where there were to be concentrated heavy loads. Under the Colosseum there is a ring of concrete footings eight metres deep. The Pantheon rests upon a solid ring of concrete 4.5 metres deep and over seven metres wide.

39 Painting from the Tomb of Trebius Justus showing Roman builders at work. (*By courtesy of the German Archaeological Institute, Rome*)

A Roman building site must have been a hive of well-disciplined activity as the walls of the building began to rise. A painting in the Tomb of Trebius Justus shows Roman masons at work (fig. 39). The brick facing has reached about three metres in height and two masons are at work on the scaffolding while two others bring baskets of bricks and mortar. A fifth man is mixing a heap of mortar.

The normal building procedure seems to have been for a pair of masons to lay a few courses of facing bricks and immediately afterwards the mortar. Because it contained pozzolana the mortar could dry even inside the brick casing (see p. 73). Thus the facing and the core rose practically simultaneously. After they had laid about 25 courses of brick they finished off that portion of the wall with a bonding course of *bipedales* which extended through the whole thickness of the wall. That they did so is puzzling because the bonding course would have been a horizontal line of weakness through the wall, as it was the concrete core which gave Roman masonry its homogeneity. It has been suggested by MacDonald that the bonding course represented the end of a day's work.

The scaffolding holes are usually directly above the bonding course. This may suggest that the wall was capped by a bonding course prior to erecting the next level of scaffolding, which of course could also coincide with the end of the day's work. In the basilica of

72

Domitian's palace on the Palatine there are between 25 and 28 courses of bricks between bipedales courses and the scaffolding holes are immediately above. The bricks are on average 4 cm high and the mortar joints between 13 and 14 mm thick. Therefore the tiers of scaffolding were about 1.4 to 1.5 metres above each other, presumably a comfortable working height for the average mason.

At this point something should be said about Roman concrete. The Romans did not possess convenient marble quarries, as did the Greeks. The commonest building materials in the vicinity of Rome were mainly soft volcanic stones (see p. 83). It was probably this factor above all which caused the Romans to adopt a mortared rubble construction which was to develop into concrete. Campania was probably the place where the first mortared walls were built. In the fourth and third centuries BC the Pompeians built walls consisting of a framework of Sarno limestone blocks with rubble between. At first the rubble was held together by clay, but by the third century a mortar of black pozzolana and lime enabled them to dispense with the framework so that the walls consisted solely of a facing of well-mortared stone and a core of rubble.

In Rome, too, as early as the late third century BC, a strong mortar had been developed, which in combination with filling and facing materials was capable of producing walls of great strength. The filling between the two outer brick facings was not just mortar, but also contained an aggregate of smallish stones (*caementa*) each about the size of a clenched fist. These caementa were placed in the core of the wall and the mortar laid over them to produce a solid, cohesive mass.

In a simple lime-mortar the quicklime (CaO) is obtained by burning limestone ($CaCO_3$). The lime is then slaked to produce calcium hydroxide, $Ca(OH)_2$ and is mixed with sand. On evaporation it forms crystals of $CaCO_3$ or calcium carbonate. So the cycle is complete. The crystals have a tendency to adhere to something rough and hard and so the addition of sand to a certain ratio actually increases the strength of mortar. Vitruvius recommended three parts of sand to one of lime (*De Arch.*, 2. 5. 1).

However, by the time of Augustus the Romans had developed a fine hard cement which used pozzolana, a reddish volcanic dust which takes its name from Pozzuoli where it was first found. The reaction of lime-pozzolana cement is quite different and far more complicated. The active ingredients of pozzolana are amorphous and vitreous silicates and aluminates, which combine with lime to form hydrated silicate of calcium and other aluminate/silicate complexes. The fact that this does not need to lose water by evaporation, and indeed incorporates it into the structure, enables it to set in damp conditions. Vitruvius recognized the remarkable properties of pozzolana: 'When it is mixed with lime and rubble it

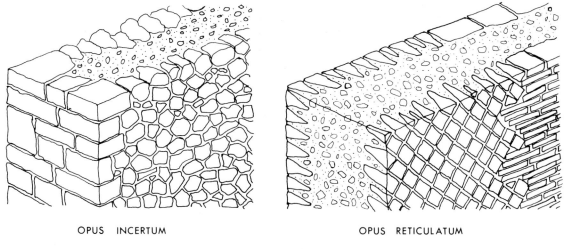

OPUS INCERTUM   OPUS RETICULATUM

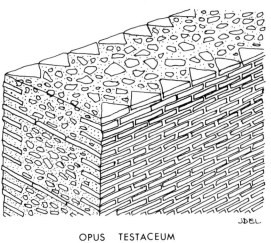

OPUS TESTACEUM

40 Diagram to illustrate Roman concrete facings. Left: opus incertum, mainly used in second and early first centuries BC. Right: opus reticulatum, mainly first century BC and first century AD. Below: opus testaceum, mainly mid-first century AD onwards

not only lends strength to buildings of other kinds, but even when piers of it are constructed in the sea, they set hard under water.' (*De Arch.*, 2. 6. 1.)

Roman concrete is usually classified according to the facing used. The three main facings are: *opus incertum*, an irregular facing of small stones, *opus reticulatum*, small stones with a square face laid diagonally, and *opus testaceum*, brick or tile facing (fig. 40).

There has been considerable reappraisal of the dating of Roman concrete recently. Writing in 1907, Delbrueck dated opus incertum to the time of Sulla (*c*. 100–80 BC), but more recent work suggests that the technique began very much earlier. In an article written in 1934 G. Gatti identified the substantial remains of concrete walling in Via Marmorata as belonging to the Porticus Aemilia (fig. 8), an enormous warehouse (see p. 19) known to have been built in 193 BC with restorations in 174 BC. As the building is of opus incertum

74

it had been suggested that it dates to an unrecorded rebuilding at the time of Sulla. However, as there are no remains underneath the surviving walls, the present building is likely to be the original one. If the remains in the Via Marmorata are correctly identified as the original Porticus Aemilia of 193–174 BC then it is clear that highly advanced concrete structures were being built a hundred years before the time of Sulla, and the period of experimentation with concrete must be moved back to the third century BC.

The more one looks at the evidence the more likely this hypothesis seems. In an article written in 1977 F. Coarelli set out evidence to explode the 'myth of Sulla' whereby so many late Republican buildings or techniques are conveniently dated to the time of the Dictator. An example of the myth is the Temple of Magna Mater on the Palatine, which is known to have been built in the years 204–191 BC, and twice rebuilt after fires in 111 BC and AD 3. On excavation three building phases were revealed: the earliest of opus incertum, the next in opus quasi-reticulatum and the latest belonging to the surviving building. Yet the excavator, Romanelli, maintained that a temple could not possibly have been built of opus incertum at such an early date, and the opus incertum must therefore date to the rebuilding of 111 BC. Coarelli notes that there was a shortage of money to finance the building of the temple in 204 BC and that opus incertum may well have been an economy. Also the concrete technique is somewhat primitive and could well suggest experimentation. The concrete core is composed of the same materials as the facing, peperino and tufa mixed, and is almost indistinguishable from the facing.

In 1940 remains of opus incertum walling were discovered at the foot of the Capitoline hill. These have been identified as a terrace wall near the Aequimalium erected by the Censors in 189 BC to support the hill. Here the opus incertum has small irregular facing pieces in grey mortar. Another structure of the same period is the viaduct erected from the Temple of Saturn to the Capitolium in 174 BC. The type of opus incertum used, with larger and better fitting pieces of stone, is closely similar to that employed on the Porticus Aemilia, which was finished at about the same time. Another example of opus incertum is the Porticus Metelli which was built in 146 BC to enclose the Temple of Juno Regina and the Temple of Jupiter Stator.

The transition to opus reticulatum may begin much earlier than was previously believed, perhaps in the last decades of the second century BC. At first the tesserae were not very regularly laid, although they were more or less square and laid along almost straight diagonal joints. This early form of opus reticulatum, which usually goes under the name of opus quasi-reticulatum, is seen in the rebuilding of the Lacus Iuturnae in the Roman Forum (117 BC), the House of the Griffins on the Palatine (*c.* 100 BC) and the Horrea

Galbana (*c.* 108 BC). The earliest example of true opus reticulatum is found in the Theatre of Pompey in Rome, which was built between 61 and 55 BC. Coarelli makes the observation that the development of opus reticulatum seems to be Roman, as no example is found of the technique in Pompeii before the Sullan colony, although Campania appears to have been the place of origin of cement work generally. Its development in Rome during the latter half of the second century BC may have been accelerated by the need to provide amenities for the rapidly growing population of Rome. Coarelli suggests that building methods may have been 'industrialized' during these years. Perhaps opus reticulatum came in as a method of standardizing components in order to speed construction work. Certainly the time of the Gracchi seems to have been a period of extraordinary expansion and energy both in Rome and in Italy (see pp. 19ff, 108ff and 121).

As early as the second century BC baked bricks or tiles were occasionally used as a building material, for example in the basilica at Pompeii (see p. 112). They were used more frequently in the first century BC, but did not oust opus reticulatum as the principal method of facing concrete walls until the time of Nero. However, there are two types of brick, baked and unbaked. The latter was used from the earliest times throughout the Mediterranean and continued to be used throughout the Roman Empire. Vitruvius (*De Arch.*, 1. 5. 8) mentions these two types of brick, baked (*coctus*) and unbaked (*crudus*) when discussing city walls. The imposing stretch of fifth-century BC walls, eight metres high in parts, found at Gela, is of unbaked brick on a stone foundation. Unbaked brick is commonly found in sites all over the Mediterranean. In a recent excavation in Benghazi many types of mud-brick turned up in buildings which spanned several centuries. In one building the bricks were predominantly 44 cm square and 6 cm high. These were presumably of the type referred to by Vitruvius as '*pentedoron*' or five palms square (*De Arch.*, 2. 3. 3). He adds that private houses are normally built of '*tetradoron*' or four palms square bricks. This, however, was in the Greek world; the Romans had a different system of brick sizes, called Lydian, which were a foot and a half long (44 cm) and one foot wide (29 cm).

In another passage about brick walls Vitruvius (*De Arch.*, 2. 8. 17) implies that mud-brick was used in Rome itself. Indeed he says that the problem of using mud-brick in Rome is that walls abutting on to public property are limited by law to one and a half feet in thickness. If such walls were built of mud-brick they could only support one storey. With Rome's burgeoning population and the demands it made upon space, high apartment blocks were an essential. The only solution was to use baked bricks which would have the necessary strength to support tall structures while conforming to the one-and-a-half-foot rule.

Vitruvius' statement is a most interesting one for a number of reasons. Firstly, it illustrates the great increase in Rome's population following the expansion of the later second century BC. Secondly, it implies that baked brick was becoming a common building material in late Republican Rome, especially for apartment blocks. Perhaps when Augustus said he found Rome in brick he was thinking as much of opus testaceum as he was of unbaked brick.

Vitruvius mentions that the best baked bricks are made out of old roofing tiles (*De Arch.*, 2. 8. 19). When roof tiles were used for facing walls the flanges were cut off and the tile cut into four triangles. Roof tiles were rarely more than 3.5 cm thick. They were bright red because they were baked very hard to make them waterproof; and they were of very fine grain. Examples of tile facings are found at Pompeii from 80 BC, the Praetorian Camp in Rome built by Tiberius and the Domus Tiberiana on the Palatine. Baked bricks, which appear as early as 13 BC in the Theatre of Marcellus, were more yellowish because they were not baked so long; they were 3.5–4.5 cm thick, and more porous to absorb the mortar and give a better bond. There were three main sizes: *bessales*, eight inches square (19.7 cm); *sesquipedales*, one and a half feet square (44.4 cm); and *bipedales*, two feet square (59.2 cm).

The bricks were cut into triangles for wall facings and rectangles for arches. Bessales were cut into two triangles with sides approximately $26 \times 19 \times 19$ cm. They were used especially at the time of Claudius, Nero, Vespasian, Titus, Trajan and Antoninus Pius. Sesquipedales were cut into eight triangles, $31 \times 22 \times 22$ cm. They were used especially under Domitian and Hadrian. Bipedales, cut into 18 triangles, $28 \times 19 \times 19$ cm, were used only under Domitian. The triangles are of very similar dimensions to those of bessales and can only be recognized by the two cut sides, instead of one. Various cutting methods were used. They could be scored and then broken, in which case the visible surface was uneven, and from the time of Claudius up to the time of Hadrian the edges were often smoothed. They could also be sawn in two, a more accurate method of cutting which was used mainly under Domitian and Hadrian. In any kind of cutting much brick was lost, and the pieces were used in the concrete fill.

Tiles and bessales were stamped as early as the first half of the first century BC. Bigger bricks were stamped from the time of Claudius. Stamps become more frequent in Flavian times (one in ten thousand during the reign of Domitian) and very frequent under Hadrian (as many as one in two or three are stamped in some cases). More bricks have been found from the year AD 123 than any other year. The earliest stamps are rectangular with a one-line inscription, giving the name of the *figulus* (brick manufacturer); later they extend to two lines, adding the name of the factory and perhaps the names of the consuls of the year. At the time of Claudius semicircular stamps

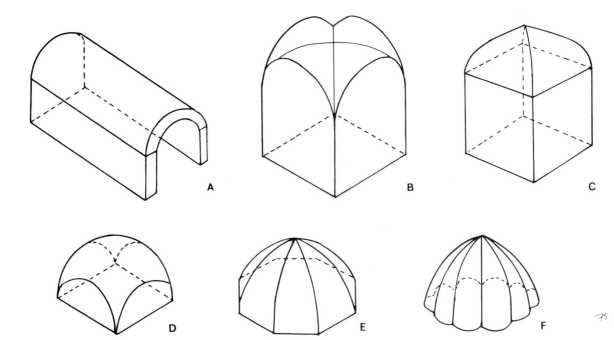

41 Roman vaults and domes: (a) barrel- or tunnel-vault, (b) cross-vault, (c) pavilion or cloister vault, (d) sail vault, (e) domical vault, (f) umbrella dome

appear. Under Domitian the shape becomes a half-moon, with a very wide internal circle. This internal circle becomes smaller and smaller until by the beginning of the third century AD it disappears entirely in some cases. The inscription can be in one line running round the circle of the stamp, or two or even three. By the time of Diocletian stamps can be octagonal or circular. Under Theodosius stamps were circular or rectangular with the name of the Emperor and his titles.

A Roman architect had to have an understanding of engineering principles when it came to building arches and vaults. It will be useful to summarize these principles at this point. A stone arch is composed of separate wedge-shaped blocks, termed voussoirs, struck from a common centre (fig. 41). An arch depends upon the compressive strength of the material from which it is made. Stone has great strength in compression, but most stones are not strong in tension. Therefore a horizontal lintel, which puts stone into tension, cannot span great distances, whereas an arch, which puts stone into compression, is capable of far wider spans. The fact that each voussoir is wider at the top than the bottom prevents it from falling vertically under the action of gravity, and forces it to transmit its thrust to its nearest neighbour. For this reason an arch can be flat or nearly flat and still stay up because of the shape of its elements. Flat or nearly flat stone lintel arches occur, for example, in the Colosseum. In these arches the thrust is almost totally horizontal and the supports at the sides need to be firmly fixed. An arch is made more stable by its curve and the larger the curve the stronger the vertical component of the thrust. The ideal arch-form is an inverted catenary. An arch has to be supported until the last voussoir is in place, and therefore arches cannot normally be erected without the use of centring.

The simplest type of vault is the barrel-vault or tunnel-vault, which in Roman architecture is a continuous vault of semicircular section (fig. 41a). A cross-vault is produced by the intersection at right angles of two barrel-vaults (fig. 41b). The cloister or pavilion vault is also the product of the intersection of two barrel-vaults, but in this case the two barrel-vaults rest on the sides of the square which defines the plan (fig. 41c). Cloister vaults are used in the Tabularium at Rome.

A dome is a vault of segmental or semicircular section erected upon a circular base. If the dome is to be erected upon a square base an intermediate member must be inserted to effect the transition between square and circle. This can be done by means of a pendentive, or spherical triangle, whose curvature is that of a dome whose diameter is the diagonal of the original square (fig. 41d). The first true pendentives occur very late in Roman work, although there is a rough approximation of a pendentive in one of the octagonal rooms on the perimeter of the Baths of Caracalla.

A domical vault is not strictly a dome. Its webs rise from a polygonal base and are separated by groins (fig. 41e). The vault in the octagonal room of Nero's Golden House starts off as this type, but it becomes a dome as it rises (fig. 54). An umbrella dome is divided into webs which are curved in section: in Hadrianic examples, such as the dome of the Serapeum at the villa in Tivoli, umbrella segments alternate with true domical segments.

In building a concrete vault the master carpenters came into their own because the shape of the vault conformed exactly to their timber framework. The earliest concrete vaults and domes seem to have been supported on a full wooden centring. When the concrete had set it formed a monolithic mass, which meant that it acted in quite a different way from a vault or dome constructed of separate stones where the pressures were mainly sideways. If concrete does form a monolithic mass it may be asked, why was there need for an arched shape? The answer lies in the nature of the concrete. In creating a monolithic mass one has produced an artificial building stone with the attendant problems of weakness in tension, and this could only be overcome in Roman times by using a curved surface. Such a surface cannot form large stresses either in compression or tension, but is either in a condition of uniform stress, as in the inverted catenary shape, or transmits its loads as bending stresses (counteracted by the stiffness of the material) or shear stresses, i.e. lateral thrusts.

In a domed building of the early Empire the envelope of the dome

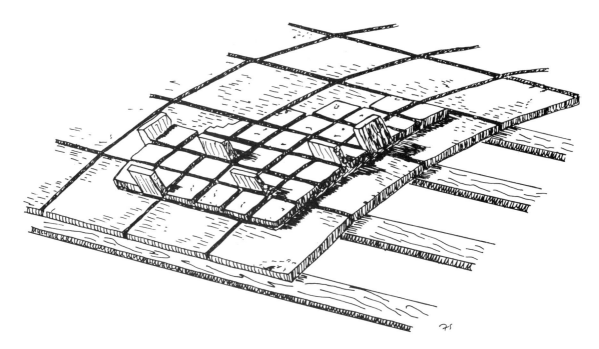

42 Diagram to illustrate tile-clad vaulting

was kept fairly thick at the haunches to counteract shear stress. The filling also was kept thick to prevent buckling. The weight of such a dome required a massive drum to support it and consequently very heavy foundations. It would have been regarded as dangerous to pierce the drum to admit light, and hence early domed rooms are lit by an oculus or hole in the top of the dome.

At this point a word should be said about wooden centring. The centring has to be capable of meeting two separate demands. One is the need for a continuous surface to give the vault its shape, and the other is the construction of a scaffolding sufficiently strong to support the formwork and the weight of the vault above.

In the case of the first problem, a continuous surface which corresponds to every curve of a complex vault would have required highly skilled carpentry. For a coffered dome like that of the Pantheon, the curved dome shape and the coffers had to be reproduced in wood. This process would have consumed prodigious amounts of time as well as timber. A simple method of cutting down the amount of timber needed was to line the vault with brick tiles. In practical terms the procedure was as follows: Rows of bessales or later bipedales were laid on the timber scaffolding instead of the full timber planking (fig. 42). The concrete was laid on top of these tiles, and the tiles remained in place when the timber supports were removed. Tile-covered vaults appear as early as the time of Nero, in his Golden House, and became common from about the time of Trajan. Good examples of them can be seen in the Baths of Caracalla and the Severan structures on the Palatine. They were not

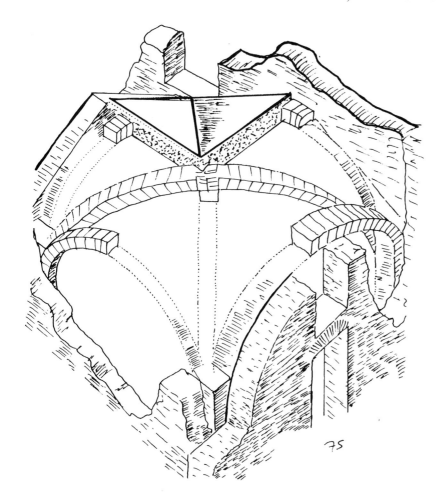

43 Diagram to illustrate a cross-vault with brick ribs

used in the dome of the Pantheon, although the small half-domed rooms in the drum are covered with bipedales.

The second problem is the construction of a scaffolding sufficiently strong to support the vault during its construction. As concrete buildings grew in scale, the weight of the vaults and domes must have created many problems in terms of foundations and support walls, as well as scaffolding. Attempts must have been made to reduce the amount of concrete used. The 'Temple of Mercury' at Baiae, which dates to the time of Augustus, uses light materials in its dome, as does the vault of the octagonal room of Nero's Golden House. In the Pantheon the filling materials of the dome were graded so that near the oculus only very light pumice is used. Also the envelope of the dome diminishes as it rises. However, if the envelope became too thin it was prone to failure by buckling. Presumably some vaults and domes did fail for this reason and no doubt Roman engineers profited from the experience. They perhaps realized that the vaults and domes which failed were not sufficiently stiff, and that

44 Part of the 'Temple of Minerva Medica' showing the brick ribs in the dome

JDEL

this problem can be overcome either by adding ribs of the same or a stiffer material, or by a cellular construction (which explains why amphorae were sometimes used with success in some cases).

The use of brick ribs in vaulting became common in the third century AD (fig. 43). They are used, for example, in the vaults of the Severan structures on the Palatine, the Baths of Diocletian and the Arch of Janus at Rome. Ribbed domes can be seen in the octagonal baths in the Villa of the Gordians on the Via Praenestina and in the 'Temple of Minerva Medica' (fig. 44). As a consequence of the use of brick ribs for stiffening, vaults and domes became thinner and lighter. The walls to support them became less massive and were often pierced by big windows. Consequently the oculus was no longer needed as a source of lighting and in late imperial buildings the dome became totally enclosed. However, despite the introduction of new, lighter domes circular buildings often needed some stabilization of the drum, especially when it had been weakened by the insertion of big windows, and niches at ground level. The result can be seen in the buttresses around the 'Temple of Minerva Medica'. A late building like the fourth-century Mausoleum of St Constantia in Rome was even more daring in its construction. As well as windows in the upper part of the drum there was an arcade at ground level. In this case the structure was stabilized by means of a barrel-vaulted annular passage, a solution which had been tried as early as the third century in the Temple of Portunus at Portus where an external vaulted colonnade runs round the circular domed cella.

Although concrete was commonly used for foundations, walls and vaults, a number of stones and marbles were used structurally as well as decoratively throughout the Roman period.

Alban stone or peperino was one of the oldest stones used for *opus quadratum* masonry. Soft, and so easily worked, it does become friable if exposed. It is a grey stone whose colour and softness make it unsuitable for subtle carved detail.

Gabine stone also has a long history as a building material. Found at Gabii about ten kilometres from Rome it is both lighter in colour and denser than peperino, and fireproof, as Tacitus affirms (*Annals*, XV. 43). It is perhaps for this reason that it was used for the offices in the south-west side of the Forum Julium and in combination with peperino for the back wall of the Forum of Augustus.

In the second century BC the first travertine quarries were opened in the plains below Tivoli. Travertine is a sedimentary limestone, very hard with a creamy texture and recognizable by its lightly pitted surface. It was used a great deal during the late Republic, especially to carry heavy loads. It was also used decoratively, especially on the façades of buildings like theatres and amphitheatres (e.g. the Colosseum) where durability was important. From the time of Augustus travertine took second place to marble as a decorative material. Its main disadvantages were that it calcinated in fire and tended to split when set vertically. It was also expensive to quarry.

Cappellaccio is the term commonly given to the grey volcanic stone which is composed of ash from the earliest volcanic activity in the Rome region. It is a poor, crumbly stone used monumentally in Rome's early period, for example in the substructure of the Capitoline temple. Later on it was seldom used for anything above ground, its main use being in foundations and sewers.

Tufa is solidified volcanic mud, easily worked, but weak under concentrated loads. Of the various tufas, that from Fidenae was one of the earliest to be used by the Romans, the quarries being opened after the fall of Fidenae in 426 BC. It is of a dark yellowish colour and contains ugly inclusions. The more attractive greyish-yellow tufa of Grotta Oscura was clearly preferred by the Romans who began to exploit it shortly after the fall of Veii (396 BC) in whose territory the quarries lay. An early example of the use of Grotta Oscura tufa is the so-called 'Servian wall' (see fig. 4). It was one of the commonest of all building stones until the end of the Republic. In the Augustan period the finely grained lithoidal tufa from the Anio region was preferred. It was used in conjunction with travertine in the platforms of temples such as that of Deified Julius Caesar, Apollo Sosianus and Apollo Palatinus. In the platform of the Temple of Castor travertine piers support the columns and the casing is Anio tufa.

The finest decorative stone as well as the strongest in tension is marble. The first marble temple in Rome was that of Jupiter Stator (146 BC). Another early marble temple was the circular Temple of Hercules in the Forum Boarium which dates to the late second century BC (see p. 20). Architectural sculptures began to be imported by wealthy individuals during the first century BC, for example Crassus, Lucullus, and Sulla who brought marble columns from the Temple of Olympian Zeus at Athens for use in the Capitoline temple. However, there was much criticism of such luxury. By 48 BC the marble quarries at Carrara in northern Italy were being exploited and marbles of every kind became a common sight in the Rome of Augustus (see p. 49). These marbles were at first landed along with other commodities at the Emporium near the Aventine. By the time of Augustus a special wharf was built for them near the later Pons Aelius. There is evidence that that whole area of the Campus Martius was devoted to workshops of stone-masons and sculptors. The din and bustle of this part of Rome is mentioned by Tibullus (II. 3. 43–4).

Of the white marbles Carrara was the most commonly used in Rome. It has a pure, white colour sometimes tending to bluish. Its crystalline structure is extremely compact, which gives it a some-what duller appearance than white Greek marbles. It is mainly its cheapness which made it popular throughout Roman history.

Of the Greek white marbles Pentelic is first found in Rome in the Temple of Hercules by the Tiber. It has the somewhat looser crystalline structure typical of Greek marbles. When chipped the micacious particles of its structure flash and glow in the light. The iron in its composition makes it weather to a soft golden tone, as can be seen in the Parthenon at Athens. Parian is a pure white marble, composed of large crystalline particles. Architecturally its use was largely confined to roof ornaments, perhaps because of its trans-lucent quality.

Coloured marbles came into use in the Hellenistic period, as is shown by the first Pompeian style, which imitates walls encrusted in polychrome marbles. In Rome coloured marble was rare until the time of Augustus. In his Forum, Augustus made extensive use of cipollino or Carystian marble. It comes from Euboea and, as its name implies, has something of the texture of an onion because of its strong veining. It is white or pale green in colour and is heavily striated with mica. It tends to split easily along the veining. In Augustan times and throughout the Empire it was commonly used for columns as, for example, in the exedras of the Forum of Augustus and in the Temple of Antoninus and Faustina in the Roman Forum. Only one example is known to me of its use in sculpture and that is in a crocodile in Hadrian's villa. The greenish hue of the marble and its strong veining make it a peculiarly appropriate stone from which to carve the creature.

Unfluted monolithic columns of grey or red granite became more common as the empire progressed. Granite is an extremely hard granular crystalline rock, and both the red and grey types used in Roman construction were quarried in Egypt.

Porphyry is a very hard igneous rock with an extremely compact crystalline structure. Its deep maroon colour near to purple gave it imperial connotations in the late Empire. It was used for columns, although generally smaller ones than those made of granite. It came from the Red Sea area of Egypt.

Green porphyry or serpentino is a bright green stone speckled with light green crystals. Quarried near Sparta, it was used in wall incrustations or in conjunction with red porphyry and other stones to produce *opus sectile* (cut stone) floor inlay. Giallo antico or Numidian marble, from Tunisia, was also used in inlay work. It is a yellow marble with red or dark veining. Rosso antico is a red stone quarried in the Peloponnese near Cape Matapan.

Of the breccias or variegated conglomerate stones pavonazzetto was commonly used for decorative purposes. Found in Asia Minor, it has a violet base with irregular white limestone inclusions. Other breccias are portasanta from Chios, with red or yellow patches on a soft grey or pinkish ground, and africano from Asia Minor, with black, grey and bright red patches.

5 The Julio-Claudians

The architectural climate in Rome changed abruptly after the death of Augustus in AD 14. The Temple of Concord, finished in AD 10, was to be the last great marble building of its kind built in Rome for some time. With the accession of Tiberius architectural fashion swung away from public monuments employing columnar orders. Instead the Emperor built a number of lavish residences for himself both in Rome and outside. Often sited in rocky or almost inaccessible locations they stimulated a renewed interest in concrete as a building material. For example, the Emperor's main residence for many years, the Villa Jovis at Capri, was perched on the top of a sheer cliff at one end of the island. Its location required the construction of enormous concrete water cisterns to store any rain that fell, and concrete buttresses were needed to stabilize the huge semicircular dining room with its dizzy panorama over the Gulf of Naples. Concrete undercrofting was also required to provide a flat platform for the large new palace he built for himself on the Palatine. The reign of Caligula (AD 37-41), too, was notorious for its architectural follies, for example the floating palaces he built for himself on Lake Nemi. One might have expected that an antiquarian like Claudius (AD 41-54) would have returned to Augustan propriety, but the architecture of the Claudian period has many odd features. His reign is notable for several heavily rusticated, stone buildings such as the Porta Maggiore, as well as a number of severely practical projects, such as the harbour at Ostia and two new aqueducts. This interest in engineering and the exploitation of concrete as a constructional medium continued into the reign of Nero (AD 54-68). In the latter part of Nero's reign the great fire destroyed much of the city of Rome. The rebuilding was done very largely in brick-faced concrete, and the new building codes, which laid down standards for new houses, are strikingly reminiscent of the Act of 1667 after the Great Fire of London. Nero's reign is memorable for the infamous Golden House, but this architectural extravaganza was in fact an extraordinarily important building. It represented a revolutionary departure in the exploitation of concrete as a building material. Terms like 'the new architecture' are commonly applied to it. The architects of the Golden House began to realize the potential of concrete in shaping architectural space. Concrete was not just used as a medium to create coffered barrel vaults, but to mould apses, niches and domes, to open up and to enclose vistas, to provide hidden lighting effects, to shape an interior from the inside rather than the outside. To use Ward Perkins' words, 'the emphasis has suddenly shifted from the solids to the voids'. Thus the reign of Nero began an architectural revolution which was to gather pace over the next 70 years, until by the time of Hadrian the concept of interior space had changed beyond recognition.

After all his other heirs had died, Augustus was succeeded by his adopted son, Tiberius, who had all the taciturn and introspective resentment of a man who had been continually passed over. He was descended on both sides from the aristocratic Claudian family, which boasted 28 consulships, five dictatorships, seven censorships, six triumphs and two ovations (Suetonius, *Tib.*, I. 2). His own career, too, was one of unbroken success, and he was even awarded a triumph for his campaigns in Germany. His private life, however, was less happy. He was forced by Augustus to divorce his wife Vipsania, whom he adored, to marry Augustus' daughter, Julia, for whom he came to feel such a passionate loathing that at the height of his career he retired to Rhodes for several years

In the barracks he built for the Praetorian guard on the eastern edge of the city between AD 21-23, it is notable that the main entrance, marked by a marble arch, faced towards the city, making it clear that the guards were to be used against the citizens of Rome and not an outside enemy. The outer walls are of interest because they represent the first large-scale use of brick-faced concrete. The barracks cover an area of 440 × 380 metres and are crossed by two roads which intersect in the middle. The building was later incorporated into the walls of Rome by Aurelian (see p. 261).

Tiberius spent little time in the capital, especially in the later part of his reign. He did, however, build the first palace on the Palatine hill, the Domus Tiberiana. This represented a sharp break with the policy of Augustus, who deliberately lived very modestly. The Farnese gardens have largely destroyed any vestiges of this palace, and little is known of its layout in detail except that the rooms were grouped around a central courtyard and that in scale the palace far exceeded the nearby house of Augustus. In AD 22 as a result of the death of Drusus, the son that Vipsania bore him, he once again withdrew from Rome, this time to Campania, where he had an imperial villa on the coast, called the 'Grotto' ('*Spelunca*' in Latin — the name still survives today in the corrupt form, Sperlonga). It was here that he was dining when the roof collapsed and he was saved by the good offices of the Praetorian prefect, Sejanus. Excavated in 1957, the villa's focal point is a large natural cavern in the rocky cliffs

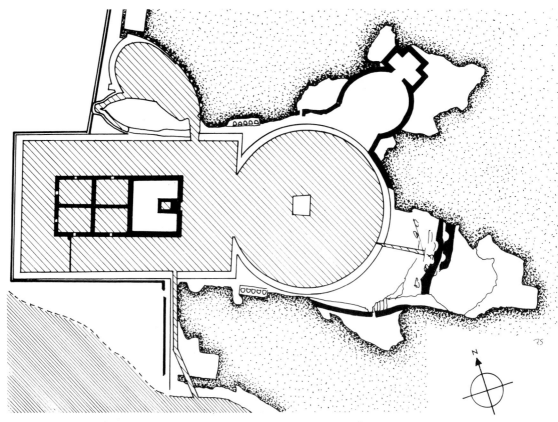

45 Sperlonga, Grotto of Tiberius, early first century AD: plan

which meet the sea at this point of the coast (fig. 45). Concrete walling and masonry flooring were added to the natural cave and two basins were scooped out near the mouth of the cavern. The inner one is circular and the outer, linked to it, is rectangular. In the middle of the rectangular pool is a masonry island with a *triclinium* (dining area) and a *vivarium* (fish-pond). In the centre of the round one is a statue base. Within the cave are two deep hollows. The left-hand one is lined with concrete walls to produce a circular room with a stage for theatrical or musical performances. The larger one, to the right, probably contained a sculptural group in white marble showing the Cyclops being blinded by Odysseus and his followers. The sculptures, carved in a theatrical Hellenistic style, are signed by Rhodian sculptors, which suggests a connection with the Emperor's stay on that island, although recently scholars have attempted to date them to the Flavian period. Seats were cut into the rock in the main cave to allow spectators to observe the performances. Tiberius' grotto at Sperlonga exemplifies the Roman delight in uniting architecture, landscape and sculpture into a single entity.

Tiberius spent most of the last ten years of his reign in the seclusion of Capri. Augustus had taken over the island as an Imperial estate and had built himself a seaside palace there. Tiberius

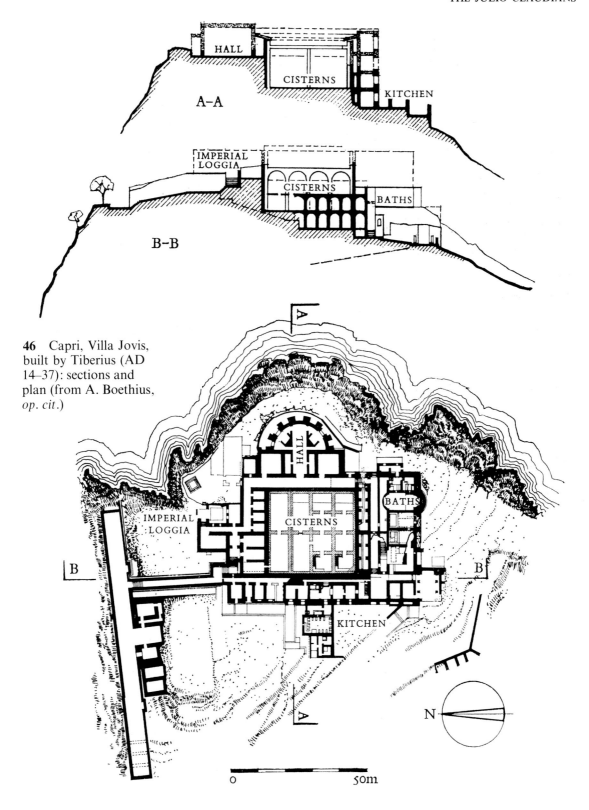

46 Capri, Villa Jovis, built by Tiberius (AD 14–37): sections and plan (from A. Boethius, *op. cit.*)

47 Capri, Villa Jovis, built by Tiberius (AD 14–37)

added several more Imperial buildings, embellished a number of natural grottoes and built the Villa Jovis, which stood on the very edge of the cliffs which ran down sheer to the sea on the eastern tip of the island (fig. 46). The cliff slopes away to south and west and a level site was created by cutting back the rock and building a huge undercrofting of concrete barrel-vaults. The inner part of this vast network was used as an immense water cistern to collect and store the infrequent but heavy rainfall. The cistern was vaulted over to form a flat square platform in the centre of the villa (fig. 47). The platform was probably covered with mosaics and perhaps surrounded on four sides with a peristyle of columns like those found in Delos and North Africa, for example the square of the cisterns at Ptolemais (p. 191).

The villa must have presented an extremely imposing aspect to a visitor who would have approached it not by the modern pathway from the south, but up the steeper Roman road paved with herringbone bricks leading from the west. The villa would have towered above him, its main rooms standing over 20 metres above the rising ground. In the south-west corner is the entrance vestibule with four green cipollino marble columns supporting the ceiling with, opposite, a niche in which stood a statue, perhaps of the Emperor. From there a mosaic-paved ramp led up past a bathing suite on the south side of the Imperial suites. On the east side was a huge semicircular audience hall flanked by lesser halls. Only the substructures now survive (fig. 48), but even they required an

immense work of cutting, levelling and buttressing. The rooms above must have commanded stupendous views of Sorrento and Vesuvius, situated as they are on the very edge of 300-metre-high sheer cliffs. On the north side is the Emperor's private suite. It is approached by a single, well-guarded corridor and kept quite separate from the service rooms and kitchens on the west side of the villa. A long corridor leads northwards to a loggia, 100 metres long, running close to the edge of the cliffs. Here the Emperor could have strolled after eating and resting in the rooms which opened off it to the south. The triclinium, with its splendid views, was a vaulted room with polychrome marble paving on its floor.

In his last years Tiberius was haunted by the spectre of impending death and it was his habit to consult soothsayers. Just to the west of the main block of the villa are the massive foundations of the observatory used by his adviser and astrologer, Thrasyllus. At the edge of the cliff to the south of the villa are the remains of a lighthouse which was used mainly for signalling the mainland opposite. The Emperor's orders could also be transmitted to a signalling tower at Cape Misenum where the imperial fleet stood ready for the Emperor's command. The lighthouse collapsed a few days before Tiberius' death in AD 37. (Suetonius, *Tib.*, 74.)

After the death of Tiberius, Caligula, the son of the popular Germanicus, was proclaimed Emperor by the Praetorian guard, and began his reign amidst general enthusiasm, but his cruel excesses resulted in his murder by his own guards after only four years as

48 Capri, Villa Jovis, showing the substructures of the audience hall

Emperor. However, during this period he did make some notable architectural contributions. According to Suetonius he completed the Temple of Deified Augustus and the rebuilding of the Theatre of Pompey which were left unfinished by Tiberius; he began the aqueducts which were later to be completed by Claudius (see p. 93). Among his wilder schemes was a plan to cut a canal through the isthmus of Corinth and to found a city on a peak of the Alps; among his more eccentric was the extension of the Palatine palace as far as the Forum and the conversion of the Temple of Castor into a vestibule to it. In his final unbalanced period he built a bridge to link the Palatine palace with the Capitoline hill so that he 'might live with Jupiter'. (Dio Cassius, Book 59, 28).

Excavations have brought to light parts of the great circus he built at the side of the Via Cornelia almost on the spot where St Peter's now stands. The enormous obelisk, now in the middle of the St Peter's Square, once graced the spina of this circus and was brought to Rome by a ship of huge dimensions. This ship was later sunk in the harbour at Ostia to provide a foundation for the Claudian lighthouse (see fig. 69).

Suetonius gives a fascinating description of the pleasure galleys Caligula built for himself:

> He also constructed ten-oared Liburnian galleys with sterns studded with gems, multicoloured sails, and ample space for baths, porticoes, and dining rooms, and with a great variety of vines and fruit-bearing trees; reclining on these ships all day long he would sail along the Campanian coast amid choral dancing and singing.
>
> (Suet., *Cal.*, 38.)

In 1928 the level of Lake Nemi was lowered to reveal two enormous pleasure galleys in the mud. They were very broad in the beam, 20 metres and 24 metres respectively, and were 72 metres and 73.5 metres long. They were 1100 tonnes in burden, ten times as much as Christopher Columbus' largest ship. Flat tiles set in mortar were found in the hulls. These were laid over the oak decking, and the pavements were of polychrome marble and mosaic. Flanged tiles were found, which suggest that there were heated floors and perhaps baths on board these sumptuous vessels. The galleys contained a number of technical devices such as pump-pistons, pulleys, and anchors.

When Caligula was murdered by the Praetorian guard his old uncle, Claudius, was proclaimed Emperor. Claudius had a strong practical streak and his reign is mostly notable, as far as building is concerned, for engineering projects like the draining of the Fucine Lake, the repair of the emissary of Lake Albano, the completion of the two aqueducts begun by Caligula and the building of the

harbour at Ostia (see p. 123). The harbour was not an unqualified success and was later superseded by the Trajanic harbour (see p. 124). A more successful scheme was the completion of the aqueduct which bears his name. Begun, along with the Anio Novus, by Caligula in AD 38 and finished by Claudius in AD 52, it is perhaps the most impressive of the Roman aqueducts. Its water came from springs in the upper valley of the Anio and reached Rome through a covered channel 68 kilometres long. For much of that distance it travelled underground, but for the last ten kilometres it was carried on the tall arches of rusticated stone which form such a conspicuous landmark in the Campagna to the south-east of Rome. It is calculated that the two new aqueducts opened by Claudius accounted for two-thirds of the total water supply available to ancient Rome. No major new aqueducts were built after the Aqua Claudia because by then Rome had the best water supply of any city in antiquity — and a considerably better water supply than modern Rome.

The Aqua Claudia and Anio Novus are carried over the Via Labicana and the Via Praenestina on the outskirts of Rome by a monumental double archway, built of heavily rusticated travertine masonry, the Porta Maggiore (fig. 49). The twin openings are flanked by three aedicules each with a pair of Corinthian half columns supporting a tall triangular pediment. The attic carries three inscriptions put up successively by Claudius, Vespasian and Titus. The masonry of the lower part of the arch was deliberately left

49   Rome, Porta Maggiore, built by Claudius (AD 41–54) to carry the Aqua Claudia and the Anio Novus over the Via Praenestina and the Via Labicana. It was later incorporated into the Aurelianic walls

50 Rome, Temple of Deified Claudius, completed by Vespasian after AD 70. Detail of the west façade of the temple terrace

rough and the columns supporting the aedicules are actually composed of a number of battered or unfinished Corinthian capitals laid one on top of the other. This curious mannerism may well have been a fancy of the Emperor and other examples of rusticated work exist from the period. The arch which carries the aqueducts over the Via Labicana is known from a Rossini drawing of 1829 also to have had rusticated masonry. The emissary which regulated the level of Lake Albano, originally constructed in the fourth century, was repaired at about this time, possibly by Claudius. Certainly the masonry around the mouth of the emissary has rustication and irregularly projecting voussoirs like those on the two Claudian aqueduct arches.

A final work which is not strictly Claudian but has stylistic similarities with these other Claudian monuments is the Temple of Deified Claudius on the Caelian hill. A portion of the west façade of the temple terrace survives in the Convent adjoining the church of St John and St Paul (fig. 50). Once again we find heavily rusticated arches, sharply projecting keystones and the device of a flat pilaster only partly carved out of rough unfinished masonry.

Claudius died in AD 54, possibly of poison, and was succeeded by Nero, who at the time was 16 years old. His reign began quietly enough, guided as he was by the firm hand of his domineering mother, Agrippina, until her murder in AD 59 gave him full power

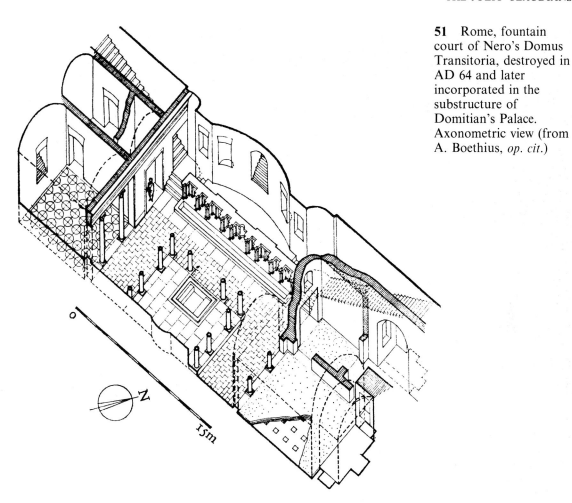

51 Rome, fountain court of Nero's Domus Transitoria, destroyed in AD 64 and later incorporated in the substructure of Domitian's Palace. Axonometric view (from A. Boethius, *op. cit.*)

to flaunt his ambitions. His singing and chariot racing gave greater scope to the wit of ancient historians than his achievements in art and architecture. Even so, important artistic developments were taking place in his reign and owe much to this versatile Emperor's patronage. Sculptors in marble and bronze, mosaicists, painters, engineers and architects and other artists of ability and renown worked for his court and many of their achievements are still to be seen. His reign is regarded as a turning point in the exploitation of concrete as a building material; his court painter, Famulus, invented a new wall painting style, known from the many examples of it at Pompeii and Herculaneum as the Fourth Pompeian Style; his Golden House contains one of the first major examples of glass mosaic on a vault; his court sculptor, Zenodorus, created the astonishing 120 (Roman) feet high bronze colossal statue of the Emperor which stood at the entrance to the Golden House; his patronage too must have stimulated the minor arts to judge from a passage in Pliny (*Natural History*, 37. 20) in which he is said to have

95

paid one million sesterces for a single bowl.

Nero built two palaces in Rome, both of which are important for our understanding of the 'Roman architectural revolution'. The first was the Domus Transitoria (or 'passageway') which linked the Palatine with the Imperial estates on the Esquiline. It was begun in AD 64 and was probably unfinished when it was destroyed by the great fire of the same year. It was built to link the villa of Maecenas on the Oppian hill, which had been bequeathed to Augustus on the death of its owners, with the Imperial palace on the Palatine. Three main portions of the Domus Transitoria survive: a fountain court, which owes its preservation to the fact that it was incorporated into the foundations of the Flavian palace, a section of the cryptoporticus or corridor running alongside the Domus Tiberiania, and the domed junction of two corridors which was later incorporated into the platform of the Temple of Venus and Rome.

A staircase leads down to the fountain court (fig. 51). On the north side of the court is a shallow semicircular recess pierced with niches and in the centre a stepped water cascade. In front of this is a row of low fountain niches ornamented with small free-standing columns which originally had bronze Corinthian capitals. The

52 Rome, domed intersection of two corridors in Nero's Domus Transitoria, later incorporated into the platform of the Temple of Venus and Rome. Restored drawing

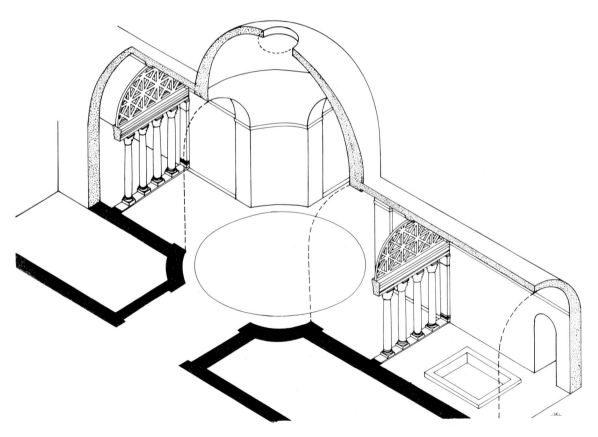

96

paving and wall inlay was in polychrome marble, porphyry and serpentino. On each side of the open court is a pair of barrel-vaulted rooms. Some of the paintings on the vaults have survived and provide us with our earliest examples of the Fourth Style. Delicate borders of relief stucco divide the vault and lunettes into small panels which are filled with medallions, plaques and figured scenes surrounded by elegant scrolls studded with blue glass. One vault is finely decorated with octagonal coffers in white relief stucco. This small complex reflects Nero's taste for refined opulence and hints of future extravagance.

A second survival of the Domus Transitoria, the Palatine cryptoporticus, reflects similar taste. A portion of the vault decoration survives and once again the vault is divided into small panels by delicate relief stucco decoration. The third survival cannot be restored with confidence (fig. 52). It is the domed intersection of two corridors. The dome was carried on four massive piers and may be presumed to have had an oculus in the middle to supply lighting. There were columnar screens at each side of the dome on the minor corridors and perhaps on the major ones too. The use of a dome at such a key crossing point, to open light and airy vistas, marks the beginning of a new concept of architectural space which was to be further exploited in the Domus Aurea.

Nero was at Antium when the great fire of AD 64 broke out in Rome. When it was over, four of Rome's 14 regions were completely destroyed and in seven there were few buildings left standing. Only four regions escaped undamaged (Tacitus, *Annals*, 15. 39), and the Domus Transitoria was destroyed in the blaze.

The fire created great opportunities for Nero, by clearing large areas of land in the city centre. Nero was not slow to take advantage of this and immediately made plans for a vast new palace, the notorious Golden House. Suetonius' description of it (*Nero*, 31) gives some impression of its splendour.

> It had a vestibule, in which stood a colossal statue of him, 120 feet high; the area it covered was so great that it had a triple portico a mile long; it also had a pool which looked like the sea, surrounded by buildings which gave the impression of cities; besides this there were rural areas with ploughed fields, vineyards, pastures, and woodlands, and filled with all types of domestic animals and wild beasts. Everything in the other parts of the palace was inlaid with gold and highlighted with gems and mother-of-pearl; there were dining rooms whose ceilings had rotating ivory panels to sprinkle flowers, and pipes to sprinkle perfumes on those below; the most extraordinary dining room was a rotunda, which rotated day and night like the heavens; there were baths through which flowed sea water and sulphurous spring water. When the palace was completed in this manner, he inaugurated it, but would only

express his approval to the extent of saying that he had 'at last begun to live like a human being'.

The grounds of the Golden House covered 50 hectares (125 acres) and filled the valley between the Esquiline, Caelian and Palatine hills. There was an artificial lake in the middle, where the Colosseum now stands. The park was so vast that a popular joke ran around Rome:

'Rome will become a palace;
migrate to Veii, citizens,
unless the palace has reached Veii too!'

(Suetonius, *Nero*, 39.)

The park was approached from the Forum along the Sacred Way which was straightened and lined with colonnaded porticoes. At the end stood a rectangular vestibule in the centre of which was the colossal bronze statue of Nero. A branch of the Aqua Claudia supplied a row of fountains built against the unfinished platform of the Temple of Divine Claudius and the waters then cascaded into the lake. Nothing of the mile-long portico, baths and other buildings survives except the Esquiline wing of the palace. Today it is damp and gloomy, buried as it is under the platform of Trajan's baths (fig. 90). Mildewed walls and faded paintings are occasionally bathed in a shaft of white light from a light-well cut into the vaulting. In these dimly lit rooms it is difficult to imagine the former splendour of the great palace. Yet in terms of painting and architecture the building was undoubtedly revolutionary. The building in general must have resembled the many villas with columnar façades depicted in Pompeian paintings, because one or two column bases of the façades still survive (no. 1 in fig. 53).

A glance at the ground plan shows up many of the building's

53 Rome, Nero's Golden House, AD 64–68: plan

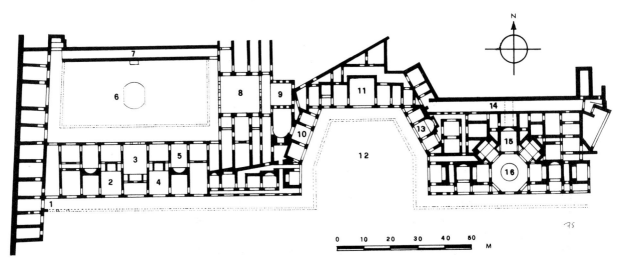

strengths and weaknesses (fig. 53). For example the octagonal room to the right (no. 16 on fig. 53) is undoubtedly a piece of architectural ingenuity. Yet its bold shape creates an architectural jumble behind. Similarly, the main suites opening off the big pentagonal courtyard in the middle of the façade are well designed and in each case have a large important room in the centre of each group. Yet once again there is a jumble of awkward-shaped rooms behind. The architect and engineer, called respectively Severus and Celer (Tacitus, *Annals* 15. 38-43), show their skill in good groupings, rhythms and novel solutions, but not in overall planning.

The group of seven rooms on the south facing the courtyard (including numbers 2-4 in fig. 53), which were perhaps suites of bedrooms, show the best organization. The shapes and sizes of the rooms repay close attention. From left to right they are medium/narrow/medium/large (room 3)/medium/narrow/medium. On the courtyard side they are from left to right short/ long/short/long/short/long/short. On the façade side there is the opposite rhythm. Notice too the way the rooms are divided: plain wall/apse/square-sided recess/square-sided recess/ square-sided recess/apse/plain wall. The biggest room of all (no. 3 in fig. 53) is in the centre, facing the courtyard. Opposite in the middle of the courtyard is a fountain (no. 6 in fig. 53). The back of the courtyard is closed by a cryptoporticus (no. 7 in fig. 53) built against the hillside. It has the dual function of corridor and sustaining wall.

Another set of rooms, unconnected with the first, faces on to the courtyard from the east. Opening directly on to the courtyard is a very large vaulted dining-room (no. 8 in fig. 53) whose lunette would presumably have towered above the peristyle of the courtyard to light the rooms behind. At both ends it had a columnar screen. At the far end opens a smaller barrel-vaulted room with a fountain at the end (no. 9 in fig. 53). The whole group is treated as a nymphaeum. Covering the upper parts of the walls and extending to the springing of the vault is a mosaic frieze 2.20 metres high. The frieze runs unbroken round the walls of both the larger and the smaller barrel-vaulted rooms, a total length of 65.84 metres. It is bordered at the top and bottom by a row of cockle shells. The vault of the smaller barrel-vaulted room is covered in brown pumice to give the rustic appearance of a grotto and in the centre of the vault is an octagonal panel filled with a mosaic of polychrome glass tesserae showing Odysseus offering wine to the Cyclops. The idea of a cave glimpsed through a garden peristyle is not new. The ensemble, like Tiberius' grotto, is another outstanding example of the skill of Roman architects in introducing nature into a domestic setting.

The pentagonal courtyard (no. 12 in fig. 53) is the focal point of the wing as a whole. The colonnade would presumably have continued around the courtyard producing four flanking col-onnades of equal length and the fifth in the centre somewhat longer with perhaps taller columns supporting a projecting pediment in the manner of villas depicted in Pompeian wall-paintings, for example the House of Lucretius Fronto, Pompeii, or the later Templum Pacis of Vespasian. Immediately behind the centre of the pentagonal courtyard was a large vaulted room flanked on each side by a symmetrical suite of lesser rooms (no. 11 in fig. 53). The big room, 'the room of the gilded ceiling', was so called because of its magnificent barrel-vault, inlaid with painted and gilt coffered panels made of moulded relief stucco. The vault is the one Raphael and other artists clambered through to make the drawings which inspired so much Renaissance stucco work.

The final group of rooms, to the east of the pentagonal courtyard, is centred around a large octagonal domed room (no. 16 in fig. 53). Here the architect had two main problems. The octagonal room and the rooms which opened off it created a series of awkwardly shaped triangular and irregular rooms behind. Secondly, the building ran very much closer to the hill on the east side than the west. The result was that there was no room for a courtyard like that on the west side. Instead the cryptoporticus (no. 14 in fig. 53) abutted directly on to the rooms behind the octagonal room. These rooms were therefore not only awkwardly shaped, but also very badly lit. The architect to some extent overcame the problem by ingeniously piercing downward-sloping light-wells into the upper part of the northern wall of the cryptoporticus. A corresponding set of light-wells was cut into the opposite, southern wall lower down. In this way shafts of light were directed from the edge of the hill into the rooms

54 Rome, Nero's Golden House, AD 64–68. Octagonal room: axonometric view from below, section and plan (from A. Boethius, *op. cit.*)

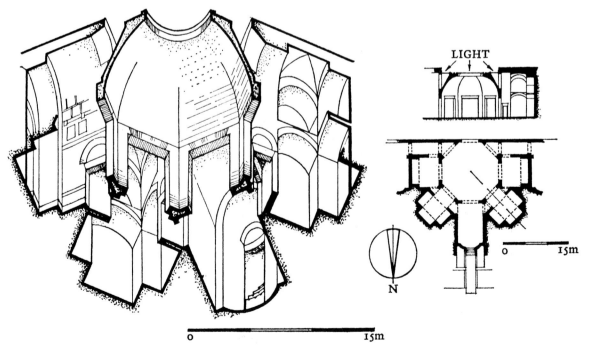

LIGHT

N

0   15m

0   15m

immediately south of the barrel vault. An equally ingenious device was used to convey water for the waterfall in the room (no. 15 in fig. 54) opening off the octagon. Water from cisterns on top of the hill was ducted across the cryptoporticus via an arched bridge.

55 Rome, Nero's Golden House: octagonal room, AD 64–68

The octagonal room is perhaps the most revolutionary architectural concept in the whole house (fig. 54). Its vault is supported on eight brick-faced concrete piers, originally adorned with stucco and marble pilasters (fig. 55). Although it begins as an eight-sided domical vault, it becomes a dome towards the top. In profile it is extremely flat and the oculus is unusually wide. When one stands under the dome the oculus is the only visible light source and yet the five rooms which open off the octagon are bathed in light. The source of this light is five light-wells left between the extrados of the dome and the five abutting rooms. Thus the architect has achieved a dramatic play of light and space. There is evidence that there was an upper storey above and it may well be here that we must imagine the rotunda which rotated night and day like the heavens, as described by Suetonius.

This, then, was Nero's greatest architectural achievement and one which was to have profound influence on the future of Roman concrete construction. The building was entirely built of brick-faced concrete. The work was done in haste, as the poor quality bricklaying and thick mortar joints shows. Indeed, it is noticeable that the brickwork of the substructures of Trajan's Baths which often cuts across the Neronian walls is easily distinguishable from the latter because it is much more finely laid – even though it was never intended to be seen. However, Nero chose brick instead of the opus reticulatum which at that time and for 50 years after his death was still quite common. He chose it because it was recognized as a material suited to rapid construction.

It was the material used for the rebuilding of Rome which followed the fire of AD 64. When the rubble of the fire-torn buildings had been tipped into the Ostian marshes, wide, straight streets were laid out and apartment blocks built of fireproof materials and without beamed ceilings. Presumably concrete vaulting and brick facing became commoner as a result. Streets were lined with porticoes and these were apparently built at the emperor's own expense. Each house, too, had to have a water tank in its courtyard to deal with future fires. We know little of the appearance of Nero's new Rome, but can perhaps imagine it by looking at the developments which took place in Ostia a few decades later. There the tall apartment blocks of brick-faced concrete, barrel-vaulted rooms and open courtyards, ranged along broad straight paved streets, may reflect a Rome which was the product of the imagination of Nero's architects. The result would certainly have contrasted sharply with the Rome of tortuous alleys and precarious tenement blocks which once provoked the ridicule of the Campanians (Cicero, *de lege agraria*, II. 96).

The career of this extraordinary Emperor ended abruptly in AD 68 when his Golden House was barely complete and the reconstruction of Rome could scarcely have progressed very far. He was forced to flee the city and only a few kilometres away on the Via Cassia he stopped to make preparations for his own death. He fastidiously ordered his servants to look for pieces of marble for his tomb. His dying words 'What an artist dies in me' are perhaps a fitting epitaph for the Julio–Claudian dynasty. It was a self-indulgent period in many ways, but the caprices of the Julio–Claudians had fostered much innovation in art, architecture and engineering. Indeed, the changes in architecture which had occurred in the half century of their rule have rightly been termed revolutionary, and as such had far reaching consequences for the future of Roman architecture.

6 Two Roman towns: Pompeii and Ostia

At ten o'clock in the morning of 24 August AD 79 smoke began to issue from Mount Vesuvius. It was the beginning of an eruption which was to engulf the towns immediately to its south and west, and in so doing encapsulate them in a layer of volcanic matter which was to preserve them to our own day. The prevailing southerly winds carried a hail of red hot volcanic stones over the towns of Pompeii and Stabiae and buried them to a depth of four to five metres. The torrential downpour which accompanied the last stages of the eruption washed a slimy ooze of ash and mud down the slopes of the mountain to cover the small town of Herculaneum to a depth of 15–20 metres. Oplontis, which lay midway between Pompeii and Herculaneum, and which is only now beginning to be uncovered, disappeared under a combination of ash and mud. Pliny the younger, whose uncle died in the disaster, wrote an eye witness account of it (*Letters*, 6. 16):

> My uncle was at Misenum and was personally commanding the fleet. On 24 August in the early afternoon my mother pointed out to him a cloud of unusual size and appearance. . . . It was not clear as we were so far away which mountain the cloud was rising from (it was afterwards known to be Vesuvius). Its appearance can only be expressed as being like an umbrella pine, for it rose to a great height on a sort of trunk and then split off into branches, I imagine because it was thrust upwards by the blast which had just occurred and then left unsupported as the pressure subsided, or else was borne down by its own weight so that it spread out and dispersed. In places it looked white, elsewhere spotty and dirty, according to the amount of soil and ashes it contained.

The volcanic matter set hard over the dead cities and at Pompeii only a few walls projected out of the crust. Using these as landmarks some of the survivors dug down to try to salvage their possessions, digging through walls as they did so. Such efforts were short-lived and soon the site was totally abandoned, only the name *civita* (city) lingering on through the Middle Ages to remind people that once there had been a town there. The towns were only rediscovered in the

56 Pompeii, general plan. 1. Triangular Forum. 2. House of the Surgeon. 3. House of the Faun. 4. Villa of the Mysteries. 5. Temple of Apollo. 6. Temple of Jupiter. 7. Meat and Fish Market. 8. Basilica. 9. Theatre. 10. Quadriporticus. 11. Stabian Baths. 12. Forum Baths. 13. Small Theatre. 14. Amphitheatre. 15. Castellum Aquae. 16. Civic Offices. 17. Building of Eumachia. 18. Temple of Fortuna Augusta. 19. Temple of Vespasian. 20. House of the Vettii. 21. House of Loreius Tiburtinus. 22. Central Baths

eighteenth century, and the first excavations were little more than treasure-hunts by miners and tunnellers whose only interest was to find works of art for the palaces of the Bourbon kings. Fortunately the Swiss engineer, Karl Weber, worked with these tunnellers and conscientiously drew the ground plans of the buildings excavated. Modern scholarship has shown his drawings to have been very precise. Until Giuseppe Fiorelli took over the excavations in 1860 anything of value was taken from the houses and any attractive paintings cut from the walls. Fiorelli was the first to attempt to preserve the houses more or less intact. It was his idea also to make plaster casts of the hollows left by dead bodies and thus vividly preserve their last moments. Of the most recent excavators, Amadeo Maiuri, who worked on the site for 37 years from 1924 to 1961, was the most energetic. He filled every blank spot on the map of Pompeii. Although the city is not yet completely excavated the present policy is to limit excavation in order to concentrate upon preserving what has already come to light.

As early as the eighth century BC Pompeii existed as a small market town, built on a spur of lava in the southern foothills of Vesuvius. Its geographical position on the river Sarno soon made it a centre of the Oscan towns around. Little is known of this early city. In the sixth century it only covered 9.3 hectares (23 acres) and its population could not have added up to more than a few hundred (fig. 56). The early town must have been under Greek influence to judge by the Doric temple in the triangular Forum. Its ground plan is rather unusual for a temple of so early a date. Its length is only just

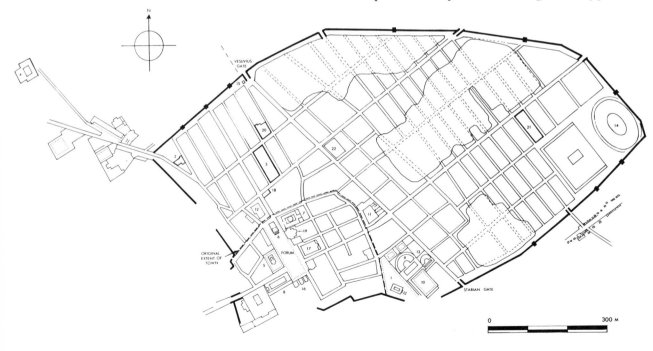

one-and-a-half times its width in contrast to the extremely elongated plans of contemporary Greek temples in Sicily and south Italy. The column count, too, is unusual, seven by eleven, unless there were six by eleven columns with a wide intercolumniation in the entrance way, a feature found in the Temple of Apollo at Syracuse, built earlier in the century (c. 565 BC). The capitals with a widely spreading echinus accord well with a mid-sixth-century date.

During the fifth or fourth century BC the town was greatly enlarged, probably in connection with Samnite expansion in the region. A new wall circuit was laid out enclosing 63.5 hectares (160 acres) and the grid was extended north and east, but it is unlikely that anything like the full area within the walls was built upon at this early stage (fig. 56). Looking at the plan of Pompeii one might guess that the gates were positioned by the military engineers and the street plan was adapted to fit the wall circuit, a common practice in ancient cities where military and civic planners rarely co-operated. The Vesuvius and Stabian gates were doubtless positioned on the lines of a pre-existing road which ran slightly east of and parallel to the old town. The three gates on the north-east side of the town were also positioned with important roads in mind.

The few blocks just north of the old town were fairly irregular and their streets mainly followed the lines of roads leading out of the city to the north. Presumably the wide street running between the Vesuvius and Stabian gates determined the axis of the adjacent streets to the east, although it appears that only a dozen or so squarish blocks were laid out at this early period. The elongated rectangular blocks, on a slightly different axis, which lie to the north-west of the old town and fill almost the whole eastern half of the city, were presumably the last to be laid out. Post-war excavations have revealed several city blocks in the vicinity of the amphitheatre with no evidence of buildings at all. Presumably they were vineyards or olive groves. Therefore it appears that even by AD 79 the city had not yet expanded sufficiently to fill the fifth-century circuit. These discoveries have modified earlier estimates of Pompeii population, which is now thought to have been at most 10,000 instead of the 18,000–20,000 originally envisaged.

The earliest surviving houses of Pompeii date to the third century BC. The House of the Surgeon is representative of the type (fig. 2). It is an atrium house (see p. 32) with a severe, plain façade built of blocks of Sarno limestone, a local porous, yellow-coloured stone with an abrasive surface. This was the most common building material at Pompeii until the end of the third century BC. In the House of the Surgeon there are two types of wall; the façade in ashlar masonry, and the interior walls of 'limestone framework': that is to say the ends of the wall are of limestone blocks and the rest of the wall is of limestone and lava rubble reinforced by big limestone blocks laid alternately vertically and horizontally. In both cases the

57 Pompeii, House of Menander: view of the atrium looking towards the front door

stones are cemented together by clay, which remained the normal bonding material until the later third century BC when mortared rubble came into use.

Houses like the 'House of the Surgeon' are often taken as typical atrium houses, but it should be remembered that excavation has shown that there was no impluvium at this early date. All the evidence points to the impluvium being introduced in the late third or early second century BC. Whether this means that the original atrium of the House of the Surgeon was completely roofed over or was an open courtyard is still to be determined (see p. 33).

Around the end of the third century Pompeii entered the so-called 'tufa period'. The term derives from a new material, the smooth dark tufa from Nuceria, which began to be used on the façades of houses. Interior walls continued to be built of limestone and lava rubble, although by the end of the second century little limestone was used and walls were almost entirely composed of a hard black lava. At the end of the third century houses still followed the old atrium plan, and by now the atrium had the familiar opening in its roof (compluvium) and water tank (impluvium) set in the floor directly beneath (fig. 57). As the second century progressed wealthy Campanians came into contact with Hellenistic ideas, just as the Romans had (see p. 19). This influence is reflected in a new feature, the peristyle (fig. 58), a colonnaded garden which wealthy Pompeians added to the back of their house, either in what had been the garden or by acquiring and demolishing adjacent houses. However,

the time-honoured atrium, replete with family busts, died hard, and it was still not extinct when Pompeii was destroyed.

Perhaps the best-known example of the atrium/peristyle house is the House of the Faun at Pompeii (fig. 59). Covering 0.43 hectares (just over an acre) it is the largest and perhaps the most finely planned Hellenistic house in Pompeii. Most of it was built about 180 BC, and the decoration throughout is in the austerely elegant First Style. Even to the end, this old style of decoration was kept up in the House of the Faun, which explains the rather noble appearance of the house. There are two entrances side by side facing the street. The left-hand door led through an entrance passage (1), with a fine stucco lararium on the wall, into the atrium (2). There were bedrooms only on the left (3–5), the rooms on the right acting as links with the tetrastyle atrium beyond (9). The tablinum (6) was framed between two big square pillars and opened on to the atrium, like the triclinium on its right (8), while a second triclinium on the left (7) opened on to the peristyle beyond. The peristyle has Ionic columns of tufa covered with white stucco and supports a Doric triglyph frieze. The oecus at the far end (13) is perhaps the finest room in the house. The famous Alexander mosaic was found there. Either side are summer dining rooms (14, 15). Behind this peristyle is a second larger peristyle which takes up the whole width of the house. The right-hand side of the house contains the domestic wing which is plainer in its decoration. Beyond the tetrastyle atrium (9) is a long passage (10) walled off from the master's peristyle. Off this

58 Pompeii, House of the Gilded Cupids: view of the peristyle

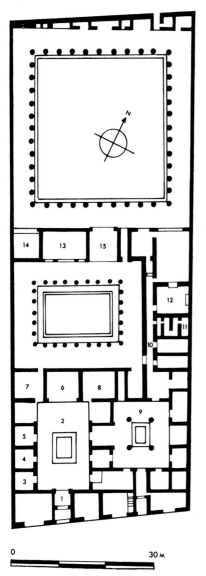

0   30 M

59 Pompeii, House of the Faun, second century BC: plan

passage opens a private bath (11), the earliest known example in Pompeii, and the kitchen (12).

The house is neatly divided into family and service quarters. At the front of the house the formal atrium and the domestic tetrastyle atrium and their ancillary rooms each take up almost exactly half the width of the house and one-third of its depth. The first peristyle and its pleasant light and airy rooms take up another third of the depth, but three-quarters of the width of the house. The service quarters are consequently darker and more cramped. Finally, at the back of the house the second peristyle took up the entire width of the block.

During the second century BC many of the roads leading out of Pompeii began to be lined with extensive suburban residences, a good example of which is the Villa of the Mysteries, situated only 400 metres outside the Herculaneum Gate of Pompeii (fig. 60). It rests upon an artificial platform of earth supported by a concrete cryptoporticus on three sides. From the road one enters first the peristyle, an arrangement prescribed for villas by Vitruvius (*de Arch.*, 6. 5. 3). On the far side of the peristyle is the large Tuscan atrium and beyond this, overlooking the sea, the tablinum. The most elegant rooms are either side of the main atrium. To the south of the peristyle is the kitchen and a small bathing suite which opens off a tetrastyle atrium. A portico of columns ran around the projecting west side of the villa which enjoys a fine panoramic view over the bay. This was pulled down in early Imperial times so that a suite of summer rooms could be added; in the middle a large semicircular room which extended to the edge of the platform, and at either end a summer house. The villa has in all 60 rooms and covers 0.56 hectares (nearly $1\frac{1}{2}$ acres), which means that it is larger in area than the House of the Faun. However, a comparison of their ground plans makes it clear that the villa has a much freer layout than the house.

Towards the end of the second century BC the entire Forum area was replanned. What it looked like before is uncertain, although excavations show that the cult of Apollo had a long history dating back as far as the sixth century BC before the Temple of Apollo was erected in its present form to the west. The original shape of the Forum was somewhat different. Also, the Temple of Apollo is not quite aligned with the present Forum and this may suggest that the latter originally had a somewhat different orientation. The Forum as laid out in the later second century BC is a masterpiece of Hellenistic planning. In shape it is a long rectangle surrounded on three sides by a double portico of tufa columns (fig. 61). The fourth side is dominated by the Temple of Jupiter, also built at this time. The floor level of the surrounding colonnades is two steps higher than that of the central area, thus effectively cutting the square off from wheeled traffic. The Forum was the focal point of the busy town, and in the second century BC a meat and fish market had already been built in its north-east corner. Its plan, with shops behind a colonnade

ENTRANCE

WINE PRESS

KITCHEN

PERISTYLE

BATH

ATRIUM

TABLINUM

SUMMER HOUSE

SUMMER HOUSE

CRYPTOPORTICUS

CRYPTOPORTICUS

0   25 M

running round all four sides of the building and the central circular kiosk, is reminiscent of the markets at Pozzuoli and Lepcis Magna (see p. 36).

The basilica belongs to the same period as the Forum porticoes and the Capitolium (fig. 62). A date before the foundation of the Sullan colony is suggested by Oscan graffiti and roof tiles stamped with the words 'N. Pupie', the name of an Oscan magistrate. The main entrance to the basilica from the Forum is on one of the short

60 Pompeii, Villa of the Mysteries, mainly second century BC with later alterations

61 Pompeii, general view of the Forum. The columns in the foreground belong to the second century BC

62 Pompeii, basilica, late second century BC

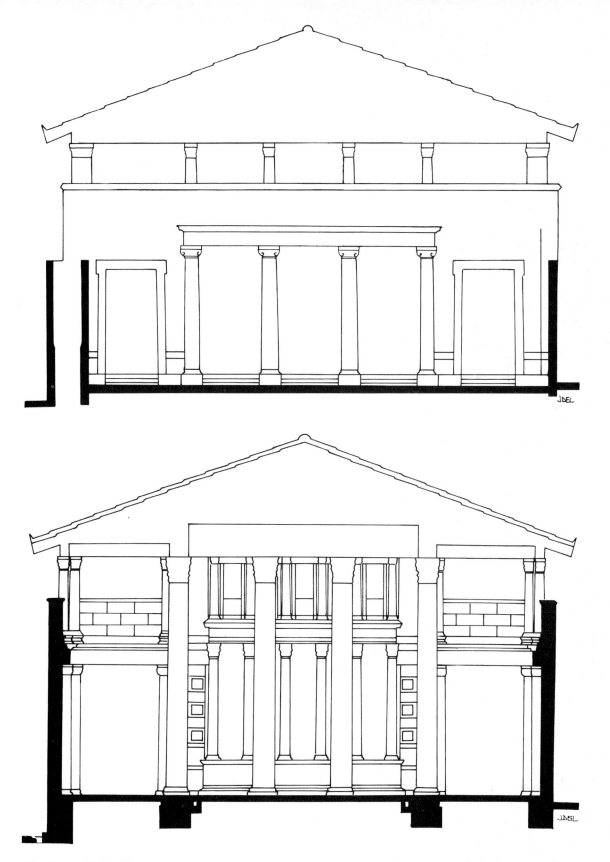

63 Pompeii, basilica, late second century BC: restored elevation and section (after Ohr, *Die Basilika in Pompeji*, Karlsruhe 1973)

sides and the tribunal for the magistrates is at the far end. The entrance façade has five doorways, one either side of a porch of four Ionic columns, and three between the pairs of columns. Internally the building is divided into a nave and aisles by 28 giant order columns whose shafts are made of brick, the earliest known example of this technique at Pompeii. A row of Ionic half-columns about half the height of the giant order is engaged into the side walls. Above these is visible the lowest part of an engaged upper order. Many fragments of free-standing Corinthian columns of the same diameter as the upper order were found near the north wall. Until recently nobody had been able satisfactorily to account for these columns and as a result no proposed elevation of the building was fully convincing. Maiuri for a time accepted Sogliano's theory that the nave was unroofed, but his excavations under the floor of the basilica in 1951 disproved the theory. A recent reconstruction of the building by Ohr solves the problem of the elevation and roofing in a somewhat inelegant fashion (fig. 63). He takes account of the fact that the fragments of Corinthian columns have the same diameter as the upper order of engaged columns, and concludes that the two belong together. This would mean that for half their height they were engaged into a masonry balustrade and above that they were free standing. Thus the building was lit by the spaces between the columns, and there was no clerestory. This solution has precedents in Hellenistic building practice. For example, the upper order of the Stoa of Attalos in Athens, which has Ionic columns engaged for half their height into a balustrade, and the columns which run around the upper part of the atrium in the Samnite house at Herculaneum. However in both these cases the entire shaft is visible on both sides. Ohr's proposed reconstruction has the balustrade masking the lower half of the shafts on the outer elevation.

The second century BC saw much other public building. Improvements were made to the Triangular Forum where the old Doric temple stood. Colonnades were built along the two sides of the triangle, but the third side, which commanded a superb panorama towards the sea, was left open. Another splendid complex, the theatre and quadriporticus, also dates from this period. The quadriporticus was a huge open area bounded on all sides by colonnades of Doric columns, 74 in all, where people could stroll during performances.

The Stabian Baths took their present form during the second century BC, although a bathing establishment had existed on the site since the fourth century BC (fig. 19). Recent excavations have shown that the trapezoidal shape of the palaestra dates back to the fourth century, as do the row of small hip baths to the north of the palaestra. In the second century a complex of bathing rooms was added to the east side of the palaestra (fig. 64). The northern rooms were for women, and the southern for men. The entrance hall leads

to the apodyterion (or undressing room), and thence to the warm and hot rooms. The small circular room was presumably the sudatorium or sweating-room originally, but became the cold-room when the underfloor heating system was installed sometime in the first century BC. Although their decoration and some of the installations were subsequently changed after the earthquake of AD 62 the basic layout belongs to that most fruitful building period in Pompeian history, the second century BC.

The first two decades of the first century BC were a period of considerable upheaval for Pompeii. During the social wars of 90–89 BC the powerfully defended city became a centre of rebellion for the Italians of Campania who were fighting to win Roman citizenship. Pompeii was besieged by Lucius Cornelius Sulla and the damage caused by his artillery can still be seen near the Vesuvius gate. In 80 BC the Pompeians were punished for their stand. Much property was confiscated from the old Italic ruling class and a colony of veterans was established at Pompeii, which was officially renamed Colonia Cornelia Veneria Pompeianorum. The number of new colonists has been variously estimated at between 3,000 and 5,000. For a time the new ruling class came from their ranks, but within a generation or two the old Pompeian families began to edge back into government. Latin became the official language and Roman measures were used for new public buildings. Oscan weights and measures (the Oscan foot is a little shorter than the Roman foot; 100 Oscan to 93 Roman feet), were gradually abandoned. Pompeii, which had hitherto been a prosperous Hellenized Italic town, was now firmly linked to the destinies of Rome.

64 Pompeii, Stabian Baths: the palaestra, second century BC, rebuilt after the AD 62 earthquake

65 Pompeii, Forum Baths: the caldarium showing the *schola labri* at the end

The new buildings put up to mark the foundation of the colony echo its new status. They were the Forum Baths, the small theatre and the amphitheatre, buildings that might be expected to appeal to the veterans newly settled in the town. The baths were similar in layout to the earlier Stabian Baths although rather smaller. They were built of opus quasi-reticulatum, a type of construction then common in Rome. Their plan in many ways resembles that of the Stabian Baths. There is the same apodyterion, tepidarium, caldarium and circular frigidarium. Beside the bathing rooms is a palaestra, and the complex also includes a smaller bathing suite for women. The main difference between the Forum Baths and the earlier Stabian Baths is the way the former fit compactly into a single insula or building block. Most of the actual bathing rooms were relegated to the centre of the block and rows of shops face onto the street on three sides. Entrance to the baths themselves is through dark passageways between shop frontages. It is perhaps in this bathing complex that we gain some idea of the kind of insulae that were being built in Rome at the time of Sulla. The circular room was probably the original sudatorium or sweating-room, like a similar room in the Stabian Baths. However the caldarium (fig. 65) was later provided with a hypocaust system with hollow walls for the circulation of hot air, and furnaces were built in the adjacent room to the west. The circular room consequently became a frigidarium or cold-room as it did in the Stabian Baths. However, the tepidarium was never given under-floor heating and until the end of the city it relied upon its old bronze brazier to heat the room.

The small theatre, probably planned as part of the large theatre and quadriporticus complex, was not actually built until the time of Sulla. One of the magistrates who built it, Marcus Porcius, is also known to have built the amphitheatre, the earliest surviving permanent one in Italy (fig. 66). It is sited in the most easterly corner of the city, presumably because it was a vacant area and also so that it could take advantage of the sloping earthworks against the city walls for the north-east and south-east sides of its *cavea* or auditorium. Artificial earthworks were dug on the north-west and south-west sides. The earthworks were supported on all sides by a continuous sustaining wall which followed the elliptical shape of the arena, although it encompassed a larger area and in fact ran underneath the seats of the *media cavea* or central part of the auditorium. Running parallel with and outside this sustaining wall was the exterior wall of the building. The circulation system of the amphitheatre was primitive. Four staircase systems were built against the outer wall and the spectators of the *summa cavea*, or highest seats, simply clambered up them and found their way to their places. Under these external staircases passageways led under the superstructure to join up with an annular passageway which followed the line of the inner sustaining wall under the media cavea. A clumsy double staircase system then sorted out those whose seats were in the media cavea from the more important magistrates, who occupied the privileged seats of the *ima cavea*.

New methods of construction appeared at Pompeii in the second half of the first century BC. Opus reticulatum came into use, and

66 Pompeii, the amphitheatre, *c.* 80 BC

115

later on was combined with brick cornering to create interesting polychrome effects. Tile facings, which were first used in the small theatre as well as in the door frames of the Forum Baths, became more common during the first century BC. The technique of alternating rows of cut tufa blocks and rows of tiles (*opus listatum*) came in at the time of Augustus, and can be seen in the Vesuvius Gate at Pompeii.

A major project of the Augustan period was the building of an aqueduct system to bring water from the mountain springs near Serino, about 40 kilometres east of Pompeii. The aqueduct brought the water down to the plains at Sarno and then split off into two sections, one serving Neapolis and the other Pompeii. The Pompeii branch entered the city at the Vesuvius Gate where it was fed into the *castellum aquae*, which divided it into three channels and distributed it throughout the town. All over Pompeii there are subsidiary water towers about six metres high with a lead tank on top. Fourteen such towers have been found. The water was carried up them through lead pipes and then a series of smaller lead pipes fed the water to individual houses and public drinking fountains in the vicinity.

The gradual Romanization of Pompeii under the early Emperors is reflected in some of the new buildings in the Forum area. A trio of brick-faced civic buildings was erected on the south side of the Forum; the west one for the *duoviri* or annually elected chief magistrates, the central one the *tabularium* or public records office and the last one the *curia* for meetings of the *decuriones* or council. On the east side of the Forum is the building of Eumachia or the wool market, which dates to the time of Tiberius, although the façade was rebuilt in brick after the earthquake of AD 62. On either side of the main doorway are semicircular apses and beyond these two square recesses. The floors of the latter are raised and lateral staircases lead up to them. It is thought that they were platforms where the auctioneers stood when selling consignments of wool. Just inside the main door, to the right, is a small room where the urine used for cleansers' work was stored in a large terracotta vessel. Inside the building is a large two-storey peristyle with honorary statues in the middle. At the end are three niches, the central and largest one contained a statue of *Concordia Augusta*. A cryptoporticus ran around three sides of the peristyle and there the wool was stored. Other buildings which reflect the Romanization of Pompeii are the Temple of Fortuna Augusta which was dedicated to the five Julio-Claudian Emperors, and the Temple of Vespasian in the Forum. There is little evidence of foreign cults in Pompeii with the exception of the cult of Isis, which was apparently established there in the early first century BC.

In the houses of the early Empire, a greater emphasis was placed upon the peristyle. An example of this is the House of the Vettii where the tablinum has disappeared and the atrium has almost become an ante-room to the large peristyle beyond, onto which all of the main rooms of the house open. Older houses were remodelled during the early Empire to admit more light. The influence was undoubtedly the splendid seaside villas which, significantly, form the subject-matter of many a Third-Style wall painting. It was during the reign of Nero that the seaward façade of the Villa of the Mysteries was opened up with a curved exedra and flanking colonnades. Two houses at Herculaneum, the House of the Stags and the House of the Mosaic Atrium, were terraced out over the old city walls, and gardens with summer belvederes faced the sea. The House of 'Loreius Tiburtinus' at Pompeii is an example of an old atrium house that was entirely remodelled at the rear. A small mosaic- and pumice-lined fountain sends a cascade of water into an ornamental canal which runs almost the whole width of the house. An open-air dining room faces onto this pleasant terraced area which was originally shaded by· vines. From the canal the water cascades down into the garden and flows down a long ornamental conduit which runs the length of the garden. That these houses echoed the spacious country and seaside villas there can be no doubt.

However, despite its apparent prosperity the early first century AD was a time of economic and social change for Pompeii. Already there were signs of a breakdown of the patrician household which for centuries had been a self-sufficient unit based on a rigid master/slave relationship. With the Imperial peace more grain was entering Italy from Egypt and Africa, and at the same time Gaul and Spain were producing more wine and oil. As a result the old independent farm households were less viable than before. Also, as the towns developed and populations increased there was a greater demand for manufactured goods. A man who had baked bread in the house of a patrician master could make more by opening a shop and supplying the entire district. Masters saw the advantage of this and set up emancipated slaves in business in return for a percentage of profits. Division of labour increased and certain goods were mass-produced. For example we know that Pompeii was famous for its garum or fish relish. These businesses made the former slaves who owned them enormously rich. Petronius' character, Trimalchio, the millionaire ex-slave, and Claudius' close advisers, Pallas and Narcissus, are representative of the type.

The disastrous earthquake of AD 62 only aggravated the town's problems. The damage was enormous and the repairs were still in progress when the city was finally destroyed in AD 79. As a result of the earthquake there were few new projects between AD 62 and 79, the Temple of Vespasian in the Forum and the uncompleted Central Baths being the main exceptions. The extent of the damage can be gauged by the number of Fourth-Style paintings found all over Pompeii. The new style came in at the time of Nero and only reached

Pompeii after AD 62, and yet there are far more Fourth-Style paintings than any other style despite the fact that they were all painted in a space of 17 years. Most buildings in the town suffered some damage in the earthquake and the repairs are evident enough. Some houses were abandoned, and only in the amphitheatre and the Temple of Isis were repairs finished by AD 79. An inscription records that a freedman rebuilt the latter in the name of his son, Numerius Popidius Celsinus, a boy six years old, as a means of securing him a seat on the town council. This perhaps reflects the changed social complexion of Pompeii in these years, when many of the older patricians had left the town and newly enriched freedmen began to win political power. It may seem curious that such a temple should have been totally rebuilt at a time when those of the official cults were still in ruins. The explanation may lie in the fact that the cult of Isis was a popular one among the very slaves who now had so much influence.

In the last years of the city many old patrician houses were bought up and subdivided, or turned into lodging houses or commercial premises. Any available room with a street frontage was turned into a small shop. Sometimes a whole house, as for example the Villa of the Mysteries, was turned over to industrial production. In other cases a few rooms of a house were made into a bakery or a fullery. The whole aspect of Pompeian streets was changing as upper storey rooms were added, and balconies and upstairs windows penetrated street façades. One might justly claim that if the eruption of Vesuvius had not occurred in AD 79 the old Pompeii, familiar to us by its fine houses and splendid paintings, might have largely disappeared within the next half century.

Ostia is another well-preserved Roman city, but it was not destroyed by a violent natural catastrophe like Pompeii. It was gradually abandoned until its buildings collapsed one by one. Precious marbles, statues and columns were torn from the decaying buildings to turn up as far away as Pisa and Salerno. For over a millennium the site was one of almost complete desolation and abandonment, until it slowly began to be uncovered in the mid-nineteenth century. The pace of excavation increased in the period 1938–42, when most of the city known today was uncovered.

As Ostia was abandoned gradually there are fewer spectacular finds than at Pompeii, where entire painted rooms, wooden shutters and furniture, and even foodstuffs, regularly turn up. Yet in many ways Ostia is a more typical Roman town than Pompeii, which had deep Oscan roots, and whose people never fully accepted Roman ways. Ostia was the harbour town of Rome, and was thus particularly well-placed to reflect the styles and tastes of the capital. Whereas Pompeii died in AD 79, at a time when architectural and artistic styles were in a process of rapid change, Ostia lived on. The

67 Ostia, general plan

town was practically rebuilt in the second century AD using all the techniques of brick-faced concrete which had been evolved in the course of the first century AD. The typical buildings of Ostia are not sumptuous houses and villas, but tall apartment blocks, baths and warehouses. While Pompeii survives as a leisured country town with elegant, sprawling houses, Ostia was an Imperial port, jammed with the functional housing blocks which must have been a feature of Rome itself. Ostia is therefore a fundamental document of the urban and social changes which took place in the later Empire, and in addition illustrates the whole life of a Roman city from the fourth century BC to the fifth century AD.

Ostia is situated on the south bank of the Tiber close to its mouth, at a distance of about 25 kilometres from Rome. The road that links it with Rome, the Via Ostiensis, leaves the capital through the Porta Trigemina and runs close to the south bank of the river for some 15 kilometres, at which point it meets high ground. This high ground was also the source of Ostia's water supply, as can be seen from the remains of brick piers belonging to an aqueduct of Imperial date. From the high ground the road descends into a marshy plain. This section of the road was laid upon wooden piles driven into the soft subsoil.

Ostia was founded as a defensive fortress to protect Rome's coastline. Marauding bands of Gauls were still active in the area after the great invasion of 390 BC, and in 349 BC Greek fleets had ravaged the coast from Antium to the Tiber estuary. Colonies composed of Roman citizens were established, at Antium in 338, Anxur in 329, and Minturnae in 296 BC. In 311 BC ships were built to patrol the coast, and *quaestores Italici* were placed in charge of naval defences (267 BC). Ostia was part of the series of coastal forts. Although the exact date of its foundation is not known, it can probably be placed between 349 and 338 BC.

The outline of the original *castrum* can still be seen, although the actual walls have largely disappeared (fig. 67). It was rectangular and covered an area of about 2.2 hectares ($5\frac{1}{2}$ acres). The usual two streets, the *decumanus* running east/west, and the *cardo* running north/south, divided the fort into four areas and intersected in the middle, the area where the later Forum was built. Traces of the four gates belonging to the fort have been found under later buildings of the town. The eastern branch of the decumanus led directly to Rome, but the roads to the south and west were somewhat more irregular. As at Pompeii, the line of these roads is preserved in the layout of the later, developed town. It has, however, been suggested that the southern branch of the cardo, which leads away from the castrum in a south-easterly direction, was in fact originally a part of the same road as the Via della Foce which leads out of the Porta Marina or west gate of the castrum in a north-westerly direction. Thus the original Via Laurentina led directly to the mouth of the river, and had to be diverted when the castrum was built. That the original road from Rome followed the line of the eastern decumanus is less likely because the latter is dictated by the siting of the castrum.

At about the time of Sulla (around 80 BC) new walls were built around Ostia enclosing an area of 63.5 hectares (160 acres), or almost 30 times the extent of the original castrum (fig. 67). Such a massive increase in the city limits must mean one of two things: either the city had already expanded beyond the lines of the old castrum by that date; or a great increase in populaton was envisaged. Unfortunately any attempt to gauge the size of pre-Sullan Ostia is hampered by the fact that not all the area around the castrum has yet been excavated, and because much of the area was totally rebuilt in the second century AD. There is very little archaeological evidence of buildings made of permanent materials before the end of the second century BC. However, some painted terracottas were found in the pre-Sullan layers, and these suggest mud-brick buildings with timber roofs. Timber was plentiful in the district and may have been a common building material in the early period of Ostia's growth. So the pre-Sullan town may have been larger than it at first appears. Also, a glance at the area south of the theatre and to the east of the Via dei Molini shows a haphazard street plan which may well date back to an earlier period of uncontrolled building activity. Certainly, towards the end of the second century BC a number of prosperous peristyle and atrium houses were built, and it is also to this period that we must attribute Ostia's first stone temple, the Temple of Hercules. It is perhaps no coincidence that the first signs of prosperity in Ostia came at the time of the Gracchi when the importation of cheap corn and the wars against the Cimbri and Teutones brought prosperity to the harbour town.

The Sullan wall circuit is trapezoidal in shape, and its line is partly dictated by the coastline and the river. The three main gates are the Porta Marina through which the western decumanus runs to the sea-shore, the Porta Laurentina through which the southern cardo runs on its way south, and the Porta Romana which marks the end of the eastern decumanus and the beginning of the Via Ostiensis. During the last century of the Republic, atrium and peristyle houses continued to be built, and porticoes on tufa piers began to appear along some of the main streets. Perhaps the most important development of the period was the rebuilding of the north-east corner of the town. The land adjacent to the river was declared public property by the Roman praetor, and the whole area re-planned on orderly lines. The regular planning of the area north of the eastern decumanus contrasts starkly with the haphazard development south of it, where private building had run amok during the Republic. Even the four late Republican temples just west of where the theatre was later built are planned in a neat and orderly

68 Ostia, plan of the Claudian and Trajanic harbours

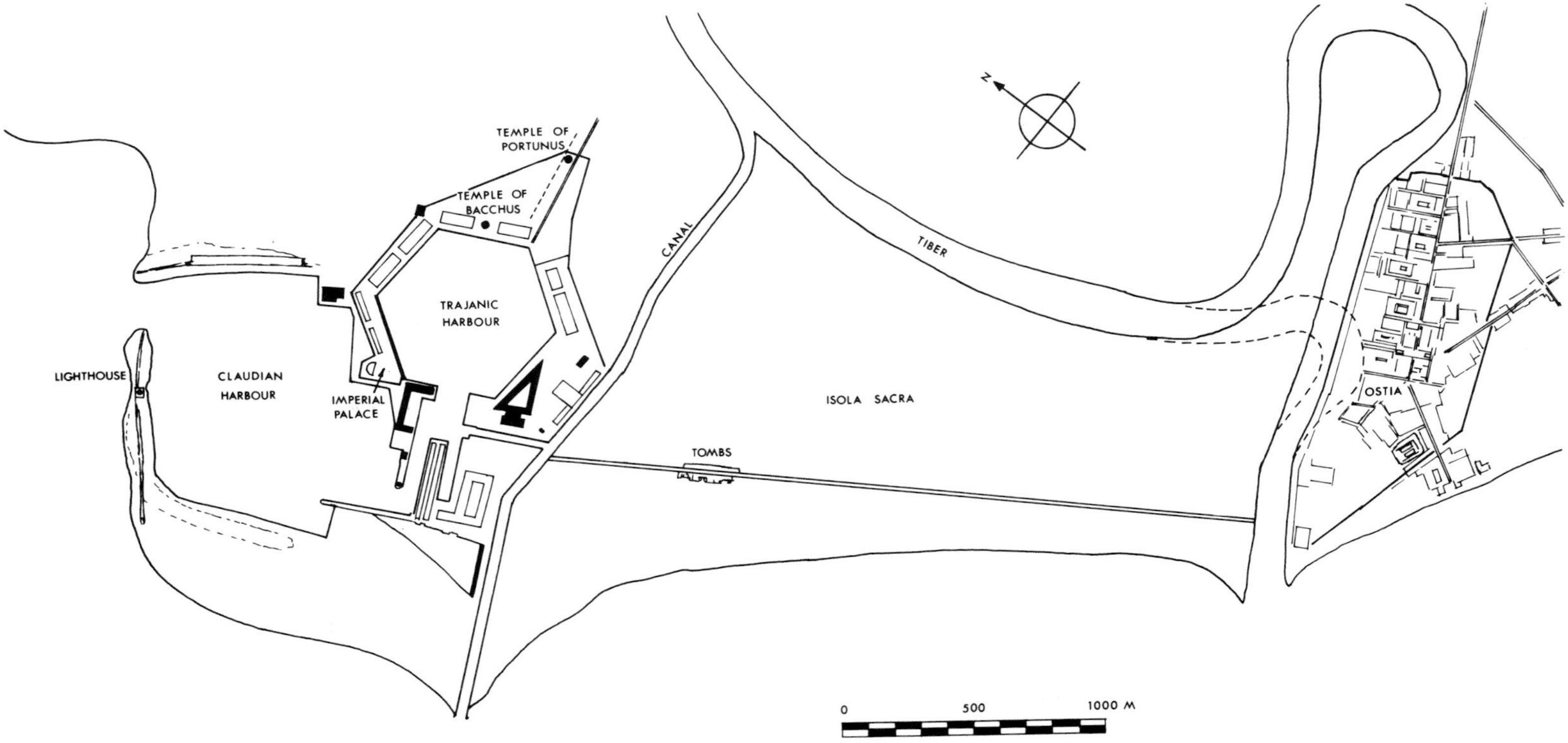

TIBER

CANAL

ISOLA SACRA

TOMBS

N

0   500   1000 M

TEMPLE OF PORTUNUS

TEMPLE OF BACCHUS

TRAJANIC HARBOUR

IMPERIAL PALACE

CLAUDIAN HARBOUR

LIGHTHOUSE

OSTIA

fashion. At some time during the late Republic or the early Augustan period the centre of the old castrum where the cardo and decumanus meet was cleared of buildings and laid out as the Forum. At the south end a temple of Rome and Augustus was built. It is hexastyle and is raised on a high podium. Like the Temple of Divine Julius in the Roman Forum it had a rostra in front of the porch, and access to the podium was by two lateral staircases. Like buildings in Rome it was sheathed in Carrara marble, and the sculptures were done by artists brought from the capital.

The river harbour at Ostia had become increasingly inadequate during the later Republic because of the bigger merchant ships used, the growing volume of shipping and the narrowness of the river (it was only 100 metres wide where it flowed past Ostia). The mouth of the river, too, was beginning to silt up and the resultant sand-bar was a hazard to shipping. Julius Caesar planned a harbour at Ostia, but the project was dropped, and it was not until the time of Claudius that the idea was revived. The reaction of the Emperor's architects was that the scheme would be prohibitively expensive, and they tried to dissuade him (Dio Cassius, 60. 11. 3). However, the Emperor persisted and excavation work for the harbour began in AD 42 at a spot four kilometres north of the harbour mouth (fig. 68). A huge shallow basin about 1,100 metres wide was cut out of the coastline and extended into the sea by two curving moles. Also, a canal was built to link the harbour directly with a bend in the Tiber. This canal had the important secondary effect of providing an extra outlet for the river and helping protect Rome from flooding. The two moles were built of enormous travertine blocks each weighing six or seven tonnes, tied together by iron clamps. In the middle of the left mole was built a lighthouse which rested upon the ship which Caligula had built to bring the great obelisk from Heliopolis for his circus (see p. 92). Pliny (*Natural History*, 16. 202) describes this ship as having carried a ballast of 800 tonnes of lentils and as having a main mast that could be spanned only by four men linking arms. A ship of such dimensions using ancient construction methods seemed an impossibility until recent excavations revealed parts of the ship and the famous lighthouse (fig. 69). The ship was 104 metres long, 20.30 metres wide and had six decks. Its displacement was 7,400 tonnes and it must have been manned by a crew of 700 or 800 men. The hulk was filled with concrete and sunk to provide the foundations for the lighthouse. Sadly, the Claudian harbour was not a success. Tacitus (*Annals*, 15. 18. 3) records that in AD 62 200 vessels in the harbour were destroyed by a storm. Other ancient sources make it clear that the Alexandrian corn fleet still continued to dock at Puteoli even when the Claudian harbour was complete, no doubt to avoid the hazardous sea passage to Ostia and the dangers that lurked even in the harbour itself. Indeed Nero planned a canal from Lake Avernus (near Puteoli) to Ostia, with the intention

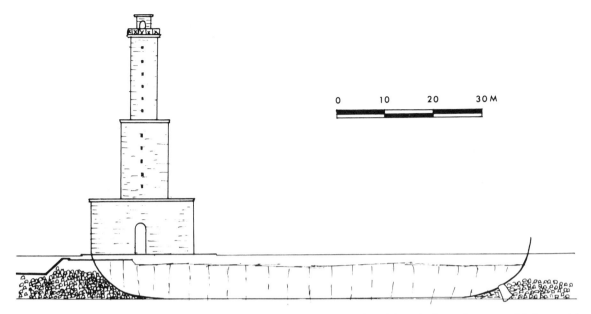

0   10   20   30 M

69 Sketch to illustrate the lighthouse at Ostia resting upon the hull of Caligula's galley (after O. Testaguzza)

of providing Rome's corn supply with a sheltered route which would avoid the stormy west coast, and the harbour at Ostia. The problems of providing a safe harbour for Rome and securing Rome's corn supply were not resolved until the time of Trajan.

Trajan excavated an enormous hexagonal basin inland of the old harbour to the south-east (fig. 68). The two harbours were linked by a canal which was essentially a rebuilding of the old Claudian canal. A second canal, again based on an earlier one, ran to the south of the harbour and linked a bend of the Tiber with the sea and the harbour. The basin itself was of huge dimensions with a maximum diameter of 700 metres. It was surrounded by large concrete *horrea* or warehouses. In type they differ from earlier Ostian warehouses in that the rooms are not grouped around a central courtyard. Instead they have two rows of rooms back-to-back, probably to save space. One of these warehouses on the south-east side of the basin had a raised floor which suggests that it was used for storing grain, and a ramp led up to the floor above. Into the embankment walls of the harbour was set a row of travertine mooring posts and there were probably facilities for over 100 ships. Along the quay were found numbered columns which probably correspond to the mooring berths. In this way gangs of men could easily be allotted to particular ships. Other monuments around the harbour basin include a building complex in which much fine statuary was found. The complex, which lies on the west side of the harbour at a point where it commands views of both Trajan's and Claudius' harbour, is often called the 'Imperial Palace'. Its position, fine reticulate construction and amenities, including a bath building, may well prove the attribution to be a correct one, although Lugli has argued that it is in fact the Forum of the town of Portus. In the centre of the north-east side is a circular temple of Bacchus who appears in the well-known Torlonia harbour relief. Nearby were found fragments of a colossal statue of Trajan in military dress. As it was so far from Ostia a small settlement grew up around the harbour and seems to have been concentrated to the south and east of the basin. The eastern area was enclosed in a tight triangular wall in the time of Constantine. At its apex was a third-century circular temple, commonly known as the Temple of Portunus. The main gate through which the Via Portuense ran lay close to the temple. Beside the road ran an aqueduct, large portions of which have recently been discovered.

The construction of these harbour facilities led to a wave of new buildings at Ostia which began in Trajan's reign and was largely completed by the time of Antoninus Pius. The volume of goods which now passed through Ostia was the reason for its prosperity, which is reflected in the more or less total rebuilding of the old town. The architectural revolution in Rome (see p. 102) had occurred at the time of Nero, but its effects only reached Ostia during the reign of Domitian, just in time for the influx of new wealth.

The western parts of Ostia were radically transformed under Trajan. The whole area between the Via della Foce and the river was rebuilt, as well as the buildings in the extreme west of the town by the river mouth. The eastern part of the town would have presented a great contrast to the brick-faced Trajanic work. The eastern decumanus was still lined with the tufa temples and houses of the Republic along with some reticulate walls of the early empire.

In the reign of Hadrian even more radical transformations took place, and half of the surviving remains of Ostia date from this period. Two areas were completely replanned: the area between the Forum and the river, and the area north of the eastern decumanus and east of the theatre. Both areas were public property and required not only clear, logical planning but also dignity. A large Capitolium was laid out at the northern end of the Forum (fig. 70). Brick-built and sheathed in marble, it was raised on a high podium, presumably so that it could dominate the tall surrounding blocks. Interestingly, the total height of the building to the apex of the gable is 70 Roman feet (21 metres), which suggests that the surrounding buildings were built to the full 60 Roman feet allowed in the Trajanic building regulations (*Epit. de Caes.*, 13).

A radical replanning of the northern cardo provided a monumental approach to the Forum from the river. The point where the cardo met the river was a landing place of importance where the Emperor or any visiting dignitary would land. The road from the river to the Capitolium was laid out on broad, straight lines and was flanked by brick porticoes. The whole adjacent area was also rebuilt at that time.

The large-scale rebuilding under Hadrian was greatly facilitated

70 Ostia, the Capitolium, *c.* AD 120–130

71 Ostia, Forum Baths: the frigidarium, *c.* AD 160

by the expansion of the brick industry (see p. 77), and by the end of Hadrian's reign reticulate work had entirely disappeared. Late in his reign another section of the town, the area east of the theatre, was rebuilt. New buildings included the Baths of Neptune and the barracks of the *vigiles*, along with a brick portico to flank the adjacent stretch of the eastern decumanus. By the middle of the second century AD the city was almost fully built up. There were few open spaces except the public gardens behind the theatre. Even the four temples west of the theatre were surrounded by buildings.

Demolition and rebuilding went on in Antonine times, but the pace had begun to slacken. Perhaps the most interesting buildings of the period are the baths. At Pompeii there were only two public baths until the final years of the city, when the Central Baths were begun. In Ostia 18 public baths have been excavated, a reflection on the changing bathing habits of Romans during the Empire. Some of them are large and imposing structures, for example the Forum Baths (fig. 75), built at the time of Antoninus Pius. The frigidarium (fig. 71) is conservative in its layout, with eight columns supporting a vaulted roof and cold plunges to north and south. However, the series of warm and hot rooms which project boldly out from the lines of the old castrum are more interesting. The most westerly is octagonal and presents four big windows to the afternoon sun, which, in the absence of heating pipes in the walls, suggests that it was a *heliocaminus* or sun room of the type found at Hadrian's villa. The oval room next to it has a bench against the walls, underfloor heating and heated walls: therefore it was probably a sweating room. Next are two warm rooms with big windows, and at the end a large caldarium or hot room. The irregular triangle to the south of the baths was left open as a palaestra. It was presumably one more welcome open space in an increasingly crowded city centre.

Other interesting buildings of the Antonine period are the School of Trajan, with its apsidal hall and long nymphaeum running the whole length of the garden. Also built at this time were the House of Diana and the Horrea Epagathiana, with its remarkable dressed-brick doorway (fig. 74). As the second century progressed the tempo of building slowed even further. A little building went on in the area between the eastern decumanus and the river. The great Granary was rebuilt under Commodus, and the Augustan theatre was rebuilt in brick and re-opened at the beginning of the reign of Septimius Severus.

At this point we should pause and look at the housing blocks and warehouses which are such a conspicious feature of second-century AD Ostia. Tall buildings had existed in Rome since the third century BC as we know from Livy's tale (21. 62. 3) about an ox finding its way up to a third storey of a house in the Forum Boarium. What was a necessity for the poor later became a fashion for the rich. By the end of the Roman Empire there were 25 insulae to every domus in

72 Ostia, insula, second century AD

73 Ostia, one block of the Garden Houses (above), and the Insula of Diana, later second century AD (below)

Rome. Insulae, or apartment blocks, also existed in Pompeii, and in its final years Pompeii was undergoing changes which might have transformed it into a city more like second-century Ostia instead of the leisured, sprawling town that has survived. However, Ostia lived on to meet the demands of the second century AD, when scarcity of space made tall buildings a necessity.

The Ostian insulae probably reflected Roman models. They were built of brick-faced concrete which was designed to be seen and not covered with stucco. The rather severe façades are often relieved by a doorway of decorative brick or a balcony (fig. 72). In the absence of good window glass, lighting was a problem which greatly occupied architects. Big windows faced the street and the inner courtyards which formed the centre of the blocks. The House of Diana is a convenient example of a typical insula (fig. 73). It will be seen from the ground plan that only the west and south sides of the building faced onto the street. The other two sides of the block abutted against other buildings and could draw no light from those sides. Therefore the architect has placed a courtyard to light the rooms on the north and east sides. On the street frontages there were shops on the ground floor and staircases led up to the apartments on the upper floors. In the centre of the courtyard was a water cistern which served all the residents. Lavatories were scarce in insulae, usually only one on each floor. The height of some of these blocks must have been considerable to judge by the Trajanic regulations banning buildings over 60 Roman feet. The number of storeys in such a block can be roughly calculated by the thickness of the walls at ground

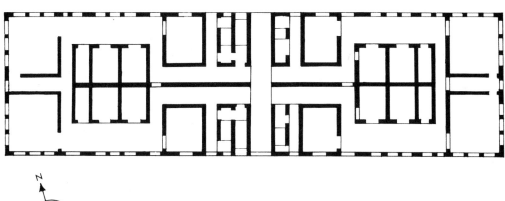

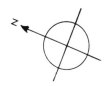

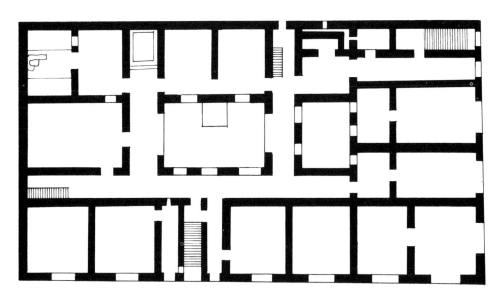

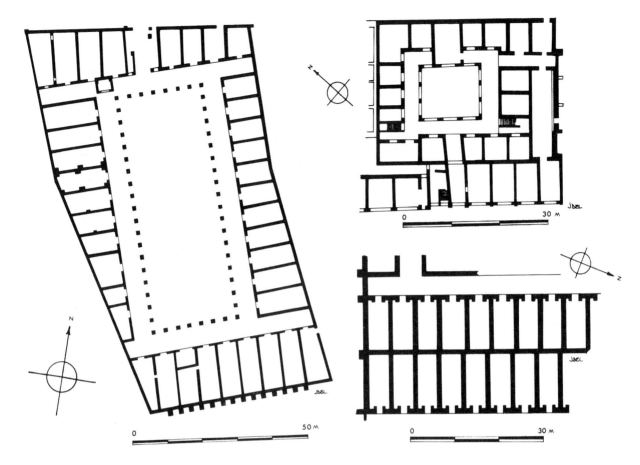

74 Ostia, Horrea of
Hortensius, granary
c. AD 30–40: plan (left);
Ostia, Horrea
Epagathiana, warehouse
c. AD 145–150: plan
(right, above); Ostia,
Antonine Horrea: plan
(right, below)

level. For example a wall 50 cm thick suggests two storeys, 80 cm four storeys and 95 cm five storeys.

The so-called Garden Houses represent an interesting planned development. Here two identical housing blocks are set in a large garden. Each block (fig. 73) is divided by a corridor into two halves and in each half are two entirely self-contained housing units back to back. Six outside staircases lead to the upstairs apartments.

There is a large concentration of warehouses, mainly on the river side of Ostia. Their capacity is clearly greater than the needs of Ostia itself would warrant. Most of them were designed to store grain until it was required in Rome. The grain warehouses usually have raised floors for dryness, and conform to two types. One type has a number of rooms on four sides of a colonnaded courtyard (fig. 74). The second type, which eventually superseded the first, has rows of rooms back to back and thus made more economical use of space. Not all the warehouses were for grain; some were for the storage of oil, wine and other commodities. Local traders and the representatives of overseas shippers had offices in Ostia. Sixty-one such offices were found in the Piazzale delle Corporazioni behind the theatre. On the floor in front of each shop is a mosaic explaining the

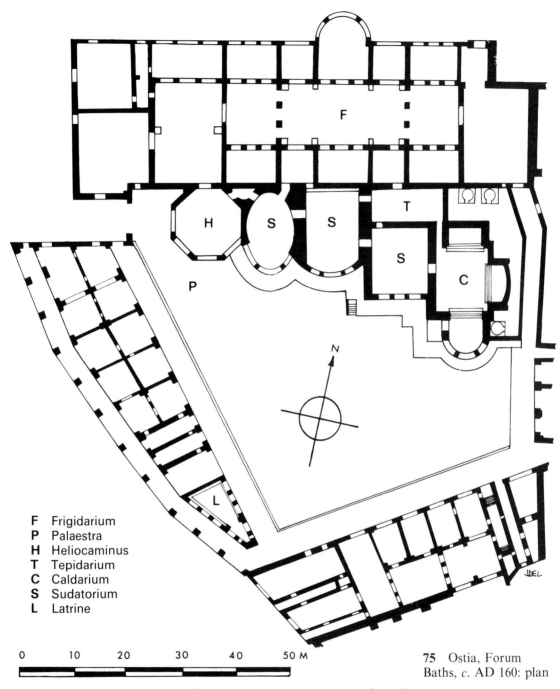

F Frigidarium
P Palaestra
H Heliocaminus
T Tepidarium
C Caldarium
S Sudatorium
L Latrine

0   10   20   30   40   50 M

75 Ostia, Forum
Baths, *c.* AD 160: plan

nature of the business. Many of them represent the corn trade and symbols associated with Africa are common. One mosaic bears the words '*stat(io) Sabratensium*' and an elephant, a reference to the town of Sabratha in Tripolitania.

As a seaport Ostia attracted a wide range of foreign traders and businessmen. The cosmopolitan nature of Ostia is reflected in the wide range of religious buildings found there. As well as a large number of conventional temples there is evidence of a flourishing Imperial cult, as well as buildings devoted to the cults of Cybele and Isis. A large number of mithraea have been found, mainly dating to the later second and the third centuries. Even a synagogue has been found dating to the first century AD with evidence that it was still in use in the fourth century AD.

Most of the Severan era was devoted to the restoration of baths and granaries, but in the middle of this quiet period an exceptionally ambitious project was begun, the Round Temple. It is difficult to explain such a scheme at this late date (suggested dates are in the region of AD 222–244). At a time of declining wealth it would almost certainly have been the product of Imperial patronage, either by Alexander Severus or Gordian III whose father lived at Ostia. The temple, sited just west of the Forum, is essentially a smaller version of the Pantheon with its circular drum, pierced by alternately round and square exedras, supporting a dome. A large, rectangular, colonnaded courtyard was built in front of the temple and provided another much-needed open space in the congested central area.

As land prices dropped in the third century, more open spaces were created, such as the small square south of the eastern decumanus and east of the Forum. A second square, the Piazzale della Vittoria, was created just inside the Porta Romana.

Ostia remained a prosperous city up to the time of the Severans, but as Imperial trade ran down in the third century people began to move to the harbour, at first called Portus Ostiae, then Portus Romae and finally Portus, when it became an independent authority. Excavations in the area between the decumanus and the river give a dismal impression of impoverishment in the late Empire. However, in other parts of the town there is evidence that many large houses were kept up and several new ones built as land values dropped and senatorial families with big households moved in. Often walls of old insulae were re-used to save money, but the new houses were quite lavish in their interior decoration and use of space. The House of Amor and Psyche is a good example of a late Imperial Ostian domus (fig. 76). A vestibule containing two rows of benches for waiting visitors leads into a wide colonnaded passage running the length of the house. To the left are three rooms with floors and walls lined with polychrome marble. At the end of the corridor is an ample *oecus* with marble-lined walls and *opus sectile* floor. In an angle was a staircase which led to an upper storey which probably only extended over the four smaller rooms. Nearly half the ground area of the house is taken up by an open garden. Against the back wall is a row of five round-headed fountain niches lined with marble and glass mosaic.

In AD 314 Constantine stripped Ostia of her municipal rights and transferred them to Portus, which henceforth became the seat of the bishopric. Even so Ostia retained a measure of prosperity throughout the fourth century. Opulent houses were still built and the baths kept in repair until the end of the century, when civic authority began to break down. By AD 414 the poet Rutilius wrote that the only glory remaining to Ostia was the glory of Aeneas who, legend says, landed there. By the sixth century only a few inhabitants lived in the ruins of buildings, half-demolished and stripped of their marble. The dead were buried in the baths and the theatre. The road from Rome to Ostia was overgrown and the Tiber a river without boats. No longer the port of Rome, little attempt was made to defend it from barbarian incursions. Finally, the area became malarial and was abandoned.

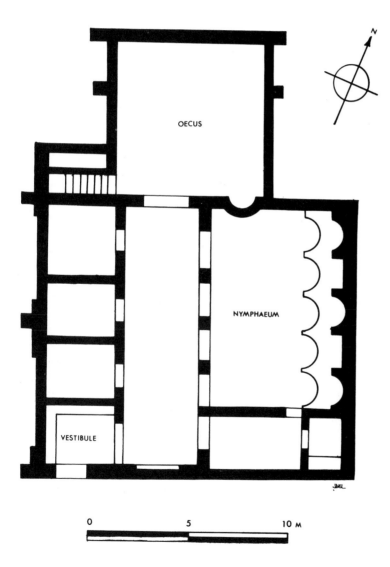

OECUS

NYMPHAEUM

VESTIBULE

0   5   10 M

76 Ostia, House of Amor and Psyche *c.* AD 300: plan

7 The Flavians

The Colosseum dominates the Flavian period. It was the biggest amphitheatre of its age or any age, and has come almost to sum up Roman architectural achievement. In spite of this, it is not a strikingly novel building when measured against the standards of the 'new architecture' (see p. 86). Rather it should be considered as a monument to sheer Roman organizational ability. Despite its enormous size, it was actually inaugurated five years after it was begun. It is also important because it reflected the outlook of Rome's new Emperor, Vespasian.

Vespasian, commander of the field forces in Palestine, was proclaimed Emperor by the eastern armies in AD 69, and marched on Rome. The new Emperor was a blunt, down-to-earth man whose solid middle-class character is well reflected in contemporary portrait busts. He was a man of the people and also proved to be a shrewd politician. The Colosseum, his greatest monument and still unfinished at his death, was a building for the people built by a man who understood something of their tastes and needs.

But this was not Vespasian's only architectural achievement in Rome. In fact in his short reign (he died in AD 79) he did more than any other Emperor since Augustus to add to the monuments of Rome's centre. He completed the Temple of Claudius on the Caelian hill and rebuilt the Capitoline temple. He also built the Temple of Peace, sometimes known as the Forum of Vespasian. It was begun in AD 71 and dedicated in AD 75, to commemorate his victory over the Jews. Destroyed in the fire of AD 192 it was restored by Septimius Severus and in one of its halls was placed the famous marble plan of Rome which measured 18.10 metres wide and 13 metres high.

The temple was an apsidal hall facing onto a large rectangular enclosure measuring 110 × 135 metres and surrounded by colonnades. The six columns of the temple façade were on the same line as the surrounding colonnades and were distinguished from the latter only by being higher. The apsed hall of the macellum at Pozzuoli had a similar relationship to the colonnade and we may see an echo of this treatment in the garden façade of the House of the Stags at Herculaneum. Presumably the lower entablatures of the

flanking colonnades would have been carried on brackets projecting from the taller columns of the temple, in the manner of a Rhodian peristyle such as are found, for example, in some Hellenistic houses at Delos. The complex was built in what was at the time the only remaining free space in the area north-east of the Forum. The area was more congested than it seems today because until the time of Domitian (see p. 147) a spur of land linked the Capitoline hill with the Quirinal and ran close to the Forum Julium and the Forum of Augustus, and another spur ran from the Palatine across to the Esquiline immediately to the south of the Temple of Peace (the latter spur, the Velia, was cut away in 1933 to make way for the road now known as the Via dei Fori Imperiali). On the site of the Temple of Peace there had formerly stood a meat market (macellum), but Nero had recently built a new market on the Caelian hill. As the Temple of Peace closely resembles meat markets such as those at Pompeii and Pozzuoli in layout it is possible that it may have followed the old market's plan to some extent.

77 Rome, Colosseum, AD 75–80

But these buildings, although important to the urban layout of Rome, must take second place to that most important of Vespasian's buildings, the Flavian amphitheatre or Colosseum (the name 'Colosseum' dates from the eighth century AD and refers to its size, or possibly is a confusion with the colossal statue of Nero which stood close by). It was built on the site of the lake of Nero's Golden House, a master stroke, as Vespasian was seen to be creating a place of public resort out of a tyrant's palace. Also, the sub-soil was very firm and compact and thus ideal for the huge weight of the building which measures 188×156 metres $\times 48.5$ metres high.

78 Rome, Colosseum, inaugurated in AD 80: plans, sections and sectional view (from A. Boethius, *op. cit.*)

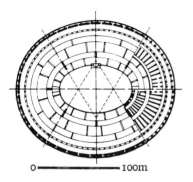

0 ———————— 100m

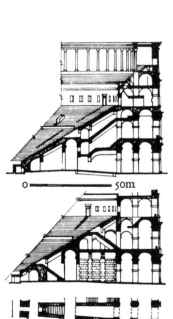

0 ———— 50m

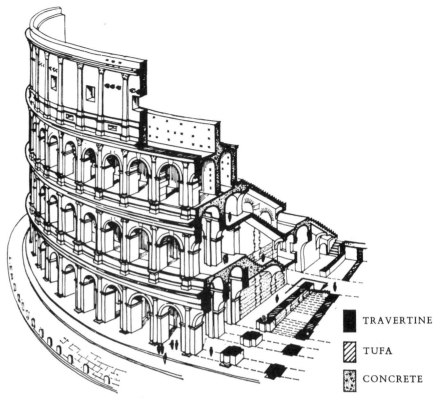

TRAVERTINE

TUFA

CONCRETE

It was the first large permanent amphitheatre in Rome, although gladiatorial spectacles had been popular in the city for over 300 years. It is estimated to have had a capacity of 45,000–55,000 spectators. The façade (fig. 77), built of travertine, has 80 arched openings at ground level, flanked by Tuscan half-columns. Above are two further tiers of openings also decorated with half-columns, Ionic and Corinthian respectively, and the top storey is decorated with Corinthian pilasters flanking alternate square openings and plain walls, originally decorated with bronze shields. Immediately behind the lowest three storeys are two rings of annular passageways from which run radial passages leading to the main annular passage (fig. 78). Further radial passages lead on to the innermost annular passage.

The system of circulation was exceptionally clear and logical. A fine triple entrance on the south side gave access to the consul's box, which was situated at the edge of the arena in the middle of one long side; a similar entrance on the north side gave access to the emperor's box which faced the consul's. The gladiators entered from

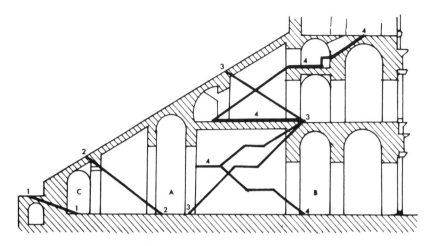

79 Rome, Colosseum:
diagram to illustrate the
staircase system (above);
and section to illustrate
the building procedure
(below) (after Cozzo,
Ingegneria romana,
Rome 1928)

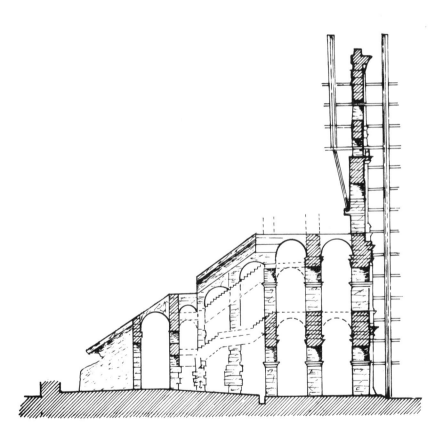

80 Rome, Colosseum: view of the seating, part of the arena and the animal cages underneath

one of the short sides and the bodies were carried out through the Porta Libitinaria opposite. Each of the 76 entrances had a number carved over the arch. Admission was by ticket and the use of wooden barriers would have ensured orderly circulation throughout the building. The door by which the spectator entered determined the segment in which he would sit. Women, banished by the Lex Roscia (67 BC) to the highest seats at the back of theatres and amphitheatres, would have gone no further than passage B (fig. 79) where staircases would take them directly up to their rows of seating within that segment (section 4). Men of the lower ranks could proceed to passage A where staircases would take them to the upper block of seating (section 3) above the big annular gallery which separated the upper classes from the lower. Men of higher rank proceeded up the staircases on the opposite side of the passage to reach the lower block of seating (section 2). Those of the highest ranks, including knights or senators, would have proceeded straight through to the innermost annular passage, C, where a small ramp led them to the arena-side seats (fig. 80).

The materials needed to build this vast structure included 100,000 cubic metres of travertine alone. It is calculated that 300 tons of iron were needed to clamp the blocks together. An army of masons, blacksmiths, bronze workers, marble workers, and construction workers must have been engaged on the building. It has been suggested that the Colosseum was built by captives from the Jewish war. However, the structure of the building is so complex that an

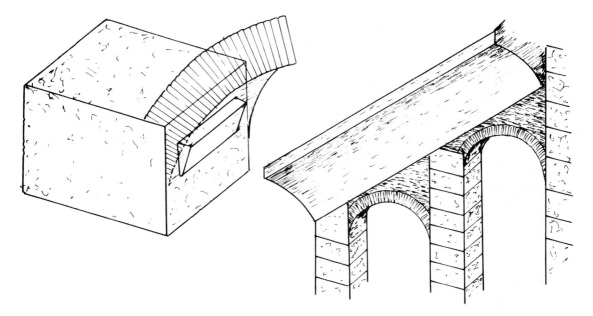

unskilled labour force could hardly have been used on the building itself, although such men could have been used in ancillary occupations such as transporting the stone from the Tivoli quarries (it is calculated that up to 200 ox-carts of stone entered Rome each day during the period of its construction). A more real problem is how such a building could have been inaugurated by Titus in AD 80 although it could not have been started by Vespasian until AD 75.

An answer has been given by penetrating analysis of the building by the Italian engineer, Giuseppe Cozzo. Cozzo showed that the enormous number of workmen required to build such a vast structure in so short a time could not physically have worked on the building at the same time if it was built by conventional methods. Therefore the architect must have worked out a method of erecting a skeleton structure in many ways analogous to modern concrete or steel-framed buildings. Cozzo shows that only the two lowest orders of the exterior were actually completed by the time of Vespasian's death, and that only the barest skeleton of the building was finished by that time (fig. 79). The method of work was to erect the outer travertine walls up to the top of the second order and the two concentric walls behind them. In the radial passages leading towards the arena Cozzo has isolated a number of travertine piers which run straight up through the structure quite independently of the walling between them. When these piers reached the point where they were to support the vaults which carry the sloping staircases a concealed springing was left in the stone (fig. 81). Instead of building the vault at this stage the pier was continued until it had reached its highest projected point, i.e. where it supported the seating. When the piers reached their full height the topmost vaults were built, but not the

81 Rome, Colosseum: drawing to illustrate the concealed springings in the travertine piers (left), and (right) the completed brick arches supporting a sloping barrel-vault (after Cozzo, *Ingegneria romana*, Rome 1928)

139

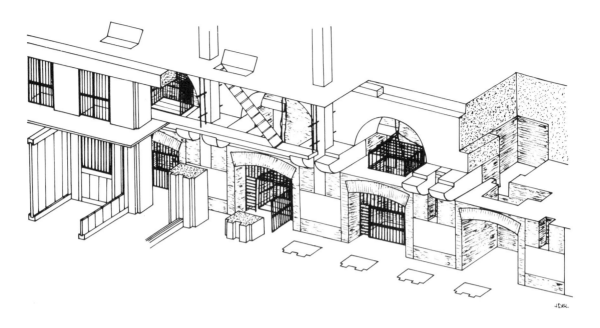

82 Rome, Colosseum: reconstruction of the system of animal cages beneath the arena floor (after Cozzo, *Ingegneria romana*, Rome 1928)

lower ones (fig. 79). Next, brick arches were built linking the piers (fig. 81) and on these were constructed the sloping barrel vaults which supported the banks of seats. Thus, in a very short time, a covered skeletal structure was put up. Meanwhile, further gangs of men could be employed filling in the spaces between the piers, building staircases and the lower sets of vaults on the springings provided. An advantage of this mixture of materials in the interior is that it extended the working season. Unlike masonry, which can be quarried and worked at any time of the year, concrete is adversely affected by extremes of temperature, and in particular below about 10° C the time taken for it to set increases and the strength obtained decreases quite remarkably. The Romans were quite aware of this, as Frontinus says they could only repair the aqueducts between 1 April and 1 November (*de aquis*, 123).

Probably work on the infilling and building of staircases had begun by the time Titus succeeded his father as Emperor, and Titus also built the third tier of the façade. The fact that the vaults at the level of the top of the second storey had been built immediately had a dual advantage. Firstly, the workmen busy on the infilling could work under cover. Secondly the top of the vault provided a flat platform on which materials for the upper parts of the building could be stored. Only the actual façade wall was built by Titus and not the concentric walls behind. This was because no vaulting could be built on the third tier at this stage. The reason for this was that scaffolding had to be built to support the topmost parts of the building. On the inner side of the piers of the third storey huge projecting corbels were left to support the scaffolding on the inside of the building (fig. 79). Despite the fact that coins of the period show four rows of arches it is probable that only three tiers of arches were actually completed when the building was inaugurated by Titus in AD 80.

The inauguration was accompanied by a sea-battle held in the old *naumachia*, built by Augustus near the Tiber according to Suetonius (*Titus*, 7. 3). This passage has often been taken to mean that the Colosseum itself was flooded for sea-battles, an interpretation based on the assumption that the Colosseum arena was solid at the time of the inauguration and that the rooms below the arena floor were built at a later date. Yet the only literary authority to state that the sea battle was actually held in the Colosseum is Dio Cassius (*Ep.*, 66. 25) and this is very possibly a confused account. It does however make good sense to suppose that the rooms below the arena were a later addition because the flat arena floor would have been an ideal place for the storerooms, huts and masonry dumps which would have been needed during the building operations.

Domitian completed the building, adding the topmost storey of the façade. In alternate bays there was a big bronze shield, and a square window. Cozzo suggests that the smaller square openings at the bottom of the bays containing the shields were used in the construction period to support the transverse beams linking the outer and inner tiers of scaffolding (figs. 77, 79). Domitian built the topmost storey of seating, *summum Maenianum*, of wood, presumably so that the thrust should not be too great.

Domitian was probably responsible for the maze of substructures under the arena. Around the edge of the arena are 32 cells in which the animals were kept. The system of caging the animals and bringing them up to the arena at the right moment well illustrates Roman ingenuity in spite of limited technology. The animals were brought in by means of underground passages under the short ends of the arena. Each segment underneath was completely separate and contained eight cages close to the edge of the arena (fig. 80). The animals were driven along a narrow passageway only 55 cm wide which did not allow them to turn around (fig. 82). Handlers could manipulate the cell doors so that they went into the correct cells, and then the doors of the cells were shut.

Inside the cell was a cage which consisted of a bottom, three sides and a top to which was attached the tackle for hauling it up to the upper level. The cell door itself provided the front of the cage and prevented the animal escaping. The projecting brackets above the cell served the double purpose of supporting the posts of the safety net at arena level and carrying the wooden beams of the intermediate floor below arena level. In the back of the upper part of each cell was a small room in which the beast handlers took up their positions immediately before the animals were due to appear in the arena. Here they could control the tackle designed to hoist the cages up to

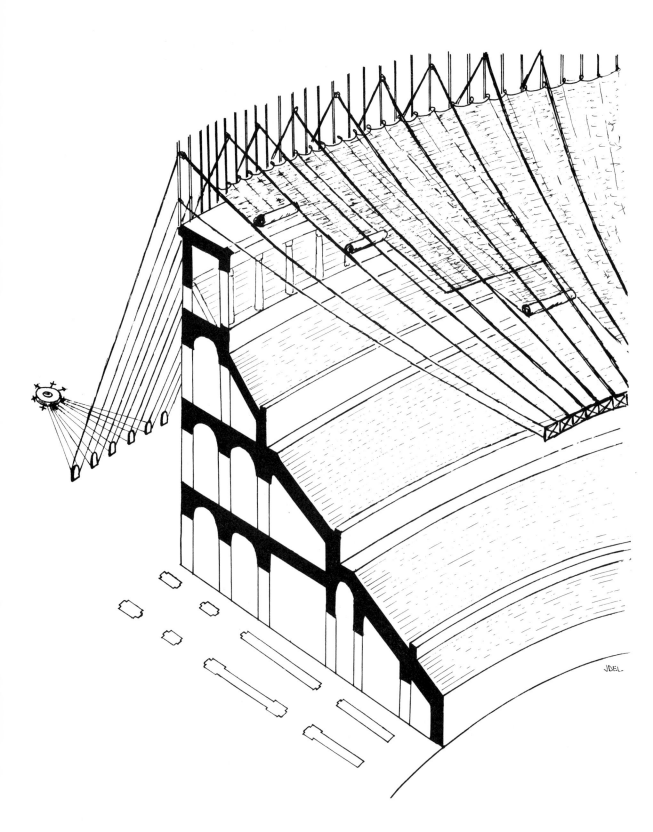

JDEL

the upper part of the cell. The system was a very neat one because the handlers could move about in perfect safety on the upper level while the animals were down below. Then at the given signal they took up position in their small rooms at the back of the cell and hauled the animal up. As the cage had only three sides the animal was free once the cage reached the upper level. Its only way of escape, however, was into a narrow passageway corresponding to the 55 cm passage along which it had been driven below. Iron gates no doubt prevented the animal wandering to the next cage. Its instinct would lead it to rush up the ramp and through the trapdoor into the light of the arena above. The operation must have been conducted very quickly and quietly. In a well-managed show all 32 animals would appear in the arena practically simultaneously.

If the animals could appear so rapidly in the arena, the scenery, which was a conspicuous feature in the centre of the arena, could appear and disappear with equal efficiency. The secret was a series of huge hinged platforms in the middle of the arena. Vast sloping masonry supports can still be seen in the wide gallery running through the middle of the arena. On these were built great hinged wooden platforms, *pegmata*, on which the scenery was mounted. They were designed so that the hinged end was immediately below arena level and the other end was about five metres below arena level. Thus, scenery up to five metres high could be built. Also, the slope meant that the effort required to haul the platform up to arena level was not very great, especially with the aid of counter weights.

One final feature of the Colosseum which is never mentioned by ancient authors is the huge *velarium* or canvas awning which protected the spectators from the heat of the sun. Such velaria are known to us from paintings like that of the amphitheatre at Pompeii, and were a common feature of theatres (e.g. Orange, fig. 142) and amphitheatres (e.g. Nîmes, figs. 140, 141). It will be noticed that in the topmost storey of the façade there are three projecting brackets in each bay, making a total of 240 for the whole circumference. The modillions which crown the parapet alternate with these and there is a vertical hole in the cornice between each modillion corresponding to the bracket below. Huge wooden poles were inserted into these holes and rested upon the brackets. The poles probably projected a considerable height above the top of the masonry. To these poles was attached the rigging which supported the velarium (fig. 83). The procedure for raising the velarium was as follows: a great rope ring was laid down in the middle of the arena corresponding to it in size, and attached to this were the supporting ropes which were threaded through pulleys on the masts. These ropes ran down to the bollards at pavement level, some of which can still be seen on the north-east side of the building (fig. 84). On each bollard was a winch around which the rope passed. The ropes were finally secured to a series of capstans around the building. At a given signal the ropes were

83 Rome, Colosseum: drawing to illustrate the working of the velarium (after A. C. Carpiceci)

143

84 Rome, Colosseum: bollards to which the winches for the velarium were attached

tightened and at the beat of a drum the ring was slowly raised into position. When the ring was in position further ropes were joined to it lower down and the strips of canvas which formed the velarium were unrolled on to the rope network beneath. A contingent of 100 sailors from Misenum was permanently billeted nearby to maintain the rigging. When it was periodically lowered and raised at least 1,000 men would have been needed. There must have been a clear space all round the building between the velarium and the top of the masonry which would prevent the awning being torn to pieces by high winds. Even so, the noise of the velarium on windy days must have been deafening, especially combined with the roaring of the animals in and under the arena.

Thus the Colosseum is not just an architectural masterpiece, but in terms of planning, engineering and organization it must rank as one of the most astonishing achievements of antiquity. Nor must we look at the building in isolation. When we consider that it sat in the middle of a complex of ancillary buildings including the quarters of the sailors, the barracks for the gladiators with its small practice arena in the centre, and the host of taverns, wine stalls, refreshment booths and the public baths built by Titus, one cannot but marvel at the creators of such a complex.

Vespasian was succeeded by his elder son, Titus, who in his short reign endeared himself to the Roman people as one of the best-loved

Roman Emperors. He inaugurated the Colosseum in AD 80 and (fig. 90) built the nearby baths which bear his name. Little of the Baths of Titus now survive, but the plan is known from a Palladio drawing. The drawing shows a building which is entirely symmetrical. The largest room, the frigidarium, is a basilical hall with a semicircular apse in the middle of one long side and four plunge baths. At either end is a palaestra. Passing through a small tepidarium one reaches a pair of caldaria. On the south side are the usual hot rooms and there is a large open space to the south of the bathing block for gymnastic exercises. Although the building is only about a quarter of the size of the great Imperial thermae of the second and third centuries, it has most of the elements of these larger baths. The main element which is lacking is the natatio or open-air swimming pool which in the classic great baths (e.g. the Baths of Caracalla) would be situated to the north of the frigidarium and flanked by apodyteria or changing rooms. However, the Baths of Titus have come a long way from the Stabian Baths at Pompeii and are only a short step away from the fully developed great thermae. Such a dynamic scheme bears the stamp of the new architecture as seen in Nero's Golden House. The fact that the baths are exactly aligned with the latter gives rise to the speculation that the Baths of Titus may be a remodelling of the famous baths of the Golden House as described by Suetonius.

Titus was succeeded by his younger brother, Domitian, whose despotic reign was remembered with dread by historians such as Suetonius and Tacitus. Yet, like many tyrants, he left behind monuments of great architectural importance. During his reign concrete rapidly developed both in Rome and Ostia as the cheapest and most efficient building material. Domitian's palace on the Palatine hill, built almost exclusively of concrete, showed how it could be used daringly to exploit space and model new architectural shapes.

His earliest monument was of a much more traditional type. The Arch of Titus which stands at the high part of the Sacred Way near the Colosseum (fig. 85) was largely built in the early part of Domitian's reign. The arch suffered much damage throughout the Middle Ages, but the *fornix* itself survived because it was incorporated into the medieval Frangipane Castle. In 1822 the Arch was isolated and skilfully restored by the architect Valadier, who used travertine to distinguish his restoration from the original portion of the Arch, which was in Pentelic marble. The much better-preserved Arch of Trajan at Beneventum is so strikingly similar that many scholars have attributed the Arch of Titus to a later date. However, as the Arch commemorates both Titus' victory over the Jews and his deification, a date shortly after the Emperor's death might be expected; also, stylistic criteria suggest that the ornament belongs to the early Domitianic period.

85 Rome, Arch of Titus, completed by Domitian shortly after the death of Titus in AD 81

The Arch has simple, elegant proportions. Slightly higher than it is wide, it has a single opening flanked by massive piers with half columns, eight in all, at each corner. The half columns stand on a high podium and support an architrave and frieze with relief sculptures showing the triumph of Vespasian and Titus over the Jews. In the spandrels are flying victories carrying trophies and in the attic is a dedicatory inscription recording that the Arch was voted by the senate and Roman people to deified Titus, son of Vespasian. The passages contain the famous relief panels showing the triumphal procession of Titus, and the soffit of the arch has coffered panels with the apotheosis of Titus in the middle. The columns which adorn the piers of the arch are of the Composite Order, which combines the acanthus leaves of the Corinthian capital with a diagonal Ionic volute above. The order probably originated at the time of Augustus when so much experimentation was taking place in the Classical Orders. An argument to support an early date for the Composite Order is the diagonal Ionic volute which was an Italian version of the order during the Hellenistic period and passed out of fashion in the early Empire. An Augustan date is also suggested by other stylistic criteria, such as the pair of rosettes rising out of the calyxes of the acanthus foliage, which are a feature of Augustan Corinthian capitals.

Another building of the early period of Domitian's reign is the Temple of Vespasian at the foot of the Capitoline hill next to the Temple of Concord (fig. 27). It has a 6×2 porch of Corinthian columns and a plain cella which abuts closely upon the Tabularium behind. Three columns have been re-erected along with a portion of the entablature with the inscription recording its dedication to Divine Vespasian. The steps up to the cella run between the columns of the porch, to save as much space as possible on the rather cramped site. A fragment of the entablature of the temple is preserved in the Tabularium and has the exuberant and rich detail typical of the Flavian period. The frieze with relief bucrania and sacrificial vessels and implements is capped by enriched egg and acanthus leaf moulding, dentils with 'spectacles' between and a prominent egg and dart (fig. 33). The modillions have heavy acanthus cladding and there is a rosette in each coffer between. The corona has a tongue moulding and is separated from the sima by a cyma reversa decorated with linked palmettes.

The stadium in the Campus Martius was also built early in Domitian's reign. The building was used for the athletic contests which he much admired. The banks of seats were ranged around an open area 200 metres long with, of course, no spina or carceres, which are features of the circus. The seats were raised on substructures of travertine and concrete, and the outside façade was decorated with two tiers of Ionic half columns, some of which can still be seen on the outside of the curved northern end. The Piazza Navona now stands on the ruins of the stadium and its buildings incorporate much of the concrete substructure.

Domitian also laid out a new forum in the narrow space between the Temple of Peace and the Forum of Augustus (fig. 23). The semicircular exedra to the south-east of the Temple of Mars Ultor further constricted the available area, but his architect skilfully overcame the problem by building the cella of the Temple of Minerva close up to the exedra. Instead of a row of free-standing columns around the open space in front of the temple a row of columns on plinths runs close to the wall and supports sections of entablature projecting from it (fig. 89). The ornament of the entablature is deeply drilled and highly ornate. The frieze is sculpted and a statue of Minerva, Domitian's favourite deity, stands in the attic between each pair of columns. The Forum was uncompleted at Domitian's death, but was shortly afterwards dedicated in the name of his successor, Nerva (AD 96–98). Another of Domitian's grand schemes, also uncompleted, was a vast new building complex to the north-west of the Forum of Augustus. This involved cutting away the spur of hill which joined the Capitoline and Quirinal. The depth of this excavation can be judged by Trajan's Column, whose top marks the original ground level. Domitian never lived to finish his project and it was left to Trajan to build the greatest of the Imperial

86 Rome, Flavian Palace: view of the lower part of the Domus Augustana

fora on the flat site that he had created. Apart from his major public monuments, it must be remembered that many of the city's apartment blocks and shops were rebuilt in the last decades of the first century AD following the two disastrous fires of AD 64 and AD 80. A glance at the city of Ostia (p. 128) as it appeared in the middle of the second century AD gives us some idea of what Rome may have looked like around AD 100.

Domitian's most enduring and influential monument was the new residence he built for himself on the Palatine hill. It remained the official home of the Emperors for the next 300 years – indeed our word 'palace' derives from it. Domitian clearly did not wish to live in the Golden House, which had been occupied only intermittently after the Colosseum and the Baths of Titus were built. Its grounds were a public park and the Esquiline wing largely cut off from the city centre. Vespasian seems to have lived largely in the Gardens of Sallust on the Pincian hill, which had become an Imperial estate, and Titus lived in the Domus Tiberiana. Domitian chose the architect Rabirius (Martial, *Epigrams*, 7.56), to lay out the new residence in a place hallowed by the associations of Augustus' house and, long before that, the hut of Romulus. However, the site he chose presented formidable problems. The western ridge of the Palatine, the Germalus, was already occupied by a venerable group of buildings and temples. Therefore Domitian chose the eastern ridge which sloped steeply away to the south-west and south-east. Rabirius overcame this difficulty by cutting a great step into the south part of the hill and using the excavated material to create a flat platform at a higher level to the north (fig. 86). The creation of the higher platform involved filling in some pre-existing monuments including the House of the Griffins, the Isiac hall of Caligula and the nymphaeum of the Domus Transitoria. These monuments thus owe their preservation to the fact that they were incorporated into the later monument. When considering the plan of the palace it should be borne in mind that the floor of the hippodrome and the lower part of the Domus Augustana are some 10 metres lower than the upper part of the Domus Augustana and the Domus Flavia or official wing (fig. 86).

There were two main approaches to the palace. The official approach was from the Via Sacra near the Arch of Titus, up the slope which led under the Arch of Domitian into the Area Palatina which the Domus Flavia overlooked. A second approach from the Forum level was through a massive vestibule, long thought to be the Temple of Augustus (fig. 27).

The official wing of the palace, known as the Domus Flavia, was on the top of the hill. The wing stood upon a tall platform with a colonnade running round the edge (fig. 87.1). Behind the colonnade were three official rooms, a lararium (fig. 87.2), a throne room (fig. 87.3) and an apsed basilica (fig. 87.4). The throne room was the largest room of the three and measured 30 metres wide by 37 metres long. The visitor entered from the north-east and in front of him at the far end of this vast room he would have seen the Emperor enthroned under a wide shallow apse. The walls either side were articulated with free-standing columns of Phrygian marble on tall plinths supporting projecting entablatures. Between each pair of columns were alternately round and square niches, each with an aedicule inside. The walls would have been sheathed in polychrome marbles and the aedicules filled with statues, and the apse under which the emperor sat enthroned may well have been covered in polychrome and gold glass mosaic.

From the throne room the visitor passed into a peristyle courtyard in the middle of which was an elaborate fountain placed at the intersection of the two main axes of the palace. The columns are of shining white marble which brings to mind Suetonius' anecdote (*Domitian*, 14.4) that Domitian had the porticoes of the palace lined with selenite, so that he might see the reflection of an assassin reflected in its mirror-like surface. On the north-west side of the peristyle an exquisite octagonal vestibule (fig. 87.5) gave access to two suites of small guest rooms, perhaps bedrooms. Four compass curves divide up each rectangle into four intriguingly shaped semicircular rooms, two with the customary recess, perhaps for beds. A similar series of curves is found in the pool in the lower part of the Domus Augustana, and foreshadows the later delight of Roman architects in creating delicately curvilinear room shapes.

The triclinium (fig. 87.6) was a room almost as large as the throne room. On the peristyle side was a screen of six huge columns of grey Egyptian granite. Similar columns stood in the corners of the room,

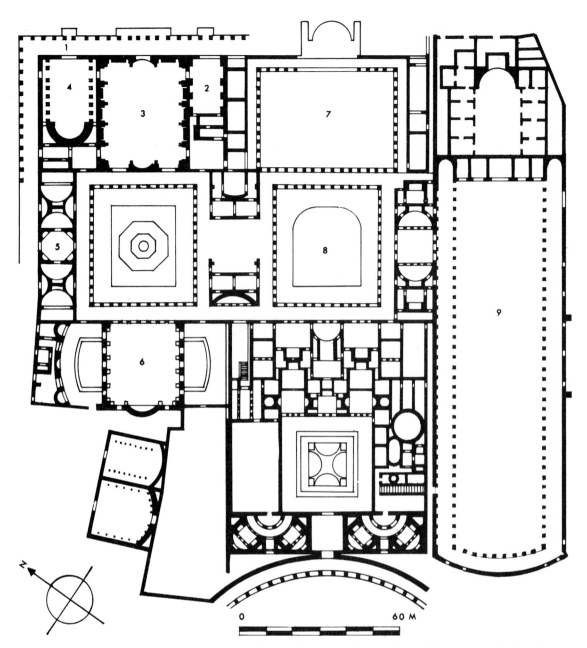

87 Rome, Flavian
Palace, inaugurated in
AD 92: general plan of
the upper level and the
hippodrome

either side of the apse at the far end, and between the five huge
windows which opened on either side of the room to admit air and
glimpses of the pair of ornate oval fountains in the courtyard
beyond. In position and general arrangements the room is similar to
room 8 of Nero's Golden House (fig. 53). In the latter, fountains also
provided a visual and aural accompaniment to the meal. However,
just as the triclinium in Nero's palace was draughty and had to be
partly walled in, so the triclinium of Domitian's palace, which was
similarly exposed to the elements, had later to be provided with
underfloor heating.

150

There is great controversy over whether the large rooms of the Domus Flavia were vaulted or covered with a flat timber ceiling. Boethius thinks that all the halls had timber roofs, Ward Perkins thinks that only the basilica could have been vaulted, while MacDonald thinks all the halls were vaulted. The latter's arguments for vaulting, which are based on literary allusions and structural criteria, are not entirely convincing. He interprets a passage from Statius (*Silvae*, 4. 2), which describes the triclinium of the palace and talks of the 'golden ceiling of the sky', to mean that a vault was implied. He points to a passage in Martial (*Epigrams*, 8. 36) which talks of the 'peak' (*apex*) and the 'pinnacle' (*vertex*) of the palace, and argues that in other passages his metaphors are celestial. Yet two books later (*Epigrams*, 10. 20) Martial uses the same term, *vertex*, of a theatre, which was presumably not covered with a barrel-vault. MacDonald also points to the buttresses built against the north-west sides as 'difficult to explain ... as supports needed for a timber roof' and shows that the throne room and the triclinium have corner reinforcements of a type which 'hardly a major barrel-vaulted hall in extant Roman architecture ... lacks.' However, the vestibule at Forum level lacks such corner reinforcement, as does the great barrel-vaulted room 8 of Nero's Golden House (fig. 53). Indeed, one searches in vain for analogies to this feature in vaulted or unvaulted structures. The 'corner reinforcements' in the throne room are nothing more than the corner responds to the niches and column bases around the walls. The corner feature in the triclinium was associated with the rows of decorative columns which ran round the edge of the interior, and the masonry platform in the north-corner of the basilica is in any case not bonded to the wall. A pertinent line of inquiry might be to relate the thickness of the load-bearing walls to the span of the barrel-vault they support. Here the evidence tends to give some backing to MacDonald's theory that the four rooms were vaulted. For example the barrel-vaulted 'room of the gilded ceiling' in Nero's Golden House has walls 90 cm thick and the vault is 9.90 metres across: room 9 which is also barrel-vaulted has walls 1.35 metres thick and the vault spans 13.60 metres. The throne room of Domitian's palace has walls 3.09 metres thick (at their widest point, excluding the column plinths) and the vault spans 30.65 metres. In each case there is a ratio of about 1:10 between wall thickness and span, a calculation which confirms MacDonald's theory. However, it may be that the ratio only applies in the case of comparatively small barrel-vaults, like the two in Nero's Golden House, and when a huge span of 30 metres is reached, other criteria may apply.

To the west is the Domus Augustana or private wing of the palace. It is approached from the north-east through two large peristyles, one corresponding to the peristyle of the Domus Flavia (fig. 87.7, 8). To the south-east of this peristyle is a fine set of rooms,

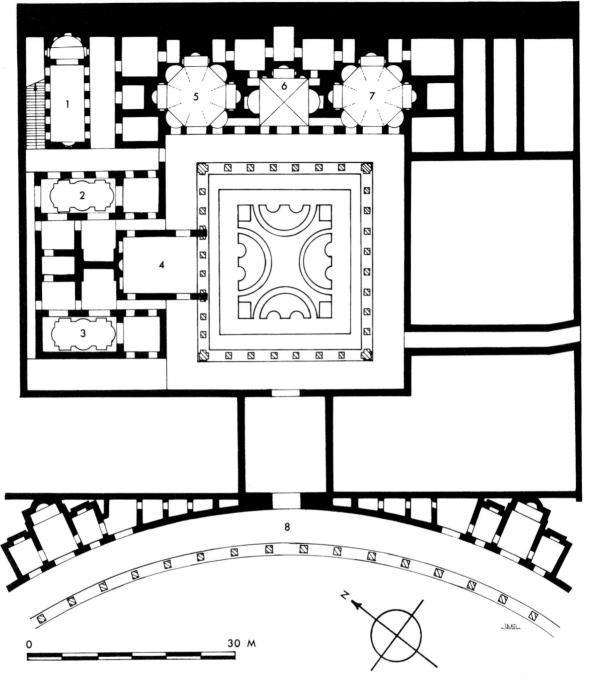

88 Rome, Flavian
Palace: plan of the
lower level

perhaps bedrooms, and to the south-west is a maze of small rooms.
Here the architect's imagination was given free rein to create a
fantasia of rooms wide and narrow, high and low, straight and
curved. Some have niches and two are exquisite octagonal rooms
lined with round-headed niches.

From this suite of rooms a single staircase leads down to the lower
part of the palace (fig. 88). The staircase is lit by a light-well at the
bottom of which is a reflecting pool whose basin is lined with
polychrome glass mosaic (fig. 88.1). Two further light-wells again

with pools (fig. 88.2 and 3) give light to the surrounding rooms which are entirely covered by the structures above. Once again the rows of service rooms behind the main triclinium (fig. 88.4) which faces onto the peristyle are logically and clearly planned and well lit. The three vaulted rooms opening off the north-east side of the peristyle (fig. 86 and 88.5–7) are fine examples of concrete planning. The central room, perhaps a dining room, is square in plan and was covered with a cross vault. Its walls are sculpted away by circular and square recesses and doorways through to the two adjacent rooms. These rooms have the classic octagonal ground plan with alternately square and semicircular niches in their sides. The remaining spaces in this intricate scheme are taken up by a series of small rooms at the back.

At the south side of the peristyle a passageway leads through to the hippodrome which is on the same low level (fig. 88.9). The row of carceres at the north-east end makes it clear that the building was based on the hippodrome rather than the stadium, although in practice it was nothing more than a walled garden. The hippodrome has a continuous arcade running round the two long sides and round the curved end. The arcade supports a concrete barrel-vault decorated with sunken coffers. Originally, the five carceres were twice their present length and ran up to the inner row of columns. At a later stage the outer half of the barrel-vaults was cut away, leaving a free passage between the inner half of the barrel vaults and the columns. The vaults of the carceres were coffered and covered in glass mosaic. When the vaults were partly demolished and bricked up the debris must have been used in the matrix of the cement because the bricking up contains glass mosaic tesserae.

The south-west part of the palace overlooks the long valley where the Circus Maximus was built. Here Rabirius created one of the finest features of the palace, the towering façade with its gently incurving columnar screen in the middle (fig. 88.8). It is from this side above all that one can glimpse the majesty of Rabirius' concept in creating a palace worthy of the rulers of the Roman world.

Rabirius was clearly given scope to innovate and the result is a complex of striking originality built by an architect whose understanding of concrete techniques clearly surpassed that of Nero's architects, Severus and Celer. The ground plan is a masterpiece of lucidity and deft planning, and the rooms of the palace represent an important step forward in the exploitation of interior space. If the Golden House was the first building of the new architecture, Domitian's palace represents its first maturity.

8 Trajan and Hadrian

At the beginning of the second century AD Rome was at the height of her power and prestige. Under Trajan the Empire reached its greatest geographical extent and the Dacian campaign brought with it the biggest influx of wealth that Rome had ever seen. The years of experimental architecture were over. Concrete was the universal material for buildings, whether designed for utility or pleasure. Mastery of concrete and seemingly limitless wealth resulted in buildings of a scale never dreamed of in earlier centuries. The new forum complex laid out by Trajan covered over three times the area of the Forum of Augustus. Trajan's new baths dwarfed the Baths of Titus. A huge new harbour was built at Portus (see p. 124) and Ostia was practically rebuilt during the first half of the second century AD (see p. 125). Trajan's Column seemed to epitomize the new age. Its cool, factual reporting of Trajan's Dacian campaigns proclaimed calm assurance of Roman superiority and security. It was a victory column in the heart of Rome. The style of its reliefs too was significant; their spirit was classical, in keeping with the high promise of the new age. How these noble, self-confident figures contrast with the anxious, dumpy little men that swarm around the column of Marcus Aurelius! They are the soldiers of Rome at the height of her power and glory.

After the murder of Domitian in AD 96, an aged senator, M. Cocceius Nerva, was chosen as the next Emperor. His chief building activity as Emperor was to complete and inaugurate in his own name the Forum begun by Domitian (fig. 89). Unable to control the army on his own he appointed M. Ulpius Traianus, the Commander of Upper Germany, as his co-regent and under his protection ruled for another year. On his death in AD 98 Trajan succeeded him.

Trajan was born in Italica in southern Spain of an old Italo-Hispanic family. A soldier by profession, he had dreams of conquering the East like a second Alexander. Following his Danube campaigns of AD 102–103 and AD 105–107 he annexed Dacia, and as a result of his Parthian campaign of AD 114–116 he added Armenia and Mesopotamia to the Roman empire. The money to finance his building projects was gold brought from Dacia. It is said

89 Rome, Forum of Nerva, dedicated in AD 97, part of the colonnade. (*By courtesy of the German Archaeological Institute, Rome*)

that Trajan brought back so much of it that the value of the metal fell. From AD 107 onwards there was an orgy of spending in Rome and as many gladiators were used in Trajan's games of AD 107 alone as in all the games held during the principate of Augustus.

One of Trajan's biggest projects was the great Baths at Rome (fig. 90). The complex was on the vast scale we have come to associate with him. The main bathing block measures 190 × 212 metres and it is set in an enclosure whose maximum dimensions are 330 × 315 metres. This places the Baths of Trajan as the first of the giant bath buildings to be built in Rome and in the provinces. The brickstamps show that the work was entirely Trajanic and that it was begun about AD 104 and inaugurated in AD 109. The architect may

BATHS OF TRAJAN

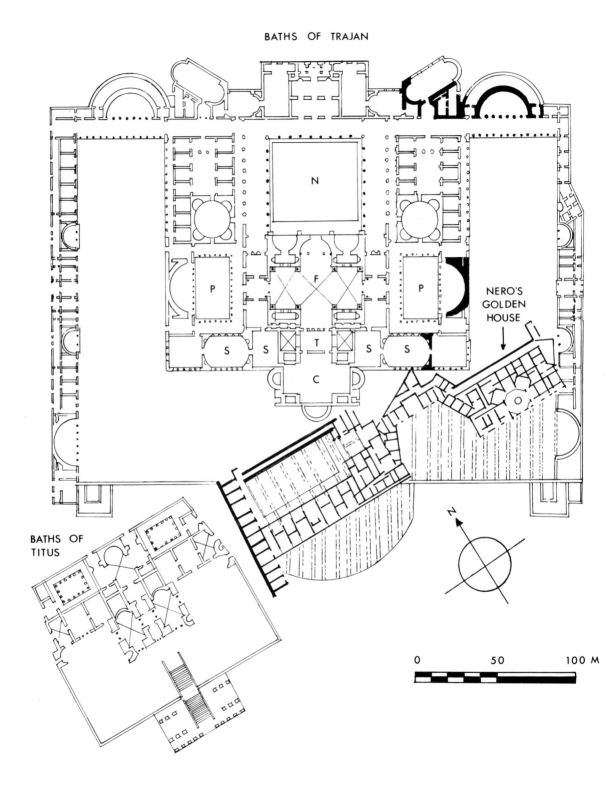

NERO'S
GOLDEN
HOUSE

BATHS OF
TITUS

0   50   100 M

have been Apollodorus of Damascus. What remained of Nero's Golden House was damaged in a fire of AD 104, and the Esquiline wing was utilized as part of the platform of the baths. Built hard against the side of the Esquiline hill, the shell of the house offered a useful extension of the hillside to take the vast bulk of the building. The orientation of the building was different from that of the earlier Baths of Titus close by. Its hot rooms faced south-west instead of due south, probably to take advantage of the hot afternoon sun.

In general layout the baths foreshadow those of the later Empire, except that the central block is joined to the perimeter wall on the north side whereas later baths such as those of Caracalla and Diocletian had completely free-standing central blocks. As we have seen (p. 39), the general arrangements of the great Imperial bath buildings had been worked out in the Baths of Titus, but the Baths of Trajan cover over three times the area of the latter. One entered them through a vestibule on the north side and beyond lay a big, almost square natatio or swimming pool, open to the sky but surrounded on all four sides by colonnaded porticoes. Then came a pair of circular rooms and two palaestrae which flanked the central hall or frigidarium. From there one went through sweating rooms into the great rectangular caldarium or hot room which had a great apse at either end. Next was a small tepidarium or warm-room, whose main function was to insulate the hot rooms from the cold rooms beyond. The climax of this series of rooms was the great frigidarium covered with three soaring cross-vaults which were given visual support by eight huge columns set around the walls of the room. In the corners were four cold plunge-baths. By placing the frigidarium in the centre of the complex the architect emphasized the two axes through the building: one through the natatio, frigidarium, tepidarium and caldarium; the other running through the curved exedra, the palaestra, frigidarium, palaestra, and curved exedra on the other side of the bath. The frigidarium was thus placed on the intersection of these two axes and became the focal point of the entire complex.

Trajan's greatest building achievement in Rome was the forum/market complex to the north of the Forum of Augustus (fig. 23). This seems to have been an entirely Trajanic project, although Domitian had already begun cutting away the spur of hill which had impeded any further development north-west of the Forum of Augustus. We also know that he began renovating the Forum of Julius Caesar late in his reign. However, it is unlikely that Trajan's forum and markets were actually begun under Domitian even though Aurelius Victor (de Caesaribus, 13. 5) suggests that they were. Domitianic brickstamps were found in the enclosure wall behind the Temple of Venus Genetrix and in the tower-like building to the north-west of the Forum of Augustus. However, the hemicycle of Trajan's market is dated by brickstamps to AD 104–110 and a

90 Rome, plan showing the Esquiline wing of Nero's Golden House incorporated into the platform of Trajan's Baths dedicated in AD 109. The walls shown solid are still visible, and the dotted lines represent the Trajanic cross-walls built to consolidate the shell of the Golden House

coin of Nerva was found in the foundations of the Basilica Ulpia. Also, the architectural ornament of the complex shows signs of the Augustan revival, which was a feature of later Trajanic buildings and continued into the early part of Hadrian's reign.

The Forum, which measured 300 × 185 metres, was entered from the Forum of Augustus. The outer wall was in the shape of a gently swelling curve and in the middle of it was a triumphal gateway with a single opening flanked on either side by three columns framing two aedicules. In the niches were statues, probably of Dacian prisoners, and above the aedicules were images in shields (*imagines clipeatae*), probably of Trajan's generals. Above was a high attic on which stood a bronze statue of Trajan in a four-horse chariot flanked by trophies with victories. These details are known from contemporary coins. Through the arch one passed into the huge area of the Forum. In the centre was an equestrian statue of Trajan and on the same axis to the right and left were two exedras. The sides of the Forum were flanked by Corinthian colonnades. In the attics were shields with heads in the middle, like those of the Forum of Augustus, but the shields were flanked by statues of Dacian prisoners instead of Caryatids. Eight of these figures can still be seen adorning the attic of the Arch of Constantine. Unlike earlier fora Trajan's Forum was not dominated by a temple at the far end, but by the huge bulk of the Basilica Ulpia set transversely across the north side. Its twin apses echoed the twin exedras at either side of the Forum. This feature had already been used in the Forum of Augustus to create a cross-accent. Here the technique is developed to give a strong series of transverse axes across the main one. As we have seen, a similar use of a strong cross-axis was also used in the Baths of Trajan.

The Basilica Ulpia was the largest basilica hitherto built in Rome. Including the apses at either end, it was 170 metres long and almost 60 metres wide. Apart from its great size, the general arrangements of the basilica were fairly traditional. Two rows of grey granite columns divided it into a nave and four aisles (fig. 91). The columns were also continued around the two short sides. The roof of the central part was presumably higher and provision was made for clerestory lighting. The general effect of the room must have been similar to the great Constantinian basilicas, such as St Paul's Outside the Walls, which is closely similar in width, although the Basilica Ulpia is actually longer. Four pieces of Trajanic relief sculpture on the Arch of Constantine are thought to have come from the Basilica Ulpia. The panels are three metres high and, joined together, make up a total length of 18 metres. The sculptures, in high relief, show the campaigns and triumph of the Emperor, and perhaps came from the attic of the basilica, although an alternative hypothesis suggests that they adorned the Temple of Deified Trajan which was added by Hadrian behind Trajan's column. Beyond the basilica, again on the main axis of the Forum, stands the column, which has an overall height of 39.83 metres (fig. 91). The actual shaft is exactly 100 Roman feet high, and is adorned with a continuous spiral of low relief sculpture, 200 metres long. The sculptures are designed to be read like a scroll, starting at the bottom with the Roman army crossing the Danube and finishing at the top with the triumph of Trajan over the Dacians. The sculptures are in effect a visual record of the campaign, the sculptural equivalent of a war note book (*commentarii*) of the kind that Julius Caesar wrote to record his campaigns in Gaul. For this reason the position of the column, between two libraries, is particularly apt. The column is raised on a high podium decorated with spoils of war in relief sculpture. The inside of the podium served as a tomb for the soldier-emperor, although the column lay inside the pomerium – an honour reserved only for those who had celebrated a triumph. The column is constructed of horizontally cut drums of Carrara marble and the jointing, which does not correspond to the windings of the spiral, is so carefully managed that one is not immediately aware that almost half the scenes had to be cut from two separate blocks of marble. Inside the column is a spiral staircase lit by the small rectangular holes which can be seen at intervals. The column was flanked on each side by the libraries, one Greek and one Roman. Each library was a rectangular room with walls lined with niches for the scrolls. Presumably the roofs of the libraries must have been accessible as viewing galleries for the upper part of the column whose details are invisible from ground level.

North-west of the column Hadrian added an enormous temple dedicated to deified Trajan. A fragment of the Severan marble plan of Rome shows that it was octastyle. It must have been on a huge scale to judge by the single surviving grey Egyptian granite column which measures two metres in diameter, larger even than the columns of the porch of the Pantheon.

The layout of the Forum, with the basilica at the far end lying across the main axis, which was later copied, for example at Lepcis Magna in the Severan Forum (fig. 121) and at Augst (fig. 144), is an unusual one, but may be explicable in terms of Trajan's career. Trajan spent most of his life as a soldier on campaign and during this time he must have lived most of his life in military camps. Recent research has shown that the layout of Trajan's Forum in many respects reflects the plan of a principia or central administrative area of a camp. In a camp the central square was flanked by a basilica and nearby were kept the military archives and the legionary standards (see p. 45). Thus, the Basilica Ulpia occupies a similar position to the basilica of a principia, and the column and libraries have a similar relationship to the standard and archive rooms of a camp. The Bibliotheca Ulpia contained important state archives and the column, as we have seen, is a narrative account of Trajan's campaigns. Seen in this light the Forum complex can be seen not

91 Rome, Trajan's Column seen through the Basilica Ulpia (AD 107–113)

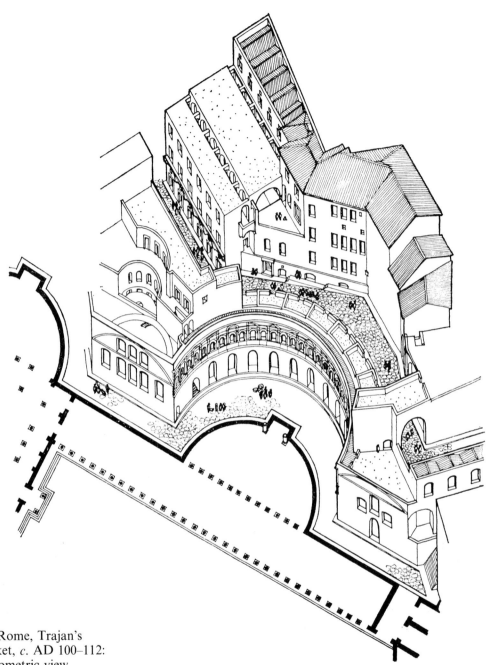

92 Rome, Trajan's Market, *c.* AD 100–112: axonometric view. Centre foreground: the hemicycle of Trajan's Forum; left foreground: one end of the Basilica Ulpia (from A. Boethius, *op. cit.*)

only as the greatest of the Roman fora, but as a singularly appropriate monument to commemorate the achievements of one of the great soldier Emperors.

The markets, although related to the Forum, formed quite a separate complex (fig. 92). The eastern exedra of the Forum echoes the big hemicycle of shops behind, but it is shut off visually from it by a high wall of peperino stone. Thus, the semicircle was never intended to be seen as whole, as it is today. This fact probably explains the low relief decoration of the brick façade (fig. 93) which springs into sharp relief when seen close to or from an angle, but which fails to dominate from a distance. (It is interesting to note that Sir Christopher Wren employed similar low relief mouldings on the south and north sides of St Paul's Cathedral, which was closely hemmed in by buildings; the present open space to the south of the building was the last thing the architect had in mind.) The markets are in many ways more interesting than the Forum, although the latter was undoubtedly the show-piece of the complex. The Romans would clearly have regarded the markets as a piece of utilitarian building in just the same way as Barlow's engine shed at St Pancras Station was 'utility' while Scott's hotel was 'art'. However, the markets, entirely built of brick-faced concrete and designed to conceal the scar left by cutting away the hillside, are full of structural and engineering ingenuity. The large hemicycle of shops is flanked at either side by a big semi-domed hall, its curve turned against the hillside to take the thrust. Behind the northern hall is another semi-domed hall at a higher level. We know that, at least later in the Empire, such halls were used as schools or auditoria. In the hemicycle are 11 extremely shallow shops on the ground floor. They are barrel-vaulted internally, but where it meets the façade each vault is concealed by a travertine doorway with a small rectangular window above. The paved street which leads around the hemicycle becomes a little wider towards the middle as the hemicycle and the exedra of the Forum are struck from different centres. A pair of staircases at

93 Rome, Markets of Trajan (AD 104–110)

the ends of the hemicycle leads up to the storey above. Here a barrel-vaulted corridor gives access to ten shops which are somewhat deeper than those on the ground floor. The corridor is lit by 26 round-headed windows. The windows form a conspicuous element of the façade, framed as they are by delicate Tuscan pilasters of brick. Above the windows is a subtle interplay of full, half and segmental pediments. The top floor of the hemicycle has been largely destroyed, but there was another corridor running round it corresponding to the one on the floor below. This was presumably a promenade gallery from which one could glimpse views of the Forum and basilica, because the shops on this level do not open on-to it, but onto the Via Biberatica behind. The reason for this arrangement is that the Via Biberatica runs gently downhill from south to north. Therefore each of the shops of the top floor of the hemicycle has a floor slightly lower than the next and thus has to have its door opening onto the street. Interestingly, this difference in height is transmitted to the shops on the floor below, and their roofs in turn become lower from south to north. This allowed the architect to keep the roofline of the hemicycle as a whole perfectly horizontal.

On the east side of the Via Biberatica opposite the hemicycle is a further complex three storeys high. This building is not divided up into shops as in the hemicycle. Instead, there are groups of rooms of different sizes, mostly intercommunicating. This suggests that the block may have been used for the administration of the complex as a whole and perhaps for the storage of some perishable items, such as foodstuffs. Some of the rooms have wall niches which suggests that they contained records.

The Via Biberatica continues northward and stops abruptly against the foundations of the modern Via Quattro Novembre. The last section of it runs straight and is extremely well preserved. The roadway is paved with basalt and on each side runs a pavement of travertine blocks. The road is lined either side with shops; the ground floor ones have balconies over the top. The shops on the west side form part of a larger block which abuts onto the hemicycle. The shops on the ground floor open onto the street, and behind them further shops open into a curved corridor which goes round the more easterly half-domed room at the northern end of the large hemicycle (fig. 92). The windows which light this semicircular corridor are round headed and the arrangement is in effect a smaller version of the semi-circular corridor running around the second storey of the large hemicycle. There are in fact some basement rooms below these and it is interesting to note that they are lit by means of light-wells over the extrados of the semi-dome in a system analogous to the octagonal room of Nero's Golden House. A similar system of lighting is employed in the market hall described below. The semi-domed room, surrounded on all sides by buildings, can only have been lit by the oculus still to be seen.

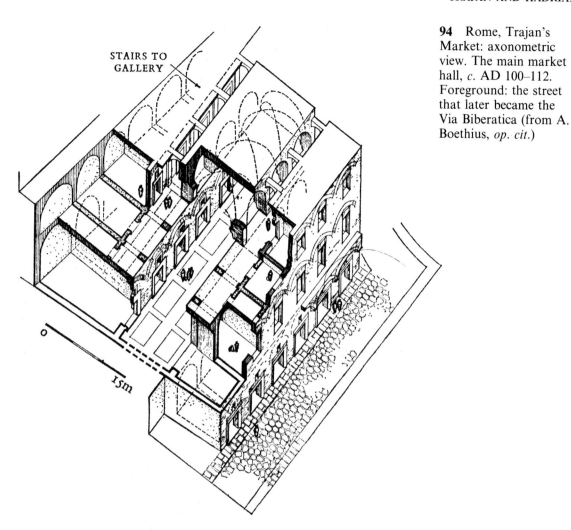

STAIRS TO
GALLERY

94 Rome, Trajan's Market: axonometric view. The main market hall, *c.* AD 100–112. Foreground: the street that later became the Via Biberatica (from A. Boethius, *op. cit.*)

On the east side of the Via Biberatica is a market hall (fig. 94). The floor level of the hall corresponds to the second storey of the Via Biberatica façade. One enters it from a staircase on the Via Biberatica. On the ground floor two rows of six-deep shops face each other across a central concourse. Such an arrangement is immediately reminiscent of the market arcade at Ferentinum and, like so much Imperial architecture, must have had its roots in Republican practice. Here, however, the hall is much more developed. There are two storeys of shops on both sides of the concourse. The upper shops are shallower because of the room taken up by the access corridor. The roofing of the central space is particularly interesting. Six cross vaults roof the space but they are not contiguous with the rows of barrel-vaulted rooms either side. Instead, a space is left between the vaults to light the corridors and shops of the upper storey and also to give extra lighting to the ground floor of the hall. To stabilize the cross-vaults two rows of seven flying buttresses run between their springings and the barrel vaults of the shops. Thus, as in the small hemicycle of shops described above, and in the octagonal room of Nero's Golden House, lighting is achieved by light-wells over or near the extrados of a vault. The markets well illustrate the Roman skill in turning the problems presented by a difficult site to entirely practical use.

The markets were a logical step in the reconstruction of the centre of Rome which had been in progress for over a century. As Rome became an increasingly important administrative hub of the Empire so the functions of the city centre multiplied. The new Imperial fora usurped central city land which had hitherto been used for trade and commerce. The Temple of Peace, for example, was built on the site of the great meat market which had been transferred to the Caelian hill. The creation of Trajan's markets was a further step in removing from the old Forum and its surrounding area the commercial and business activity which was traditional to the old Forum but inappropriate to its new dignity as the official centre of the Roman Empire. It has been calculated that the complex gave Rome some 150 new shops and offices, and walking round them one cannot fail to be struck by their similarity to modern planned shopping centres.

Trajan showed concern for the economy of Rome and Italy in several other respects. His harbour works (see p. 124) and the new markets reflected the need to protect Rome's corn supply and the distribution of an ever-increasing flood of goods and services. Trajan also involved himself in improving communications throughout Italy. He continued the repairs to the Via Appia which had been begun by Nerva, and milestones also record repairs to the Via Aemilia in AD 100, Puteolana in AD 109, Sublacensis in 103–105 and the Via Latina in AD 105. A new roadbed was built for the Via Appia where it crossed the Pomptine marshes. The Salaria was repaired in AD 110 and improvements were made to the Via Clodia and Via Cassia. The road from Beneventum to Brindisi was entirely re-made and bore the name Via Traiana. To mark the beginning of the new road a triumphal arch was erected at Beneventum. The Arch is strikingly similar in design and scale to the earlier Arch of Titus in Rome, but Trajan's Arch, built about AD 117, is better preserved than its counterpart at Rome and all the sculptural panels survive (fig. 95). The panels facing the city refer to the Emperor's work in Italy, while those facing the countryside deal with the provinces. The division was an apt one as the new road led to Brindisi, the port for ships bound for the eastern Mediterranean. Where the road ends, opposite the harbour at Brindisi stood two tall columns of white marble, one of which survives. Its capital is elaborately carved with the heads of Jupiter, Mars, Neptune and Minerva on its four sides. Framed between the two columns can be seen the narrow harbour mouth through which ships sailed for Greece and beyond.

While all these ambitious building projects were in progress Trajan went on campaign after campaign. In the summer of AD 117 he returned to the eastern provinces, but his health was clearly failing, and he was worn out. In July he left for Rome and put Hadrian in charge of the army in Syria, but was never to see Rome again. He died in Selinus in Cilicia and just before the end he declared his adoption of Hadrian.

Hadrian was a very different type from his predecessor, a man who had had dreams of marching to India as another Alexander. He was clearly aware that a huge eastern inland empire would not only cause security problems, but change the whole nature of the Roman Empire from a coastal entity to a continental one. His ideal was a secure, self-sufficient Empire where peace, prosperity and security reigned. Soon after his succession he relinquished some of Trajan's eastern conquests and was with difficulty persuaded to retain Dacia where Romanization was already well under way. His reign was in general a peaceful one except for the continued revolt of Jews in the eastern empire which he repressed with savage ferocity. It is calculated that in the Jewish wars of the years AD 130–135 580,000 men perished.

Hadrian spent a large proportion of his reign in the provinces, a fact which caused resentment in Rome. His education was Greek and he made no concealment of his admiration for the Hellenes. Indeed he showed them more favour than he did the Romans. His aping of Greek fashions (he introduced the Greek fashion of wearing a beard) and his preference for the Bithynian boy, Antinous, who was constantly in his company, showed that his tastes were distinctly un-Roman. Although he endowed the capital with new buildings his interest in the provinces was just as great. From AD 121 to 125 and again from AD 128 to 133 he was out of Rome visiting Gaul, Germany, Raetia, Noricum, Britain, Spain and Morocco. In the east he visited Africa, Asia Minor, Syria and Egypt. In AD 134–35 he spent time in Palestine. All over the Empire his presence is attested by bridges, roads, baths and other public monuments; while cities were rebuilt and new ones founded. Rome, which had for so long imported works of art, craftsmen and wealth from the provinces, began to export its own art and as a result provincial cities grew in wealth, splendour and power. By the end of the second century AD Rome's status was beginning to be gradually eroded away until it became just one among many prosperous cities vying for Imperial patronage; the phase known as the Late Empire had begun.

The architectural achievements of Rome must from now on be seen in a wider Mediterranean context. After Hadrian great building projects were few and far between in Rome. The reasons are not difficult to seek. Apart from the changing status of Rome within the Empire, such a frenzy of building had occurred in the capital during the first 150 years of the Empire that there was diminished scope for new projects. In addition, the days of the great campaigns of conquest, which brought to the capital masses of slaves and booty, were over. Never again was Rome to have such opportunities for large-scale looting as she had enjoyed during the late Republic and early Empire. Trajan's Dacian campaign, which enabled the Forum/markets complex to be built, was Rome's last great haul. Indeed it was so great that the money lasted throughout Hadrian's reign and provided the apparently limitless resources needed to build the Pantheon, and his architectural extravaganza near Tivoli, Hadrian's Villa.

The Pantheon (fig. 96) is one of the great masterpieces of Roman architecture and the fact that it is so exceptionally well-preserved enables us to experience its effects at first hand. The building survives because the Byzantine Emperor, Phocas, gave it to Pope Boniface VIII in AD 608 to turn into the church of Santa Maria ad Martyres. It was erected early in Hadrian's reign, as is shown by the brickstamps which fix the date between AD 118 and 125, to replace Agrippa's Pantheon of 27 BC. However, the inscription over the portico records the original builder, Agrippa, in accordance with

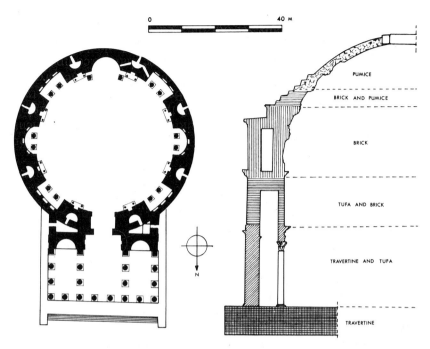

96 Rome, Pantheon, AD 118–128: plan and section showing filling materials

Hadrian's policy of not putting his name to any monument except the temple of his father, Trajan (*Historia Augusta*, Hadrian 19).

Agrippa's Pantheon was a traditional columnar temple of comparatively small dimensions, 19.82 × 43.76 metres. It says much for the scale of Hadrian's Pantheon that Agrippa's building could almost have fitted inside it. For a temple to have such a vast domed interior was quite unusual. The function of a Roman temple was different from that of a Christian church in that the congregation did not worship inside it. So, normally speaking, a Roman temple had a fairly cramped cella. The Pantheon, dedicated to all the gods, gave its architect the opportunity to make a play of interior space and create the physical embodiment of the universal cosmos. While such modelling in concrete was not unusual in a domestic context or in a bath building, it was unusual to find it in a temple. This may have been the reason for the octastyle porch which gives the impression of a traditional temple, such as that of Mars Ultor (fig. 32). It should also be borne in mind that there was a colonnaded enclosure in front of the building and that this would have tended to mask the rotunda, as would the tall square-sided block behind the porch which towers up to the full height of the pediment. Also the ground-level in front of the building was lower in antiquity (the staircase leading up to the porch is entirely under modern ground-level) which would have made it more difficult to glimpse the dome.

The porch has 16 granite columns (fig. 97), eight on the façade and four rows of two behind, dividing it into three aisles. The central aisle leads to the main door and the side aisles each terminate in an apse, in which stood statues of Augustus and Agrippa. It has been

97 Rome, Pantheon: the porch (AD 118–125)

suggested that part of the entablature above the columns comes from the original Agrippan building. However, there are no dentils in the cornice, a feature which no Augustan architect was likely to omit (see p. 67). Also, the profiles of the mouldings, particularly the egg-and-tongue, are an early second-century type. The balance of the evidence points to the fact that the porch was entirely built at the time of Hadrian, including the inscription: *M[arcus] Agrippa L[uci] f[ilius] Co[nsul] tertium fecit.* Another inscription on the architrave below mentions a restoration by Septimius Severus and Caracalla, in AD 202. A study of the fixing holes in the pediment reveals that it was decorated with an eagle with a crown. The pediment itself is extremely tall in proportion to its width. It is over one-and-a-half times the height that Vitruvius prescribes (*De Arch.,* 3. 5. 12).

The proportions of the interior are based upon simple solid geometry. The diameter and height of the rotunda are exactly the same, 43.2 metres, and the dome springs 21.6 metres above the pavement, which means that a sphere of the same diameter as the rotunda would exactly fit inside the building.

98 Rome, Pantheon: cutaway
drawing to show the structure of the
drum

99 Rome, Pantheon:
interior showing the
dome (AD 118–125)

The drum rests upon a ring of heavy concrete, with a travertine fill, 7.30 metres wide and 4.50 metres deep. Externally the walls of the drum are divided into three horizontal zones each capped by a cornice. Internally there is a lower cornice corresponding to the lowest external one and the dome springs at the level of the middle external cornice. The width of the drum is 6.15 metres and as the dome rises the concrete envelope diminishes in thickness until it is only 1.50 metres wide at the oculus. The materials used were carefully graded so that heavier materials were used in the concrete fill of the foundations and walls, and lighter materials in the dome (fig. 96). Up to the lower cornice the wall fill consists of travertine and tufa; up to the middle it is tufa and brick; up to the topmost external cornice the fill is entirely brick. As the dome rises the fill becomes lighter until, near the oculus, it consists mainly of light volcanic pumice.

Internally the building is divided into eight bays four of which are square-sided and two apsidal (fig. 96). The other two bays are represented by the entrance doorway and the apse in the wall opposite. In each bay is a pair of free-standing Corinthian columns of giallo antico flanked by a pair of square piers. The columns carry a horizontal entablature which runs around the whole interior, only breaking off at the doorway and the apse opposite, both of which carry arches which break into the wall area above. The upper part of the wall is punctuated by 14 blind windows, which structually are the product of the cross-walls under the arches. The decoration of this zone was removed in 1747 and the present aedicules alternating with square panels were substituted (fig. 99). A portion of the original decoration, known from prints, has been reconstructed just to the right of the central apse. The overall effect would have been busier than the present rather staid arrangement, with four slender

170

Corinthian pilasters of black marble between each pair of windows and a broad socle underneath.

The actual structure of the drum bears little relationship to its decoration. It is composed of eight piers (fig. 96) supporting eight round-headed arches which run through it from its inner to its outer face (fig. 98). The arches correspond to the eight bays of the interior and extend up to the upper cornice of the interior and the middle cornice of the exterior (fig. 96). The two columns in each bay support three pairs of small arches which partly brace the main arches over the bays and also help support vertical walls which define the windows above. Between each pair of main arches is a segmental arch. These do not run through the whole width of the drum, but only act as relieving arches over the windows between the eight bays. Above each of the eight main arches is another arch which externally extends to the level of the third cornice and internally into the dome to the height of the second row of coffers. These arches too run through the drum from the inner face to the outer. The drum can thus be seen as an arched structure resting upon eight massive piers, a system designed to cut down weight and minimize the effects of differential settlement.

The architect has also left voids in the piers between the bays in the form of half-domed chambers, one corresponding to each of the three external levels of the drum (fig. 96). These were doubtless intended to reduce what would otherwise have been a dense mass of concrete, which would have taken a long time to dry and which would certainly have fractured upon drying. Indeed in the curved wall of one of these half-domed rooms there is an enormous crack, but there is a very much smaller one in the corresponding room above. This implies that the cracking took place as the concrete dried out. When one layer was dry the workmen presumably went on to add the room above despite the crack. As that room dried the same weakness caused a crack there too but one which was on a smaller scale.

It is worth noting that there are relieving arches on all three external levels of the drum corresponding to these half-domed chambers. It was thought by Cozzo that the middle row of these arches corresponded to the segmental arches between each bay of the interior. However, it is geometrically impossible for them to join to form a continuous vault like the main arches which they rest upon. Cozzo also believed that there were segmental arches linking the main arches on the storey above, that is to say between the second and third external cornices, and that these ran through the drum to join the arches on the exterior. However, recent studies suggest that there are no such arches on the interior. Therefore it seems likely that the three tiers of relieving arches on the exterior, which correspond to the piers on the interior, must be in connection with the half-domed chambers.

The complex system of arches in the drum and the lower part of the dome probably not only gave stability to the structure but also facilitated construction because, as in the Colosseum, various gangs could be employed on different segments of the building and at different levels simultaneously. While work was in progress on the drum other men would have been employed cutting and carting the forest of timber needed for centring the dome. As the dome is a solid concrete structure the only way it could have been built is by means of a full timber scaffolding whose profile had to correspond to every curve of the coffers. The amount of timber needed for this operation goes a long way to explaining the reason why the Romans began to adopt tile-clad vaults in the later Empire (see p. 80).

The dome contains five rows of 28 coffers which, according to Renaissance drawings, were decorated with relief stucco mouldings and a bronze rosette in the centre of each. The steps of each coffer are shallower on their lower edge and steeper on the higher, which suggests that they were struck from a common centre somewhere towards the middle of the room at floor level. This produces the optical illusion that the dome is wider than it actually is. The oculus in the top of the dome is 8.30 metres wide and was never glazed. Rainwater fell directly on to the pavement below, which was lightly crowned so that the water ran into drainage channels towards the edge of the floor.

The Pantheon has been one of the most influential ancient buildings from antiquity up to our own day. The domed rotunda preceded by a pedimental porch was much copied, but the sheer majesty of the original was never equalled. The secret perhaps lies in the pureness and clarity of its proportions. The interior is composed of two quite simple geometric shapes, a cylinder below and a dome above, both of the same diameter and the same height. The controlling axis of the building runs through the middle of them, and is thus a vertical line from the centre of the floor to the middle of the oculus. As the latter is the only source of lighting for the room, one's eye is inevitably directed towards it. Through its circular opening a shaft of white light enters and strikes first the walls, then the floor, and later in the day, the dome, a pattern dictated by the immutable laws that govern the motions of the celestial bodies. It is perhaps appropriate that a building dedicated to the whole Pantheon of gods should admit only light from the heavens above, and not the noise and sights of the city around.

Hadrian's most extravagant and expensive project was the villa he built near Tivoli. The vast complex stretches for a kilometre on an elevated plateau to the south-west. Presumably none of the great elevated sites further up the hill, such as the sites of the so-called villas of Brutus and of Cassius, would have been big enough to accommodate Hadrian's grandiose concept. Yet although the villa

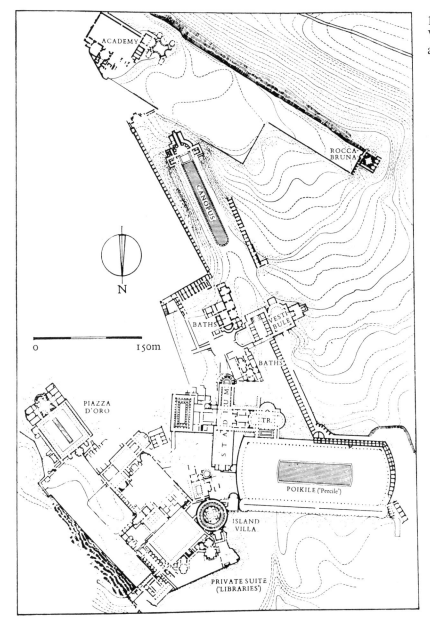

100 Tivoli, Hadrian's Villa, between AD 118 and 134: plan

is comparatively low-lying it still commands a view of Rome; standing in the villa today one can still make out the dome of St Peter's on the horizon. Hadrian began work on the project early in his reign, about AD 118 and as the plan expanded he began to incorporate into it buildings which echoed those of Greece and the east (fig. 100). Walking along the Canopus canal lined with copies of the caryatids of the Erechtheum, strolling through the Vale of Tempe or the Stoa Poikile of the Athenian agora he could recapture

101 Tivoli, Hadrian's Villa: the Island Villa (AD 118–134)

the atmosphere of his beloved Greece even in Italy. It is not clear how much of this vast complex was actually planned when the villa was begun, but at any rate the flattish site chosen suggests that the original scheme was an ambitious one. The villa is centred around a moderate-sized Republican villa which may have been owned by the Empress Sabina. Much of the original fabric of this villa, which dates to the second and first centuries BC, was incorporated into Hadrian's Villa. The most conspicuous survivals are the nymphaeum on the north-west side of the library court and a cryptoporticus which runs off the south-east side. To the east of the courtyard is a long paved corridor with five rooms opening off each side, and a large reception or communal room at the end. Each of the ten rooms was probably a bedroom as there are three recesses in each, probably to take three beds. The pavements are in each case of black and white mosaic, plain mosaic where the beds would have stood and more elaborate geometric pattern in the centre. The complex has been identified as a guest wing to house visitors. To the south of the courtyard on a higher level is a large complex of nymphaea and courtyards, including the well-known courtyard of the Doric piers. The white marble piers which are rectangular in plan and fluted support a barrel-vault which runs round all four sides of the open courtyard.

Beginning with this complex based on the original villa the architect built a series of buildings loosely related to each other and each following a different alignment dictated by the terrain. The main parts of the villa to be discussed are: (1) the Poikile; (2) the Island Villa; (3) the Piazza d'Oro; (4) the stadium/triclinium; (5) the

174

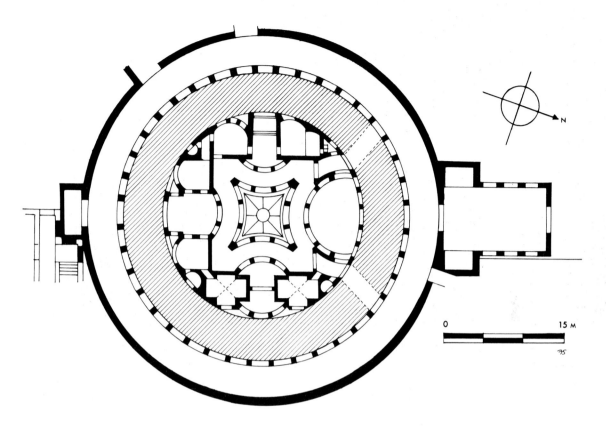

small baths; (6) the large baths; (7) the Canopus/Serapeum; (8) the peripheral buildings.

The Poikile is a huge peristyle courtyard measuring 232×97 metres with a large pool, 107×26 metres, in the middle. Although a fairly flat site was selected for this vast complex the ground slopes away to the south-west. In that corner the site was artificially levelled by a terrace of earth, and buttressed by rows of concrete barrel-vaults. These vaults provide about a hundred small rooms which were used either to house guards or domestic staff. The two shorter ends of the peristyle curve outwards gently in the manner of the outer wall of Trajan's Forum. All four sides are lined with colonnades, and on the north side there is a double colonnade with a wall between. The two short ends have curved turning points. This feature and the fact that the space between the two ends is exactly a stade (200 metres) long suggests that this side of the Stoa Poikile was built in imitation of an enclosed running track or *dromos* common in Greek cities, e.g. the Stoa of Hercules and Hermes in Cyrene. The layout of the whole area with the pool in the centre and the large open space in the middle suggests that the complex might well be an imitation of the Lyceum or Academy in Athens rather than the Stoa

102 Tivoli, Hadrian's Villa: plan of the Island Villa

Poikile. The original Stoa Poikile or painted stoa in Athens is at present being excavated and first reports suggest that it in no way resembles the so-called 'Poikile' in Hadrian's villa.

From the east end of the dromos one passed through an apsed library into the Island Villa. One of the most delightful features of the whole villa, it is essentially an island retreat where the emperor could escape from the ceremony of his huge abode. The Island Villa is circular, and moated. Around the moat runs an annular passage roofed with a barrel-vault supported on the inside by Ionic columns (fig. 101). The island is divided by semicircles into four main groups of rooms around a courtyard (fig. 102). The curves of the four groups of rooms produce convexities at the sides of the courtyard and these are transmitted to the peristyle in the middle of the courtyard. Bridges across the north side of the moat lead into a semicircular vestibule which opens on to the central peristyle courtyard. To the east is a small bedroom suite with two bedrooms linked together by twin semicircular columnar courtyards. There are tiny semicircular latrines in the angles by the bedrooms. Opposite the vestibule on the south side of the peristyle is a dining room with a smaller room either side. The fourth corner of the villa is taken up by a small bathing suite with a cold plunge bath whose bottom is actually below the water level of the moat outside. The spatial and light effects of this tiny architectural jewel must have been splendid. The white columns of the annular passage must have sparkled in the sunlight reflected by the water of the moat and contrasted with the dimness of the passage itself. On the island one must have moved continually from light to shade, from the columns of the open-air vestibule to the roofed peristyle. Within the peristyle was the quaintly shaped open-air courtyard with its fountain in the centre glowing with light. From there one would have caught glimpses of light, darkness and water through the columns all round. In all this must have been one of the most architecturally complete and satisfying delights of the whole villa.

The Piazza d'Oro is a richly decorated peristyle court preceded by an octagonal vestibule with a round-headed niche in every side apart from the thoroughfare (fig. 103). The room is covered by an eight-sided umbrella vault. Such no doubt were the 'pumpkins' for which Apollodorus of Damascus criticized Hadrian (*Dio Cassius*, 69. 4. 1–5). There is no attempt to fit this complex shape into a square and the outer walls are frankly dictated by the shape of the interior, a logical conclusion of the 'new architecture'. Beyond the vestibule is a rectangular courtyard with a long pool running down the centre. On all four sides is a double colonnade whose floors are paved with fine ochre and yellow-toned mosaics, hence the term 'Piazza d'Oro'. There are half as many columns running down the middle of the colonnades as there are on the façades, an arrangement commonly found in Greek and Hellenistic stoas. The pavilion

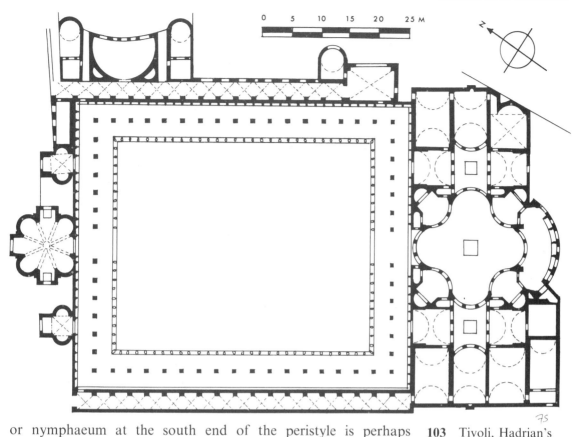

or nymphaeum at the south end of the peristyle is perhaps architecturally the most significant of the group. The main room can perhaps best be described as octagonal with alternately concave and convex sides. Its sides are in fact open colonnades and the room itself was likely to have been unroofed. One concave side is the entrance and the side opposite leads into a big semicircular nymphaeum with a boldly curving back wall lined with alternately round and square fountain niches. The four convex sides open on to four intriguingly shaped rooms each of which terminates in a semicircular exedra. The other two concave sides lead into small *diaetae* or summer rooms with fountains in the middle of the floor. The columns, some of which have been re-erected, are Corinthian and of white marble. Once again this complex would have offered vistas of light and shade, and the sight and sound of water from almost every direction cannot fail to have enhanced the effect.

The state dining room, the hippodrome and the elevated block with its courtyard and pool behind form a single, axially-planned composition, with the hippodrome dramatically cutting across the main axis rather in the manner of the basilica in Trajan's Forum. The tower block must, in my view, represent the official imperial apartments. Access to the block is strictly limited to one main staircase up from the hippodrome direction. It leads into a narrow

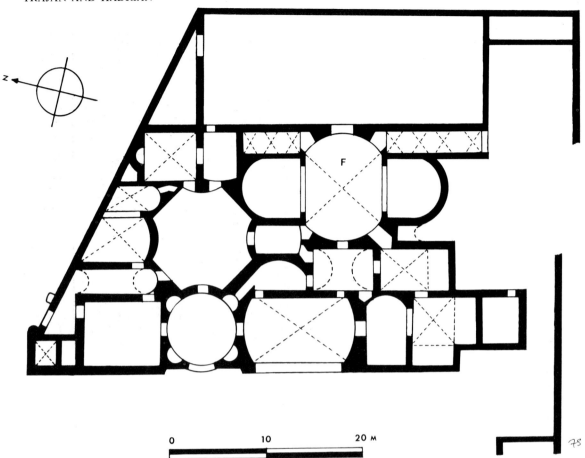

0   10   20 M

104 Tivoli, Hadrian's Villa: plan of the Small Baths

passage where other service corridors from the cryptoporticus below converge. The climax of the whole complex, secure and commanding splendid views of the Tivoli hills, is the completely secluded peristyle courtyard with a pool in the middle. To the west of this is a suite of large rooms, the largest residential rooms in the villa, and the only ones in the entire villa with provision for underfloor heating. They are also extremely well equipped with lavatories, and command by far and away the best views, not only of the villa, but also of Rome in the distance. These factors seem to suggest that this is where the emperor actually lived while he resided at his villa.

Beneath this suite of rooms is the hippodrome, an architectural conceit similar to that in Domitian's palace, and beyond, the state dining room, perhaps the finest of the Imperial series so far, its layout being more developed than that in Nero's (p. 99) or Domitian's (p. 149) palace. Three exedras flank the square covered dining area, each containing a semicircular garden. On the fourth side is a huge ornate fountain set in an open rectangular peristyle. The roar and flash of its waters must have made a mighty impression on the diners within. The idea, of course, comes from Domitian's

dining room, but here fountains and open courtyards surrounded the diners on all four sides. The decor, too, was elaborate. Fine inlaid polychrome marbles adorned the floors; the walls were encrusted with white Proconnesian marble and the columns were of extraordinary elaboration. The bases and capitals are worked with tremendous intricacy and precision in spiral, leaf, guilloche, cable and scroll patterns. Today, after a rainstorm, the fragments of these columns glow and sparkle with a sharpness that Hadrian must have admired when they were first cut.

The Small Baths are closer to the main palace block than the Large Baths, and may have been the Emperor's private bathing suite. The intricacy of the architecture suggests that the Emperor himself may have had a hand in the planning of them (fig. 104). Their layout is tortuous, the result of a laboured attempt to make rooms of ingenious shape fit together into a compact whole. Along the east side is a small palaestra flanked to the west by the frigidarium with two apsidal plunge baths each side. The room is covered by a cross vault which resolves itself somewhat clumsily into a pair of shallow apses at either end. From there one passes via the tepidarium into a series of hot rooms facing west. To the east of these is a large octagonal domed hall from which smaller bathing rooms open. The hall is an architectural *tour de force* in that each alternate side is convex, an irregularity transmitted from three of the abutting rooms. The result is hardly harmonious and the transition from drum to dome must only have been managed with great difficulty.

The Large Baths have a more conventional layout and the spaces

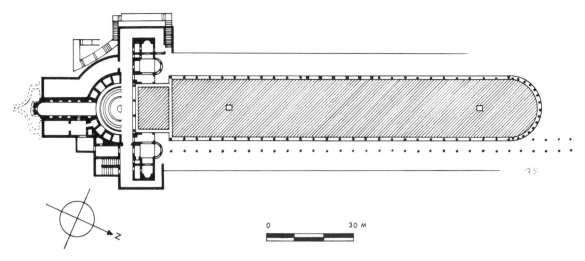

0   30 M

106 Tivoli, Hadrian's Villa: plan of the Serapeum

have greater clarity and better proportions. The cross-vaulted frigidarium with its semicircular and rectangular plunges is particularly impressive (fig. 105). The columnar screen in front of the semicircular plunge has recently been restored and the columns support three semicircular arches which cut into the lunette above. To the south of the frigidarium is a heated room whose cross vault is decorated with extremely delicate stucco reliefs. To the west of the frigidarium is a *heliocaminus*, a circular room with big windows facing south-west in order to take advantage of the heat of the late afternoon sun.

107 Tivoli, Hadrian's Villa: columns around the Canopus

The Canopus/Serapeum complex is one which above all others closely recalls buildings the Emperor saw during his travels. The long lake is like the canal from Canopus to Alexandria, and the

semicircular half-domed nymphaeum at the end follows the general line of the Serapeum (fig. 106). All round the pool are columns, some supporting alternate arches and lintels, although the columns are evenly spaced, which results in unfortunate misproportions. On the long sides of the pool is a host of statuary copied from Greek originals, the Amazons, Mars and the caryatids of the Erechtheum. The Serapeum is perhaps architecturally the most interesting part of the group. Its half-dome is built against a steeply sloping hillside, and behind is a barrel-vaulted passageway encrusted with pumice and glass mosaic to give the dim impression of a grotto. Fountains must have roared in this passageway much as they still do today in the grottoes of the nearby Villa d'Este. Water reached the building by an aqueduct from the hill above. Most of the water, however, was kept high up to flow to other parts of the villa including the two bath complexes. It parted into two branches carried on the tops of the walls of the back passageway and around the sides of the dome at the level of its springing. From there it was carried to the other parts of the villa on supports which now no longer exist, but which must have formed part of the complexes on either side of the pool. The dome looks as if it was designed by Hadrian himself, as it is composed of segments alternately of umbrella and domical section. The entire surface was covered with blue and green glass mosaic. Underneath there are niches which must have contained fountains, and a large semicircular masonry couch on which guests could recline in the midst of an aquatic fantasy. The whole area was effectively an open-air triclinium (*triclinium aestivum*).

Amongst the peripheral parts of the villa is the so-called Academy, a largely open-air building whose ground plan is reminiscent of the octagonal hall of the small baths. There were also

108 Tivoli, Hadrian's Villa: Temple of Venus

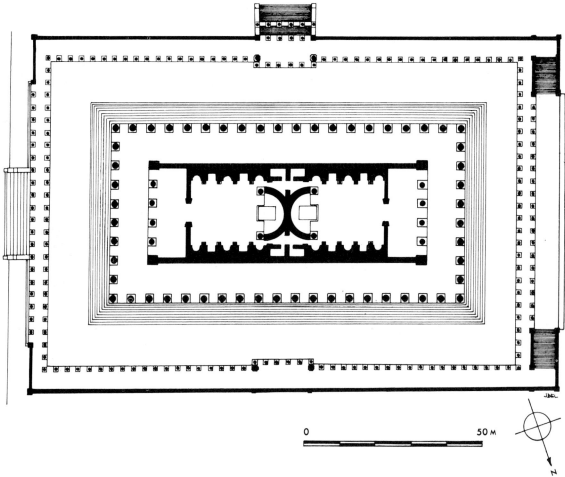

0   50 M

two theatres, the *inferi* or entrance to the underworld and a delightful copy of the Temple of Venus at Cnidos (fig. 108).

This was the greatest Roman villa ever built, and the largest in extent. Echoes of its courts and halls appear in later villas, but never on the same scale. The villa is justly a monument not only to an emperor's eccentricity, but to the ruler of an empire whose prosperity had reached its zenith.

The last building of Hadrian is a more unhappy project. He personally planned a large temple to Venus and Rome on a high piece of ground between the Colosseum and the Temple of Peace (fig. 109). It was an enormous temple, on the same scale as the ancient giants, the Temple of Artemis at Ephesus and the Heraeum of Samos. A decastyle, peripteral temple, it measures 52.5 × 105 metres and thus has a perfect double-square stylobate. However, the columns do not rest upon a lofty podium, but on a low flight of steps all around, a fact which caused a quarrel between Hadrian and Apollodorus (Dio Cassius, 69. 4. 3). The story is that Hadrian was already at odds with Apollodorus even when Trajan was alive

0   1   2
M

because he had told him to 'go away and draw your pumpkins', presumably the umbrella vaults that Hadrian took such pleasure in when planning his villa. When Hadrian submitted his plans of the Temple of Venus and Rome to Apollodorus to show that 'it was possible for a great work to be conceived without his help' Apollodorus criticized it on the grounds that it should have been placed in a higher position and that a hollow space should have been made beneath it to 'receive the machines'. The machines referred to may well mean the devices and scenery used in the nearby Colosseum (see p. 143). Hadrian was so angry that he had Apollodorus executed.

It takes little hindsight to see that Apollodorus was right and that indeed the temple is too squat. In this case Hadrian, the phil-Hellene, was trying to produce a Greek stylobate temple while using tall Roman orders. The finished temple must have been similar in scale and overall effect to the Olympieion at Athens, which Hadrian also built (see p. 237). The details of the temple are important and interesting because the style of the ornament and the fact that the marble used is Proconnesian indicates that an Asiatic, possibly Pergamene, architect was involved in its building. The entablature does not survive in its entirety, although Canina reconstructed it from fragments that he says still survived in his day. His drawings show a two-stepped architrave capped by an astragal, ovolo and cavetto (fig. 110). A plain frieze with consoles supports a cornice with corona and sima separated by an ovolo. The sima has an arrangement of palmettes and lions' heads. This entablature is closely similar to that of the Traianeum at Pergamon and suggests that Hadrian may have brought in an architect from Pergamon,

111 Rome, remains in the Piazza di Pietra of the Temple of Deified Hadrian, dedicated in AD 145

109 TOP LEFT Rome, Temple of Venus and Rome, dedicated AD 135: plan

110 BOTTOM LEFT Rome, Temple of Venus and Rome: entablature according to Canina

112 Rome, Mausoleum of Hadrian (now Castel Sant 'Angelo) completed in AD 140. In the foreground is the Pons Aelius inaugurated in AD 134

perhaps after his quarrel with Apollodorus. This new type of entablature represents the first major break with the orthodox Corinthian order as evolved by the architects of Augustus – in Rome at least. It was not destined to last long, but two other major monuments had similar features. Strictly, they are not Hadrianic buildings as both were finished after his death, but as both commemorate him they should be mentioned here.

The Temple of Deified Hadrian in the Campus Martius was begun about AD 139–140 and dedicated in AD 145. Almost a whole side survives to form an imposing feature of the modern Piazza di Pietra (fig. 111). Like the Temple of Venus and Rome, it has a two-stepped architrave and the cornice is supported by plain consoles instead of modillions, but the frieze in this case is pulvinated. The sima has a similar arrangement of palmettes and lions' heads. Once again the same architects must have been at work.

The last monument to Hadrian was his Mausoleum on the east bank of the Tiber, finished, along with the bridge which gives access to it, in AD 140 (fig. 112). The enormous cylinder of tufa 64 metres in diameter faced with marble on a square base was once covered with a mound of earth with a triumphal monument capped with a bronze quadriga in the centre. The marble entablature of the square base has details which are the hallmark of Pergamene architects. The solidity of its construction is attested by the fact that it served as the chief place of refuge for the medieval Popes, and is now known as the Castel Sant'Angelo. However, for the student of Roman architecture it is still the Mausoleum of the Emperor Hadrian, and bears silent witness to Rome at the height of her power.

9 North Africa

Moving from east to west across the North African Coast, one passes successively through Egypt, Cyrenaica, Tripolitania, the province of Africa Proconsularis, Numidia and Mauretania.

Egypt

The Pharaohs had ruled Egypt for two and a half millennia before it passed under Hellenistic rule in the fourth century BC. The older Egyptian capitals along the Nile were supplanted by the new city of Alexandria on the Delta, and it is to Alexandria that we must look for evidence of a Roman style of architecture in Egypt, because in the older cities any new building adhered strictly to Egyptian styles.

Sadly, little is known about Hellenistic or Roman Alexandria and that little is rarely studied, but one or two buildings deserve mention in an attempt to illustrate Egypt's contribution to architecture in the region. The most significant architectural remains of Alexandria are a group of rock-art tombs excavated in this and the previous century, the tombs of Shatby, Moustapha Pasha and Anfoushy. Most of these tombs date to the third century BC, but such was the architectural conservatism of the area that their architectural details remained influential into the Roman period and turn up in modified form in the adjacent province of Cyrenaica. Tomb I in the necropolis of Moustapha Pasha illustrates some of the characteristics of Alexandrian architecture (fig. 113). It appears to have four Doric half-columns supporting a standard Hellenistic Doric entablature, and there is a doorway between each pair of columns. However, looking more closely one sees that the outer columns are not really half-columns at all, but pairs of quarter columns united to form what Ward Perkins describes as 'heart-shaped' piers. This very aptly describes their plan. Heart-shaped piers and quarter columns engaged into antae appear to have been an Alexandrian invention and turn up with great frequency in both Cyrenaica and Tripolitania. Another feature of the tomb is the pilasters flanking the doorway. As Lyttelton says: 'The invention of pilasters was to prove extremely important in the development of baroque façades, for pilasters represent a complete divorce between structure and

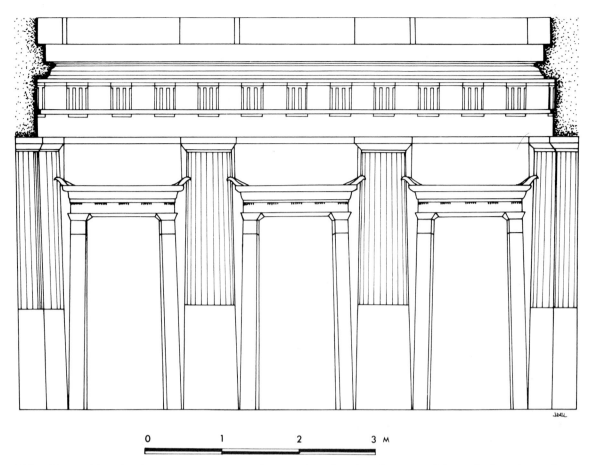

0 1 2 3 M

113 Alexandria, Tomb I of the Necropolis of Moustapha Pasha, third century BC. Reconstruction of the south wall of the court (after A. Adriani, *Annuaire du musée greco-romain*, 1933–35, Alexandria)

appearance, and mean that the visual composition of a façade can be built up without any limitation imposed by the necessity to combine structure and decoration.' The doorways themselves are of a type which proved extremely influential in Cyrenaica later on (fig. 119). The doorways become narrower towards the top although the flanking pilasters are of even width from top to bottom. Their capitals are a rectangular panel capped by a reel ornament with two fillets hanging down at either side. The same unusual type of capital turns up with great frequency throughout Cyrenaica. The architrave is plain, but has five sets of guttae on its upper edge. There are however no triglyphs in the rather perfunctory frieze. This feature too is common in Cyrenaican doorways. Perhaps the most interesting feature of the doorway and the one most difficult to illustrate is the fact that the jambs are slightly splayed outwards and the entablature rakes upwards. This striking perspective effect is echoed in doorways at Cyrene, Berenice and Ptolemais.

Among other architectural features which may have originated in Alexandria mention should be made of the segmental pediment, early examples of which appear in the necropolis of Anfoushy dating perhaps from the first century BC.

Alexandria seems to have employed the modillion as a decorative feature for cornices from an early date. A modillion cornice was found in the third-century BC Tomb III of the Moustapha Pasha necropolis. Alexandrian modillions are usually flat and narrow with a single groove running along the underside (fig. 116). This kind of modillion can be seen in the House of the Faun at Pompeii and at Palmyra. Another type of modillion is flat, square and completely hollowed out. It is edged by a deep groove. Sometimes hollowed-out modillions alternate with the single groove type. Both kinds of modillion are commonly found in Cyrenaica, for example in the Palazzo delle Colonne at Ptolemais.

Cyrenaica

Libya is composed of two distinct provinces, Tripolitania in the west and Cyrenaica in the east. Between them is the Syrtic gulf which is hazardous to shipping, and, as it cuts deeply into the North African land mass, the desert extends right up to the coast along most of its length. Thus the two provinces are separated by a double natural barrier. Historically too they developed quite separately. The Phoenicians had established trading stations on the Tripolitanian coast from early times, at Sabratha, Oea (Tripoli) and Lepcis Magna, but both the Phoenicians and the Greeks had avoided the Cyrenaican coast because of its proximity to Egypt which did not encourage foreign merchants. All this changed in 663 BC when a new government was established in Egypt. As a result the Greeks were allowed to set up trading posts on the Nile Delta and shortly afterwards established the colony of Cyrene (630 BC).

Cyrene stands on the highest point of the *gebel* or mountain range which runs along the Cyrenaican coast from just east of Benghazi to the Egyptian frontier and, as well as having a high annual rainfall, commands spectacular views down to the sea about 18 kilometres away. Cyrene soon became a flourishing city and its monuments were as splendid as those of any major city of the Greek mainland. At the lower end of the town is the Sanctuary of Apollo, while higher up on one ridge is the Temple of Zeus and on the other the agora along with most of the civic monuments of the town (fig. 114). Cyrene was one of the great cultural centres of the Greek world and famous for its artists, writers and philosophers. It was committed to Roman protection by the will of its ruler and passed to them in 96 BC. Cyrenaica was never a wealthy province and there were few major building projects during the period of Roman rule. Instead, existing buildings were adapted to suit Roman taste.

At the end of the Augustan period an inscription records that M. Sufenas Proculus rebuilt the old Hellenistic gymnasium and adapted it to the new Imperial cult. The building is a rectangular enclosure measuring 81 × 52 metres and surrounded on three sides

114 OVERLEAF Cyrene, general plan

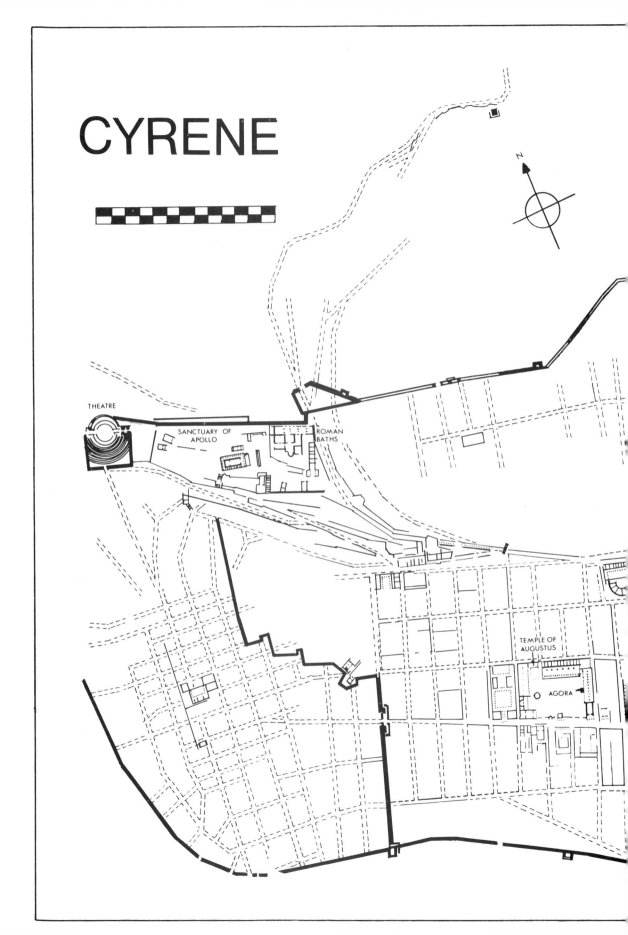

CYRENE

THEATRE

SANCTUARY OF
APOLLO

ROMAN
BATHS

TEMPLE OF
AUGUSTUS

AGORA

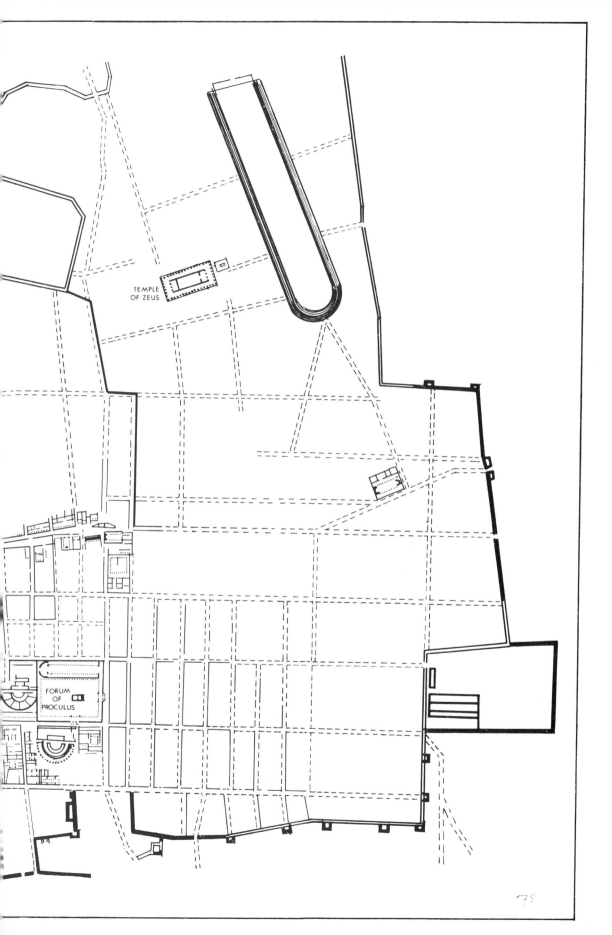

TEMPLE
OF ZEUS

FORUM
OF
PROCULUS

115 Cyrene, the basilica, built at the time of Trajan (AD 98–117) with the Forum of Proculus behind, an Augustan remodelling of the original Hellenistic gymnasium

by colonnaded porticoes. The fourth side may originally have housed a stoa. Proculus does not seem to have modified the Hellenistic building to any extent as it still retains its slender Doric columns, their lowest third faceted, and the upper two-thirds fluted. The façade of the building in fine isodomic masonry is pierced by two doorways, each with a tetrastyle Doric portico both on the outer and inner sides. At the time of Trajan the stoa was replaced by a basilica (fig. 115) with two rows of plain unfluted columns dividing it into a nave and two aisles, with an apse at the end. The overall appearance of the complex cannot have been very different from what it was in Hellenistic times and reflects the conservatism of the region.

At the time of Trajan, a large bath building was constructed in the north-east corner of the Sanctuary of Apollo close to the old retaining wall, presumably in a spot where there was an assured water supply. As was the case with many baths in the eastern Empire it only half-heartedly followed Roman fashions. Most of the work is in cut-stone and there is frequent use of columns. The plan lacks both the complexity and symmetry of Roman models. It can, however, be considered the most thoroughly 'Roman' building in Cyrene. As it encroached upon the sanctuary area a new propylon had to be built, to the north-west of the old one. It was totally inoffensive, with its four unfluted Corinthian columns and gateways behind, and, as usual, it was all of local honey-coloured stone.

A more unusual and dangerous transformation took place in the Greek theatre at the end of the sanctuary platform. The stage buildings were swept away and extra banks of seats were built in their place, thus transforming the theatre into a circular amphitheatre. The new seats, perilously poised over the edge of a steeply sloping hillside, have long since collapsed into the gorge below.

In AD 115–116 the Jewish revolt broke out, and as a result Cyrene was left in ruins. Trajan's successor, Hadrian, began the work of restoration. The Temple of Apollo was rebuilt with columns of the Doric order, but their shafts were left unfluted. Damage to the Temple of Zeus must have been more serious because the outer colonnade was never completely rebuilt. Instead work was confined to the interior. Two rows of cipollino columns were set close to the side walls and a massive platform built at the far end of the cella to support a gigantic new seated statue of Zeus.

All in all the architectural history of Cyrene was one of continuous adaptation of old buildings to new purposes, but with few innovative projects. One of the most striking examples of make-do and mend is the statue of a female figure whose breasts were clumsily removed to turn it into a male body so that the head of an Emperor could be substituted.

Cyrene's port, Apollonia, is mainly distinguished for its splendid Byzantine churches and palace. Its major pre-Byzantine survival, the theatre, was remodelled by Domitian, who added the typically Roman columnar stage buildings. Further along the coast Ptolemais, as its name implies, a Ptolemaic foundation dating to later third century BC, has provided us with several important buildings of the Roman period. The town is situated on the coastal plain between the *gebel* and the sea. At this point the plain is less than two kilometres wide and the mountains behind the city supply the huge and impressive water cisterns to the south. These cover an area 66 by 70.60 metres and are composed of a huge system of underground vaults, which, above ground, form a large concrete terrace flanked on all four sides by a Doric colonnade. The city's amenities also included a hippodrome, two theatres, an odeion and an amphitheatre.

Two villas uncovered at Ptolemais are of particular interest. One, the 'Palazzo delle colonne' excavated by Italian archaeologists before the war and sited in the centre of the town at the intersection of the two main streets, is a huge late Hellenistic peristyle house (fig. 117). The main rooms are grouped around a peristyle with heart-

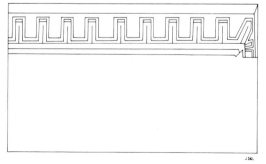

116 Cyrenaican modillions found at Ptolemais. The square, flat, hollowed-out type (left) and the narrow type with a single groove running along the underside (right)

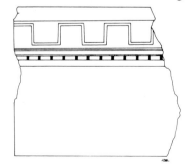

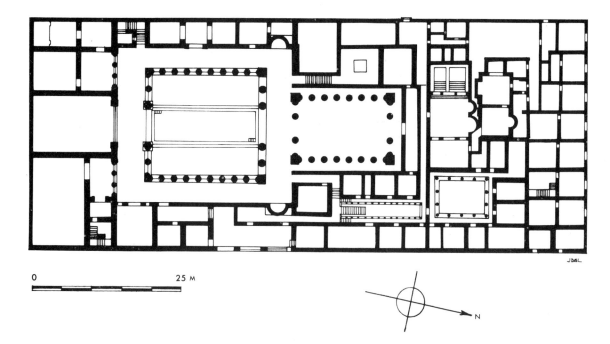

117 Ptolemais, Palazzo delle colonne, late second or first century BC: plan of both levels

shaped angle piers. A large *oecus* with an internal colonnade running close to the walls lies to the north. The columns have acanthus leaves around the lowest part of the shaft, and the leaves have wide oval holes between the touching segments, a feature found on the acanthus column at Delphi and the propylon to the Bouleuterion at Miletus. The upper order of the north side of the peristyle court has a decorative arrangement of small Corinthian columns and pilasters to form three highly ornate aedicules (fig. 118). The central aedicule has a round-headed niche set between two pairs of pilasters. The pairs of pilasters support a pediment which is broken by the head of the niche. The outer aedicules each have a pair of pilasters supporting a hollow pediment. Flanking them are single columns supporting steeply raking quarter pediments. The scheme is reminiscent of the tombs at Petra, such as the Khasne, but in the Palazzo there is no close relationship between the upper and lower orders. The dating of the building has given rise to much controversy. Parts of it, like the colonnade of the oecus, appear to be late Hellenistic, while the upper order of the peristyle may be Augustan, which would make it one of the earliest known examples of the type of fantastic architectural composition which was to enjoy such vogue in the eastern provinces during the next three centuries.

The other villa at Ptolemais, excavated by the Oriental Institute of Chicago, is a little later than the Palazzo and somewhat plainer in its decoration. The main rooms are grouped around a peristyle, and there is in addition a private suite of rooms surrounding a small tetrastyle atrium. One small suite of rooms is divided by a screen of

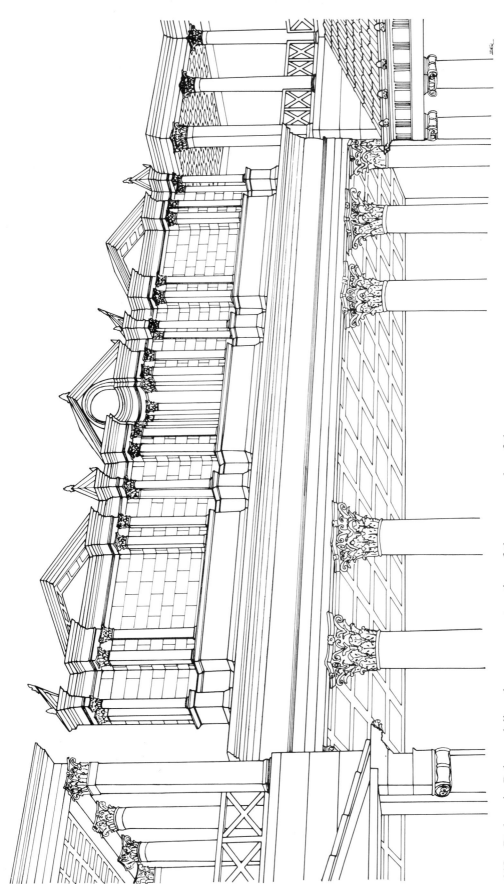

118 Ptolemais, Palazzo delle colonne: reconstruction of the upper order of the north side of the peristyle court. (?) Augustan

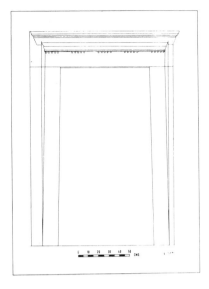 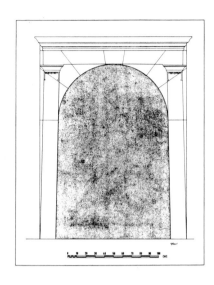

119 Berenice (Benghazi), reconstruction of a lintelled doorway (early first century AD) and an arched doorway (early second century AD)

four Ionic columns with an arch between the central pair and lintels between the outer pairs. The central intercolumniation is wider than the outer pair and as a result the proportions are correct (in contrast to the Canopus of Hadrian's villa, see p. 180). The arrangement is similar to that of the façade of the Temple of Hadrian at Ephesus (fig. 161).

Mention should be made of recent excavations on the site of Berenice, a Hellenistic foundation which now lies under modern Benghazi. The plans and architectural details of the buildings uncovered show that they were closely influenced by their larger neighbour, Ptolemais. The subtleties of Ptolemaic doorways were repeated in coarser form (fig. 119) and represent a further dilution of the same Alexandrian influence which inspired the architecture of Ptolemais and Cyrene.

Tripolitania

The interior of Tripolitania is mostly desert, and its inhabited areas are concentrated into the coastal strip between Sabratha and Misurata and in the eastern *gebel*, the precipitous edge of the Saharan plateau where the rainfall is highest. Today the climate is a harsh one. For much of the year the scorching *ghibli*, or south wind, brings heat and sand from the desert. Most of the year's rain falls in a brief few days and converts the dried-up river beds, or *wadis*, into raging torrents. The result is that much of the water drains rapidly away before it can irrigate the land, and carries away the topsoil in its course. Conditions may have been less rigorous in Roman times. We know, for example, that horses, cattle and elephants lived there, animals which could not survive today. The countryside produced a prodigious quantity of olive oil and provided crops of wheat and barley as well as wine. The Sahara desert had probably not spread so far north, and there were more trees. This fertility was due in no small measure to the Romans themselves, who took every precaution to conserve rainwater by means of dams, aqueducts and the underground cisterns which are such a feature of Roman houses in north Africa. However, one ever-present menace was the shifting sand dunes, and it is to the dunes which finally engulfed Lepcis Magna and Sabratha that we owe the remarkable preservation of these two cities.

Tripolitania came under Roman protection when Carthage, the chief Phoenician city in North Africa, was destroyed in the Third Punic War (146 BC), and it was annexed to the Empire a hundred years later. Lepcis Magna seems to have fared well under the rule of Augustus. During the late first century BC and the first half of the first century AD substantial additions were made to the Old Forum which lay near the sea to the west of the harbour (fig. 121). The Forum was laid out on strictly rectangular lines except for the north-east side which remained oblique, perhaps because of the alignment of an earlier building. The three temples which dominate the north-west side of the square were all built at this time. They have the high podium characteristic of Italian buildings; the emphasis is frontal and the columns run round three sides only. The central temple, the Temple of Rome and Augustus (dedicated between AD 14 and 19), has a rostrum in front of it, approached by a pair of narrow staircases one each side, an arrangement reminiscent of the temple of Divus Julius in the Forum Romanum. Lepcis Magna grew rapidly in size during the first century AD. The main axial street, or cardo, was twice extended by a total of 600 metres, and buildings sprang up in quick succession along it. A market, similar to that at Pozzuoli, with a circular kiosk inside a rectangular porticoed courtyard was built in 8 BC. A *chalcidicum*, or monumental portico, was built in AD 11–12, and the theatre in AD 1. The fact that the latter was built at the expense of a private citizen, Annobal Rufus, seems to indicate a general prosperity in the region. The large auditorium, 90 metres in diameter, was skilfully built, its lowest part resting on a natural slope supplemented by an artificial earthwork, and the upper part of the seating resting on rings of concrete and masonry vaulting. The stage with its lofty podium is decorated with a row of niches and contains the slot into which the curtain was lowered before each performance. Behind rises the magnificent stage wall, or scaenae frons, with its three tiers of columns curving into three bold recesses. The marble columns to be seen today are Antonine replacements of the original Augustan grey limestone.

Until the time of Hadrian limestone was the standard building material at Lepcis. The Arch of Trajan (AD 109–110), a four-sided

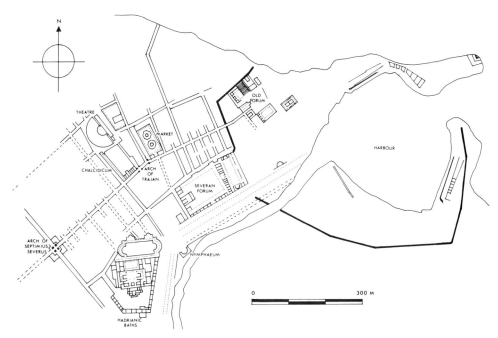

120 Lepcis Magna, general plan

121 Lepcis Magna, Severan Forum and basilica, dedicated in AD 216: plan

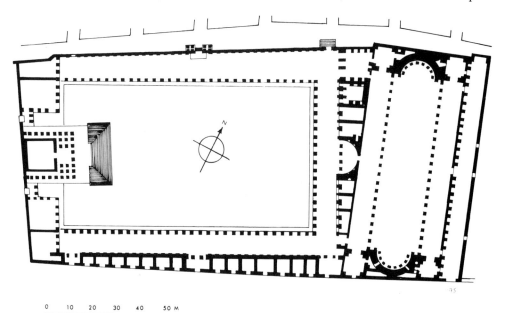

arch standing over a cross-roads, was one of the last buildings in the city to be built entirely of this material. In the reign of Hadrian marble came into use on a large scale. It came from Greece and Asia Minor and is similar to that used in several Hadrianic projects in Rome. The most important building of the period is the Hadrianic Baths. Dedicated in AD 126–127 they come comparatively early in the series of great symmetrical bath buildings, of which the first example was the Baths of Trajan at Rome (AD 109). The warm rooms face south and on the north side is a big open-air swimming pool. The rooms are arranged in an axial sequence: swimming pool (natatio), cold room (frigidarium), warm room (tepidarium), hot room (caldarium) and sweating rooms (sudatoria) to the sides. The frigidarium is the largest room of all and lies across the main axis. Because of its position in the centre of the complex, with rooms on all sides, it had to be lit by means of a clerestory, which meant that it was also higher than the surrounding rooms. Although little of the vaulting or the upper parts of the walls has survived the open-air pool and most of the plunges are substantially intact. The pool measures 27.80×14.55 metres and is 1.75 metres deep, with three steps leading down to the water on all sides. Covered colonnades provide shade on three sides, and along the fourth is a row of deep round-headed arches, their soffits gleaming with brightly coloured glass mosaic. The high vault of the frigidarium was once covered with mosaic, and three large fragments with scrolls, vine tendrils and foliage patterns picked out in bright green and yellow glass perhaps belonged to this vault. The tepidarium has a richly marbled plunge bath flanked at each side by a screen of two Corinthian columns of grey marble. Of the hot rooms special mention should be made of the sudatoria where many of the original heating installations have survived. Hot air was passed not only under the floor, but also through rows of terracotta tubes lining the walls.

The splendours of the Hadrianic Baths were only a prelude to the magnificence to come. At the end of the second century AD Lepcis Magna was one of the wealthiest cities in the Roman world. It was also the birthplace of the Emperor Septimius Severus, who reigned AD 193–211. During his reign he was immensely liberal towards the city of his birth. He endowed it with an entire new quarter, comprising a monumental nymphaeum, a new forum and a basilica, flanked by a broad colonnaded street linking the Baths of Hadrian with the harbour, which he also embellished. The Severan monuments of Lepcis are of more than purely local interest. They would scarcely have been out of place in the capital itself and are more complete as a group than any contemporary monuments in Rome. It is as a group that they should be discussed because that was the way they were conceived.

The surviving part of the colonnaded street is 450 metres long and over 50 metres broad, a width only exceeded by the streets in some

122 Lepcis Magna, Severan Forum: part of the arcade. Dedicated AD 216

Roman towns in Syria. On either side were porticoes supported by columns with Pergamene capitals. Since the Hadrianic Baths were aligned on a strict north/south axis which ran diagonal to the rest of the grid plan while the new forum was aligned to the existing grid, the new colonnaded street had to change direction abruptly by the palaestra of the baths. A monumental nymphaeum was built at the intersection to divert the eye. The use of monuments as elements in town-planning was a device well-known to Hellenistic architects and one with which the Romans were equally familiar. The nymphaeum was a spectacular structure. It had a big semicircular fountain basin, screened by a high semicircular back wall of concrete faced with masonry, and elaborately decorated with niches and columns of red granite. Half of the back wall has collapsed, but, interestingly, it remained in one piece as it fell, a positive demonstration of the monolithic quality of Roman concrete.

Along the north-east side of the street stands the Forum (fig. 121), a big rectangular enclosure, measuring some 100 × 60 metres, surrounded by a high masonry wall of a rather severe, almost military character. Indeed the Forum was converted into a fortress in Byzantine times. Around the inside of the Forum ran an arcaded portico with alternate Medusa and Nereid heads set in the spandrels (fig. 123). Against the south-west wall stood a large temple, raised on a lofty podium and approached by a monumental staircase. The temple had columns around three sides only, in the manner of the Temple of Mars Ultor in the Forum of Augustus. The basilica lay opposite, an arrangement reminiscent of Trajan's Forum and, like the Basilica Ulpia, it has an apse at each end. The nave is flanked each side by a double-storeyed aisle of Corinthian columns with red granite shafts (fig. 123). The interior decoration is of exceptional richness. Each apse is flanked by two pairs of white marble pilasters with deeply undercut vine scrolls inhabited by mythological figures. The sculpture was probably the work of artists from Aphrodisias. A complicated arrangement of detached columns runs round the drum of each apse – with a pair of giant-order columns in the centre and a two-tier arrangement either side – a somewhat unsatisfactory effect which may be due to a modification of the original plan. The building had a wooden roof with the very considerable span of 19 metres.

In gratitude for his favours the citizens of Lepcis Magna erected a Triumphal Arch in honour of the Emperor. It seems to have been built somewhat hastily, perhaps so that it could be finished in time for the Emperor's visit to his birthplace in AD 203. It is four-sided and stood at a cross-roads. The fact that the floor is raised seems to indicate that it was not for wheeled traffic. Its decoration is exuberant. On either side of the main passageway stood Corinthian columns supporting steeply raking half pediments. At the corners of the arch are pilasters richly decorated with vine scrolls inhabited by cupids and birds. They were again probably the work of the sculptors from Aphrodisias who worked on the basilica. In the attic were the famous series of reliefs commemorating the triumph of Septimius Severus and his sons.

Before passing on to the other cities of Tripolitania a word should be said about the Hunting Baths at Lepcis Magna, a small bathing complex built towards the end of the second century, and of

123 Lepcis Magna, Severan basilica, dedicated AD 216

124 Lepcis Magna, the Hunting Baths, late second century AD

exceptional interest in the history of concrete (fig. 124). The complex consists of a compact set of rooms: a barrel-vaulted frigidarium with an apse each end; a cross-vaulted plunge opening off the frigidarium to the north; an octagonal tepidarium preceded by a similar octagonal vestibule, both domed; and a barrel-vaulted caldarium. All these rooms were of concrete. The building seems to have been planned completely from within, and from the outside no attempt was made to conceal the array of barrel-vaults, domes and apses. Its excellent state of preservation both inside and out makes it tolerably certain that the exterior was designed to look much as it does today and was not treated with pedimental roofs and Classical Orders, a fact which may cause us to reconsider our views about the external appearance of later Roman buildings.

Sabratha did not enjoy the same Imperial favours as Lepcis, with the result that its growth was slower, although more sustained. Its building stone was a friable honey-coloured limestone coated with stucco. The buildings needed constant maintenance and marble was only slowly introduced as buildings were repaired or rebuilt on more regular lines. It was not until the second century AD that a new quarter was laid out near the sea to the east of the old Forum area. The most important monument, the late second-century theatre, was actually bigger than that at Lepcis (fig. 125). In most essentials the two theatres are similar, but because of its better state of preservation it was possible for the Italian archaeologists who excavated Sabratha before World War II to make a comprehensive restoration of the scaenae frons, with spectacular results.

The third main city of Tripolitania, Oea, corresponds to modern Tripoli, and unlike Sabratha and Lepcis, has been continuously occupied since Roman times. As a result little of the Roman town has survived above ground, except for the fine four-sided Arch of

Marcus Aurelius. It was built at the private expense of Caius Calpurnius Celsus and dedicated in AD 163. It is entirely of marble and was probably the work of Greek craftsmen (fig. 126). Perhaps the most interesting feature of the arch from an architectural point of view is the dome which covers the crossing. Four lintels, one at each corner, convert the square at the crossing into an octagon, which supports the dome of three rows of stone voussoirs topped by an octagonal keystone. This is thus yet another proof that techniques for covering a square with a dome existed well before Byzantine times.

125 Sabratha, the theatre showing the *scaenae frons*. Late second century AD

126 Oea (Tripoli), the Arch of Marcus Aurelius, dedicated in AD 163

The Severan dynasty saw Tripolitania at its height. Septimius Severus had conferred upon Lepcis the privilege of *ius italicum* which effectively gave it the same status as cities in Italy. In gratitude the city voted to supply Rome with free olive oil in perpetuity. In future this was to prove a heavy burden for the dwindling resources of Lepcis. When the dynasty of African Emperors ended with the murder of Alexander Severus in AD 235 the Empire was plunged into 50 years of continuous civil war, which brought with it economic ruin for Italy as well as North Africa. The splendours of Lepcis, which were not based on any sound economic foundation, brought her to collapse sooner than Sabratha, which had enjoyed no such lavish favours.

Africa Proconsularis and Numidia

To the west of arid, semi-desert Tripolitania are the rolling plains of Tunisia, the mountainous strongholds of Algeria and what is still today that remote and exotic country of Morocco, walled in by the massive Atlas mountains. Most of what is now Tunisia was the territory of Carthage, the most powerful Phoenician trading city on the North African coast. To the south and west lay Numidia, ruled by the local kings who caused Rome so much trouble in the late Republic. Further to the west were lands which had had little contact with the higher civilization of the Greeks or the Phoenicians and never acquired more than a veneer of Roman civilization.

As a result of the Third Punic War (149–146 BC), Carthage was destroyed and the area around it became the Roman province of Africa Proconsularis. For a long time Numidia was a dependent kingdom, but by Augustus' reign it was incorporated into the Empire; and by the time of Trajan all North Africa was taken over. Of Carthage itself disappointingly little survives, largely because of its proximity to modern Tunis. Perhaps the most notable remains are the Antonine Baths (AD 145–162), which are on almost the same scale as the later Baths of Caracalla in Rome, the main block being actually a little wider than that of its Roman counterpart. They are magnificently sited by the shore, with the frigidarium nearest the sea. This side of the building is joined to the perimeter wall in the manner of the Baths of Trajan (see p. 157). The layout of the natatio, frigidarium and flanking palaestrae is fairly conventional, but the five octagonal heated rooms swell out from the main block in a gentle curve reminiscent of the contemporary Forum Baths at Ostia (fig. 75). The Antonine Baths suggest that Roman Carthage must have been a large and prosperous city. Perhaps the extensive international excavations in progress at the moment will reveal comparable monuments.

Along the road leading south from Tunis to Zaghouan can be seen the remains of one of the most impressive of Roman aqueducts. It is 80 kilometres long and provided Carthage with most of its drinking water. It was built by Hadrian, partly of stone and partly of

brick, although it has been extensively repaired on several occasions.

Further south is the town of Thysdrus (El-Djem), whose famous amphitheatre (fig. 127) is such a conspicuous monument for some distance around. It owes its preservation to the fact that it was for centuries a place of refuge for the people of the area. It was probably built by Gordian I in about AD 238, and he was proclaimed Emperor in it. A very large building (149 metres long), it is mainly of stone construction with some concrete in the vaulting. A glance at its façade shows how pervasive was the influence of the Colosseum in dictating the overall appearance of Roman amphitheatres.

Tunisia is so full of Roman sites that it is difficult to do justice to them in a brief survey of this kind. However, two might well be singled out for mention, Thugga (Dougga) and Bulla Regia.

127 Thysdrus (El Djem), the amphitheatre, *c.* AD 238

128 Thugga (Dougga), Capitolium, AD 166–167

129 Bulla Regia, House of the Hunt: underground peristyle

130 Thamugadi (Timgad) founded AD 100, general view showing so-called Arch of Trajan

Dougga is a magnificently situated hill-town, originally the capital of one of the old Numidian kingdoms. In Roman times it must have resembled a hill-town of mediaeval Italy, with its winding streets, alleys and staircases. Many of the buildings, notably the Licinian Baths, are dramatically sited and command splendid panoramas over the plains below. The Capitolium (fig. 128) occupies a fine position on rising ground and overlooks an irregular forum sloping away in front. The temple itself has a fairly traditional appearance, with its tetrastyle porch of fluted Corinthian columns. The side and back walls are plain, but their construction should be noted. They are an extremely fine example of the use of orthostats with '*petit appareil*' (small stones) filling between. This type of construction was very common throughout North Africa.

Bulla Regia deserves mention because of its unusual houses. At

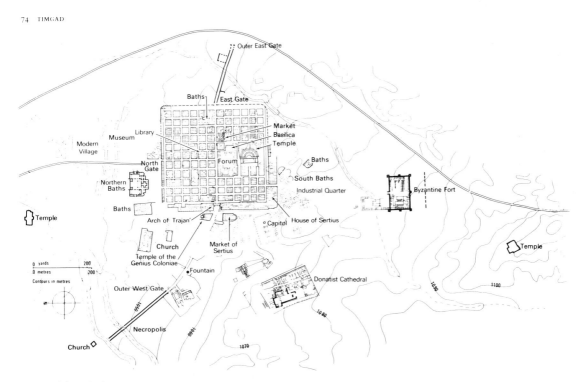

ground level the rooms are grouped around a big peristyle garden. Directly beneath the peristyle are a number of underground rooms disposed around an open court which corresponds to the peristyle above. The rooms are lit by light-wells as well as from the court itself (fig. 129). Many of the houses are equipped with fountains at the lower level, and must have been a haven of coolness in summer as well as being warm in winter.

Moving further west we leave the parts of the world which already had a developed urban civilization, and enter the mountainous regions of Algeria. Towards the end of the first century AD a number of military colonies were established in those areas. Thamugadi (Timgad), founded by Trajan about AD 100 as a colony of military veterans, is sited on the edge of the high Algerian plains. It was built partly to control the passes to the wild country to the south, and partly to spread Roman civilization in a semi-barbarous part of the Empire. To find a Roman city in such a remote part of the world is in itself surprising (fig. 130), but even more striking is its perfect layout (fig. 131). It is an exact square, measuring 1,200 Roman feet on each side, divided into city blocks, each 100 Roman feet square. The two main streets, cardo and decumanus, intersect in the middle, and where they meet is the Forum with its curia, basilica, main temple and rostrum, as well as a public lavatory with elegant arm-rests in the shape of dolphins. Near the Forum, on slightly rising ground is the theatre. The town developed rapidly

131 Thamugadi (Timgad), general plan (from M. I. Finley, *Atlas of Classical Archaeology*, London 1977)

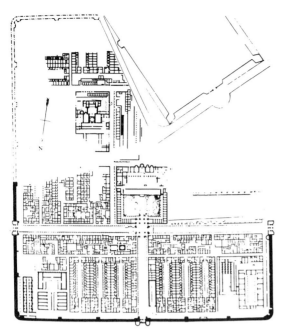

132 Lambaesis, Camp of the Third Legion, Augusta: plan (from P. Romanelli, *Topografia e archeologia dell' Africa romana*, *Enciclopedia Classica*, III, X, VII)

during the second century AD, and as there was no room in the existing street plan for new public buildings, the large public baths and the new Capitolium were built outside the original street plan, to the north and south-east respectively. One of the most conspicuous monuments of the town is the fine triple arch with its segmental pediments. It is known as the Arch of Trajan although it must date to the later second century AD.

Twenty-five kilometres to the west of Timgad is Lambaesis, the permanent camp of the Third Legion, Augusta (fig. 132). It is a rectangle measuring 550 × 450 metres and covers an area of just over 24 hectares (61 acres). It was rebuilt in its present form by Hadrian and was designed to accommodate 6,000 men. As it was a permanent camp the buildings are of masonry, and some are of monumental scale. In the middle is the principia, approached from the north by the Via Praetoria, a 20.7-metres-wide street flanked either side by porticoes. Crossing the camp in an east-west direction is the equally wide Via Principalis. These two roads were paved while the other roads of the camp are of beaten earth. Where the two main roads intersect is the monumental entrance to the principia, which is extremely well-preserved. It is in effect a large four-sided gate with three sides facing onto the two main roads and the fourth forming part of the principia behind. The sides which face the Via Principalis have a large entrance in the middle and a smaller entrance for pedestrians either side. The side facing the Via Praetoria has a similar arrangement, but with the extra elaboration of six free-standing columns on pedestals supporting projecting entablatures. Windows in the upper storey suggest that the building may originally have been roofed, and perhaps contained a guard chamber above in the manner of city gates. Beyond the monumental entrance is an open square surrounded on three sides by colonnades. On the fourth side, opposite the entrance, is an aisled basilica behind

133 Cuicul (Djemila): general plan (from M. I. Finley, *op. cit.*)

which are five small chambers, perhaps for the legionary standards, camp records and the treasury. Not all the camp has been excavated, but the two-thirds of it that has been uncovered contains many familiar buildings: houses for the commander and his officers to the east of the principia; barracks for the soldiers on the north side; and more spacious quarters at the north end of each barracks block for the centurions. In the north-east corner there are stables; and immediately to the west a courtyard surrounded on three sides by porticoes with a block of ten rooms opposite. Possibly the latter was used for meetings of the ten cohorts which comprised the legion. In the north-west corner is perhaps the valitudinarium or hospital. South-east of the principia is a big bathing establishment.

Forty-five kilometres to the north-west of Timgad is the military colony of Cuicul (Djemila), which was founded about AD 96 or 97. In appearance it could not be more different from Timgad, built as it was at the end of a narrow tongue of land with a gorge either side. All round are rolling hills of unsurpassed beauty. The town's layout is as regular as the terrain allows (fig. 133). In the middle is a rectangular forum, with its curia, capitolium and basilica. The nearby macellum or meat-market is often cited as a classic example of the type, with its shops grouped around a peristyle court with a circular kiosk in the middle. During the second century AD the town expanded southwards up the ridge. A new space outside the walls grew into a new forum, larger than the old one, dominated by the Arch of Caracalla (AD 216) and a temple to the Severan dynasty (AD 229) (fig. 134). The temple and the open space in front of it bring to mind the Capitolium at Dougga (fig. 128), reminding us that the influence of Italy was strong and direct in this part of the Roman world. Timgad and Djemila were both new foundations and their buildings, the basilica, the macellum, the baths and all the rest come directly from the repertory of Roman architects in Italy.

However, in the field of religion some indigenous types of building persisted. Although the gods worshipped in Roman Africa bore Roman names, they were still the same old native deities to those who worshipped them, and although the temples had a classical veneer, they did not invariably follow a Roman plan. There were the big, official temples, such as the Capitolium at Dougga and the Severan temple at Djemila, but there is also a second type of North African temple, which is a blend of the 'Punic' and 'Roman' types. It consists of a repository for sacred objects with a small sacred precinct opening off it. An example of this type of classicized local shrine is the Temple of Cereres at Thuburbo Maius.

Mauretania

Mauretania did not become a fully fledged Roman province until the time of Trajan and the second century was a period of rapid growth. However, although the towns follow Roman fashions one

cannot help feeling that their builders had an imperfect acquaintance with classical forms. Volubilis in the western part of Morocco was an old Mauretanian city which had enjoyed a period of Phoenician influence. It was much remodelled in Roman times and the centre included a forum, capitolium and basilica. A whole new quarter was laid out in the later second century with a colonnaded street running through it. This quarter of the city possesses a particularly fine series of peristyle houses with well-preserved polychrome mosaic floors and elaborate fountains in the middle of their gardens. Although the town is superbly sited and the houses have great charm, there can be no doubt that a Roman architect from the capital would have been dismayed by the debased Corinthian capitals and poor proportions of many of the monuments. It is in a town like Volubilis that we become aware of the cultural gap that existed between the great civilized centres of the Roman world and the fringes of the Empire. This is not unexpected in a province which had had so little contact with the more developed regions of the Mediterranean. However, it does underline the fact that the Roman Empire embraced a wide spectrum of nations, religions and cultures. That Roman architecture is as homogeneous as it is, and the very fact that we can apply the term Roman architecture to buildings throughout this culturally disparate Empire, is in itself a tribute to Rome as a civilizing power.

134 Cuicul (Djemila), view of the Severan Forum, showing (left) Arch of Caracalla and (right) Temple of the Severan family

10 The European Provinces

The European provinces include Spain, France, Britain, Germany and the Balkans.

Spain

The Spanish peninsula is the largest in the Mediterranean, accessible on three sides to the sea, but with a forbidding, arid interior. It is rich in metals and attracted traders from the earliest times. In 550 BC Greeks from Massilia (Marseilles) founded the colony of Emporion (Ampurias) on its north-east coast, while the Phoenicians set up trading posts in the south, Gades (Cadiz) and Carthago Nova (Cartagena). A clash over Spain brought about the second Punic war between Rome and Carthage, as a result of which Rome gained control of the peninsula. In 206 BC she set up a colony of Italians in the south on the river Guadalquivir and called it Italica. During the rest of the Republican era the Romans were engaged in a long and bitter struggle to subdue the interior. In 133 BC Numantia, a main centre of Spanish resistance, fell after a long siege, but the north coast was not subdued until the time of Augustus, when a series of colonies was established.

The old Greek town of Emporion was made a veterans' colony by Julius Caesar and expanded to accommodate 10,000 people. Soon the new town had a forum, basilica and an amphitheatre just outside the walls. Two fine late Republican houses have been found on the east side of the city. In style they are more Hellenistic than Roman, with their peristyle gardens and elegant fountains. The owners even had a stretch of the city walls pulled down to give them a better view over the sea, a situation analogous to Herculaneum where the House of the Stags was built out over the city walls to command a view of the coast.

Italica, the oldest Roman colony in Spain, was the birthplace of the Emperors Trajan and Hadrian. It was laid out on a grid plan with colonnades flanking the streets (fig. 135). The houses, which mostly date to the second and third centuries AD, have their rooms arranged around peristyle courtyards. Features of these houses are swimming pools and rich mosaic pavements. The town also has an

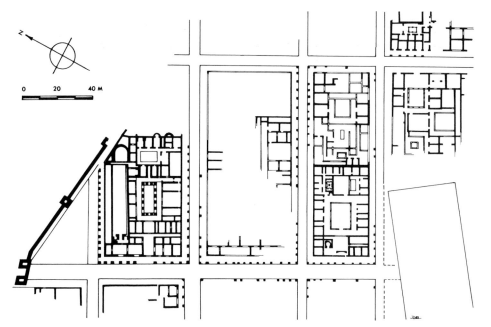

0   20   40 M

amphitheatre, built by Hadrian, which measures 160 × 137 metres and held 25,000 spectators.

135 Italica, general plan

Merida (Emerita Augusta) was founded by Agrippa in 25 BC as a colony and capital of the new province of Lusitania. By the third century AD its walls enclosed 50 hectares (123 acres), and it was one of the largest cities of the Empire. It had a splendid series of monuments including a theatre (18 BC), an amphitheatre (8 BC), three aqueducts, two bridges and a circus. The theatre is particularly impressive with its *scaenae frons* decorated with two tiers of polychrome marble columns. Its amphitheatre seated 15,000 and its circus was two-thirds the length of the Circus Maximus in Rome. The largest of the three aqueducts is still an impressive sight. It was constructed of small square stones laced with brick and survives to a height of 25 metres in parts. Also impressive is the bridge over the Guadiana, 760 metres long with 60 arches.

Some of the most notable monuments of Roman Spain are its bridges and aqueducts. Trajan built the famous bridge over the Tagus at Alcantara in AD 106 (fig. 136). The architect, as an inscription records, was a Lusitanian, Gaius Julius Lacer. It has the distinction of being the highest bridge in the Roman world, being 47 metres high. The arches gradually become wider towards the middle, so that the river can be crossed in a single span without setting the abutments in the stream (see p. 42). The two most famous aqueducts in Spain are at Segovia and Tarragona. The aqueduct at Segovia brings water from Riofrio, 17 kilometres away. The last kilometre of its route is the most dramatic, where it has to carry the water across a deep valley into the town itself. For this

136 Alcantara, bridge over the Tagus, built by Gaius Julius Lacer in AD 106

137 Segovia, aqueduct, first or early second century AD

purpose a bridge of 118 arches, 813 metres long, was built. The water channel is 30 metres above the ground at its highest point, and is carried on two tiers of arches (fig. 137). The lower tier is unusually tall and its piers extremely slender. It was probably to give the appearance of strength to this light structure that the unmortared granite blocks were left rough. Another impressive aqueduct crosses a valley, three kilometres outside Tarragona. It is 217 metres long and has a total height of 42 metres.

France

The south of France was particularly attuned to Roman civilization because of its long contact with the Greek colony of Massilia (Marseilles). Gallia Narbonensis (Provence) was annexed by the Romans in 121 BC, but there was no great building activity until the late first century BC. After his conquest of the three Gauls (58–51 BC), which correspond to modern France and Belgium, and parts of Germany, the Netherlands and Switzerland, Julius Caesar began to settle his retired legionaries in the south. Colonies were founded at Arelate (Arles), Arausio (Orange), Augusta Raurica (Augst), Nemausus (Nîmes), Lugdunum (Lyon) and Forum Julii (Fréjus). The Augustan peace also brought prosperity to local towns like Vasio (Vaison-la-Romaine) and Vienna (Vienne), as well as old Greek foundations like Massilia (Marseilles) and Glanum (St Rémy).

The influence of Rome on Gaulish architecture was strong and direct. City walls and gates bear close analogy to those of northern Italy. Baths, such as the late first-century BC ones at Glanum, have a similar layout to the Forum and Stabian Baths at Pompeii, which were presumably the type fashionable in Rome at the time. The theatre at Orange (fig. 142), the amphitheatres at Arles and Nîmes (fig. 140) and the Maison Carrée at Nîmes (fig. 139) were closely influenced by monuments in the capital, and the arch at Orange is actually the earliest triple arch to survive. However, although the Gauls were quick to accept Roman fashions, some buildings of a sacred character were largely unaffected by Roman taste. Traditional temples with a tall cella, usually surrounded on all sides by a low open portico, continued to be built all over Gaul, Britain and Germany, sometimes in simple materials, and sometimes monumentally with classical details. Some bath buildings, too, had an irregular layout dictated by the presence of a sacred spring, as at Aquae Sulis (Bath) (fig. 147).

Nemausus (Nîmes) was founded as a veterans' colony in 28 BC and in 16 BC a circuit of stone walls was built to enclose an area of 223 hectares (550 acres). At its peak its population has been estimated at 50,000. The walls are 2.5 metres wide and there are 19 towers along them of which the largest is the Tour Magne, a 40-metre-high octagonal tower, built at the highest point in the town as

138 Nîmes, Pont du Gard, late first century BC

a look-out. Another fine gate in the circuit is the Gate of Augustus (16–15 BC) which has two arched passageways for wheeled traffic, flanked by two smaller passageways for pedestrians. In the court-yard behind stood a statue of Augustus. In type it is essentially a simpler version of the great city gates of northern Italy, such as at Turin and Verona.

One of the most finely preserved aqueduct systems in the Roman world is that which brought water to Nîmes from springs 50 km away. It was built by Agrippa between 20–16 BC. Most of the channel is below ground or carried on a low wall and the water runs down a slope which has been calculated as 1 in 3,000 over the whole distance. To carry it across the gorge of the river Gardon, the famous 'Pont du Gard' was built, 269 metres long and 49 metres high (fig. 138). The proportions are simple: four units for the central arch, three for the lateral arches and one for the upper tier of arches, and six for the overall height. The bridge is slightly curved against the flow of the stream, and the wide central arch spans the stream itself so that no abutments are actually in the river bed. The bridge is built entirely of stone, with no clamps or mortar, some individual stones weighing up to six tonnes each. The many projecting bosses are left to support scaffolding for maintenance of the bridge. When the water arrived in Nîmes it flowed into a large circular basin with a settling tank and a series of outlets through which the water was fed to the various parts of the town.

Nîmes also possesses one of the best preserved of all Roman temples, the 'Maison Carrée ('square house') which dates to the Augustan period, and was dedicated to Rome and Augustus (fig. 139). It has a hexastyle porch of Corinthian columns standing on a high podium and it is pseudo-peripteral. The length and breadth of the stylobate are in the ratio of 2:1; and the podium, columns and entablature are related in the ratio of 2:5:2. In style the building seems to be strongly influenced by contemporary buildings at Rome.

139 Nîmes, Maison Carrée, begun *c.* 19 BC

140 Nîmes, amphitheatre, probably late first century AD

The acanthus scrolls in the frieze are reminiscent of the Ara Pacis and the channelled masonry is like that of the Temple of Mars Ultor.

Another notable monument of the city is the splendidly preserved amphitheatre, designed by T. Crispius Reburrus. It owes its survival to the fact that its honeycomb of passageways and chambers was used as a refuge in the Middle Ages. Its two-storeyed façade has

141 Nîmes, amphitheatre: the holes into which the masts for the velarium were inserted

openings flanked by pilasters and half-columns in the manner of the Colosseum, but the strong vertical emphasis suggests that it is a little later in date. The 120 holes for the masts which supported the velarium are still intact (fig. 141).

Arelate (Arles) was the earliest Roman colony to be founded after the conquest of Gaul (46 BC). Its two most conspicuous monuments are its theatre and amphitheatre, both well preserved. The theatre is probably older and was perhaps built shortly after the founding of the colony. There is some dispute about the date of the amphitheatre, although the architect was the same T. Crispius Reburrus who designed the one at Nîmes. In scale and detail it was almost the twin of the Nîmes amphitheatre, it too owing its survival to the fact that it was used as a fortified retreat in the Middle Ages.

Arausio (Orange), founded as a colony in 36–35 BC, possesses two monuments of special interest in the history of Roman architecture, the Arch of Tiberius and the theatre. The arch, built about AD 26, to commemorate the defeat of Julius Sacrovir who had led a rebellion in AD 21, is the first known triple arch. The arch of Augustus in the Roman Forum had a central arched opening, but was flanked by two lintelled passageways and cannot be regarded as a true triple arch. The arch at Orange has a large central arched passageway flanked by two lower arched passageways either side. The three arches are framed by four Corinthian half-columns standing on high pedestals, supporting a continuous entablature. Between the top of the side arches and the entablature are sculpted panels showing spoils of war, and in the attic are further relief panels. The arch has all the essential ingredients of the great triple arches of the later Empire, but lacks some features, such as free-

142 Orange, theatre, late first century AD

143 BELOW Vaison, House of the Silver Bust, late first century AD: plan

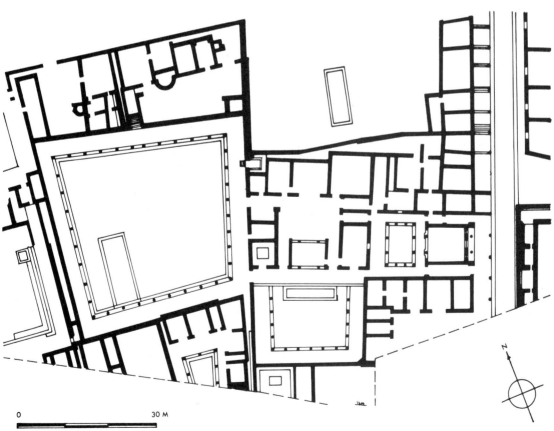

0   30 M

standing columns, victories in the spandrels, and the dedicatory inscription in the attic.

The theatre at Orange, probably built in the later first century AD, has an extremely well-preserved *scaenae frons*, 37 metres high. Its back wall survives practically intact, but most of the 76 columns which once adorned it have disappeared. However on the analogy of the finely reconstructed theatre at Sabratha (fig. 125) they must have been arranged on three tiers with aedicules emphasizing the three doors leading onto the stage. The exterior of the theatre is plainer in its design (fig. 142). The outer wall originally had a covered loggia at ground level. Higher up is a low-relief arcade and at the top a double row of projecting brackets designed to support the poles on which the *velarium* was hung.

Vasio (Vaison-la-Romaine) has been described as the Pompeii of Provence, mainly because of the excavation work of J. Sautel. There was a local hill town near the present site, and in 20 BC, taking advantage of the Augustan peace, the inhabitants moved down to found the town on its present flat site. It possessed a basilica, a large theatre and a praetorium, but is mostly famed for its fine peristyle houses. One of these, the House of the Messii, has a bath, latrine and many fine frescoed rooms, dating to the first century AD. In another, the House of the Silver Bust (fig. 143), the street façade is lined with a portico and there are shops behind. An entrance portico gives access to a columnar atrium beyond which are the principal rooms of the house. A peristyle garden with a small pool lies to the south, and a much larger peristyle is a complete private bathing suite.

While the elegant houses of Vasio give us some insight into the luxurious living conditions of wealthy Gauls, Glanum (St Rémy) shows us the older, Hellenistic type of house belonging to an earlier phase of Provençal history. It was settled by Greeks in the third century BC, and still preserved its bouleuterion and many Hellenistic houses, with peristyles and pebble mosaic floors, into Roman times. The town was sacked, perhaps by the Cimbri, in the late second century BC, but was revived by the Romans in the early first century BC. The baths probably belong to this early date. Glanum's most important monuments are the Mausoleum and the Arch of the Julii which date to about 40 BC. The Mausoleum, built by a Gaul enfranchised by Julius Caesar, has a square base adorned with reliefs of famous scenes from Greek mythology. The second storey is four-sided, with a pair of columns framing an arched opening on each side. The top storey consists of a ring of columns supporting a conical roof under which stands a statue of Julius. Like the arch of Tiberius at Orange, the Glanum arch is remarkably advanced for its date. In many respects it resembles the Arch of Titus, with its single-arched passageway flanked by piers framed by attached columns. The upper parts of the arch are missing.

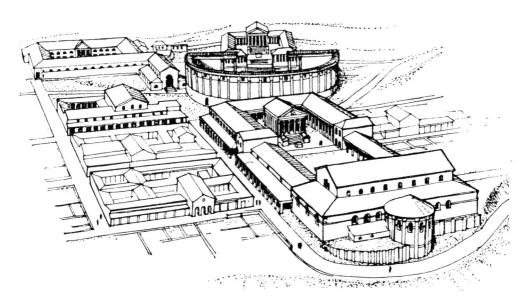

Of the many other towns of Gaul to deserve mention are Lugdunum (Lyon), founded by Munatius Plancus in 42 BC, with its well-preserved theatres, and Vienna (Vienne), with its large theatre, odeon, circus and well-preserved Temple of Augustus and Livia. The town of Augusta Raurica (Augst), near Basel, was also founded by Munatius Plancus, in 43 BC. The centre of the town was rebuilt in the mid-second century AD on regular lines (fig. 144). The basilica, forum and temple are built as a single complex over three city blocks. At one end is a large, hexastyle temple, the Capitolium, flanked on three sides by colonnades. In the middle is the forum area, and along the fourth side is the 64-metre-long basilica. The arrangement is immediately reminiscent of Trajan's Forum in Rome (fig. 23) and the Severan Forum at Lepcis Magna (fig. 121).

144 Augusta Raurica (Augst), restored view of the centre of the town, mid-second century AD with later modifications (from A. Boethius, *op. cit.*)

Britain

In AD 43 the Emperor Claudius invaded Britain with four legions and by AD 47 had overrun most of the south and east part of England. The revolt of Boudicca in AD 60 was a setback, but soon the Romans pushed their conquests into Wales (AD 78) and as far as the Moray Firth in Scotland (AD 84). The conquest was followed by the establishment of a network of military forts joined by a road system. Gradually the forts were replaced by civilian settlements, either colonies composed of Roman veterans or towns built as centres of tribal areas. Colonies like Colchester (AD 49), Lincoln (*c.* AD 90) and Gloucester (AD 96–98) had the dual purpose of consolidating Roman power and Romanizing the surrounding region. Native towns, such as St Albans and Canterbury, were often laid out on a Roman grid plan and enjoyed many amenities such as baths and theatres. The Celtic aristocracy was rapidly Romanized and as early as the first century AD villas, such as Fishbourne, were built on Roman lines. Over 600 villas are known in Britain, most of them dating to the third and fourth centuries AD.

Londinium (London) was founded as a port for trade with continental Europe. The town was sited on the north bank of the Thames at the lowest point where the river could be bridged. Burnt in the revolt of Boudicca, it was rebuilt in Flavian times and probably about that time raised in rank to a *colonia*. It is likely that some time in the late first century AD it became the provincial capital. At this time a huge forum was built covering an area of 3.2 hectares (eight acres) flanked by a basilica over 150 metres long. To the south-west of the Forum a Governor's palace was built about AD 85. At the beginning of the second century, a fort covering 4.45 hectares (11 acres) was built in the north-west corner of the city, and in the early third century a city wall was built incorporating the fort. A mithraeum was discovered in 1954 by the Walbrook stream. Built in the second century AD, it is divided into nave and two aisles by a row of columns and has an apse at the end. The nave had an earth floor and the aisles wooden ones.

Verulamium (St Albans), situated near the river Ver, some 50 kilometres north of London, was a native centre before the Roman invasion (fig. 145). Its subsequent development was typical of many non-colonial towns. In the first years following the invasion it became a military post, and soon afterwards a civilian settlement. Its grid plan was laid out before the revolt of Boudicca, although it suffered badly in the uprising because most of its buildings seem to have been of timber. The town was slowly rebuilt and some public monuments were made of stone, although houses continued to be wooden. In AD 155 a fire swept the town and afterwards stone

145 Verulamium, as it would have looked in the later second century AD: plan (from J. Wacher, *The Towns of Roman Britain*, London 1975, after S. S. Frere)

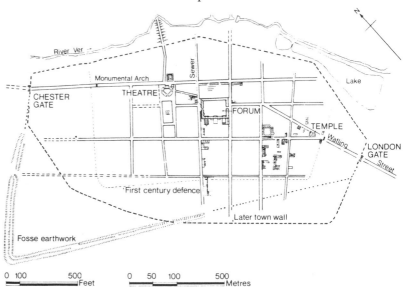

became more common in house construction. Many of these houses had painted walls and fine mosaic floors. During the second century the theatre was built as well as the two fine stone gateways known as the London and Chester gates. The city seems to have declined in the third century AD, when there was little building activity. However, the theatre was enlarged in the fourth century and houses were built and expanded. The discovery of a finely jointed wooden water pipe dating to the middle of the fifth century testifies that the town was still enjoying civilized amenities even at that late date.

Camulodunum (Colchester) became the capital of Cunobelinus in AD 5 and as such was a prime target in the Claudian invasion in AD 43. After the invasion a legionary fortress was built there, but it was supplanted by a veterans' colony in AD 49 and the defences pulled down. East of the colonia a huge classical-style temple of Claudius was built on a podium measuring 24×32 metres. The building of this temple sparked off the rebellion of the Queen of the Iceni, Boudicca. The town suffered severely in the rebellion and reconstruction was slow, the temple being restored only about AD 100. In the second century the town began to prosper and an area of 44 hectares (108 acres) was enclosed in walls measuring 2.64 metres thick on a 3-metre base. Many fine houses have been found dating to this period and the city seems to have been provided with running water and a sewerage system.

Calleva Atrebatum (Silchester) was a pre-Roman settlement and formed part of the realm of Cogidubnus after the Roman invasion (fig. 146). In Flavian times the Forum, measuring 43×40 metres, was built, flanked by a 84.5-metre-long basilica. At this time the grid plan was laid out, although the large number of buildings which do not conform to it suggest earlier settlement. Other buildings include an amphitheatre and public baths. On the basis of the capacity of these, the town probably only had a population of about 1,000 people.

Eburacum (York) seems to have begun as a fort in Flavian times or earlier. By the late Flavian period it became the headquarters of the Legio Hispana and the fortress was enlarged to cover 19.5 hectares (48 acres). The original defences were of turf and timber, but these were replaced by stone fortifications in AD 107–108. Parts of the *principia* have recently come to light under York Minster and substantial parts of the walling, and an elaborate stone sewerage system, survive. A civilian settlement grew up around the fortress and in the early third century AD its status was raised to colonia. When Septimius Severus divided Britain into two provinces, York became the capital of Britannia Inferior. Severus died in York in AD 211. It was also the place where Constantius I died and Constantine the Great was proclaimed Emperor.

Before the Roman conquest Aquae Sulis (Bath) was probably a spring sacred to the native goddess, Sulis, the equivalent of Minerva.

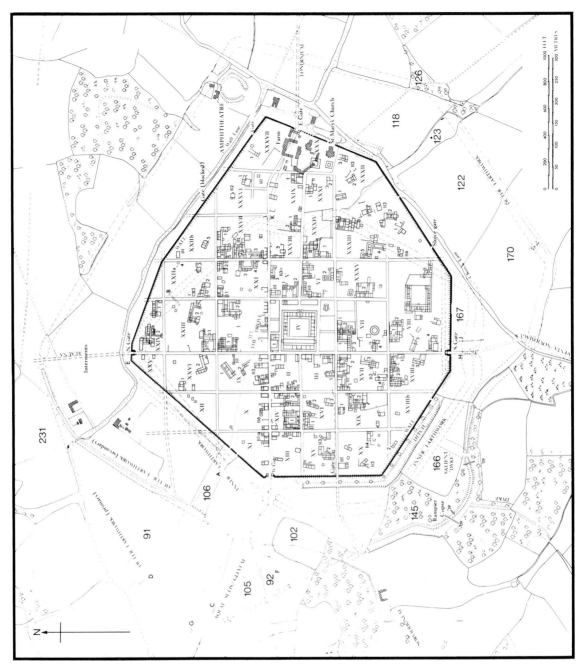

146 Silchester, general plan (from J. Wacher, *op. cit.*, after W. H. St John Hope and G. C. Boon)

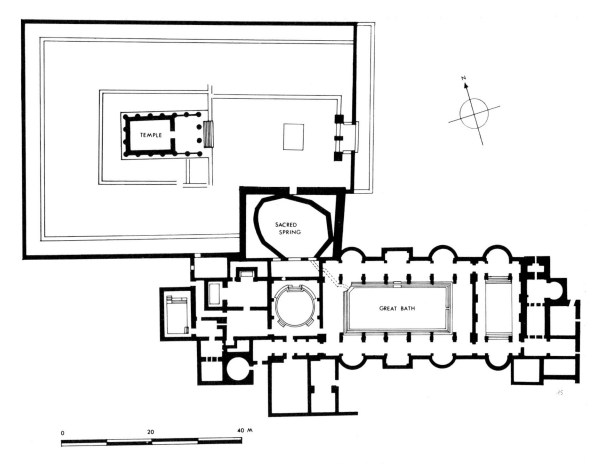

TEMPLE

SACRED SPRING

GREAT BATH

0   20   40 M

In Roman times it became a fashionable spa and the whole area around the spring was considerably developed. North of the spring a Temple to Sulis stood inside a colonnaded courtyard measuring 53 × 75 metres (fig. 147). The temple itself was raised on a tall podium with steps leading up to it. The façade had four Corinthian columns supporting a rather ill-proportioned entablature (fig. 148). The very high pediment contained a relief head of Medusa in a shield carried by flanking victories. The proportions of the podium are 2:1 and the cella was decorated with half-columns in the style of the Temple of Portunus at Rome (fig. 9) and the Maison Carrée at Nîmes (fig. 139). Bath must have been a cosmopolitan town, with visitors from all over Britain and a good number of Roman residents, which may explain why the temple is so Roman in appearance and so unlike the normal Romano-Celtic type of temple.

The baths themselves were laid out, probably close to the sacred spring, towards the end of the first century AD. A vestibule at the south led to the bathing chambers. To the east was the large swimming bath which measured 22 × 8.9 metres, with two smaller cold plunges beyond, and to the west the hot rooms. The swimming bath was lined with lead and covered with a wooden roof supported on 12 large masonry piers. Later, a second set of hot rooms replaced one of the smaller cold plunges and a laconicum was added to the

147 Aquae Sulis (Bath), Temple of Minerva and Roman baths, mid-second century AD: plan

223

148 Aquae Sulis, Temple of Minerva: reconstructed façade (from B. Cunliffe, *Roman Bath discovered*, London 1971)

hot rooms on the western side. A large circular cold bath replaced the vestibule to the west of the great bath. In the late second century AD the swimming pool was covered with a large barrel vault. In the fourth or fifth century the area became prone to flooding and the baths were abandoned.

Of the many hundreds of villas found in Britain the most famous is perhaps that at Fishbourne, which in scale surpasses any other. It was probably built for the loyal, pro-Roman king of the Regnenses, Cogidubnus, who tried to Romanize the area in the early years of Roman domination. The villa was not the first building on the site.

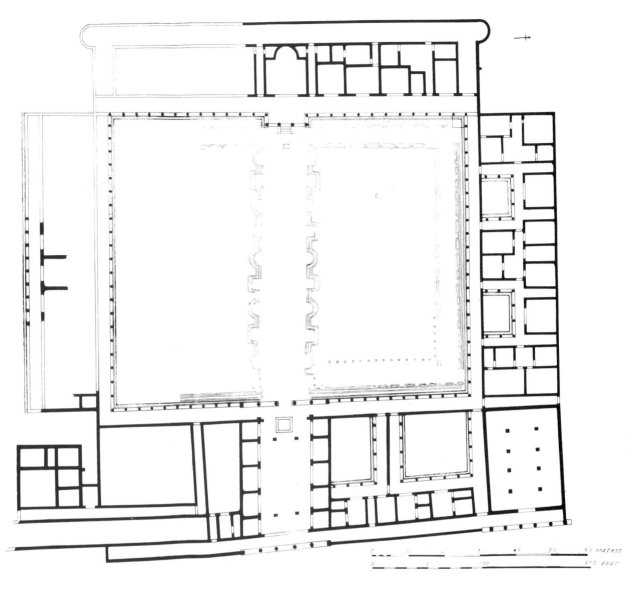

In the years immediately following the conquest the site was a supply depot, and then a timber house of some pretensions was built there. In the 60s AD a masonry building took the place of the wooden one, and it was not until AD 75 that the great villa was laid out. Presumably the earlier buildings proved unsatisfactory for Cogidubnus, whose title, *rex et legatus Augusti in Britannia*, entitled him to greater style. The huge villa, which perhaps served as his residence in old age, was an astonishing creation both for its time and its place, covering as it does over four hectares (ten acres). No comparable villa of the first century AD has been found in Europe outside Italy. The villa has four wings built around a huge formal garden. In the

149 Fishbourne, Roman palace: general plan (from B. Cunliffe, *Excavations at Fishbourne*, London 1971)

centre of the east wing is the vestibule with a hexastyle porch and a pool at the far end. To the north are suites of rooms set around two peristyle courtyards and in the corner is a basilica. There is a bath building in the south-east corner, and the private rooms of the king were ranged along the south wing. In the north wing was a set of guest chambers with fine mosaic pavements disposed around two peristyle courtyards. In the middle of the west wing was an apsed audience hall where official receptions took place.

The only Romano-British villas to approach Fishbourne in size were built in the fourth century AD. Chedworth is one of a number of Cotswold villas in the region of Corinium (Cirencester). It originally consisted of two buildings and a separate bathing suite, but by AD 300 these elements were united into an inner and outer courtyard. Fine mosaics were laid in the dining room and a second set of baths added.

Hadrian's Wall was the largest single project ever undertaken by the Romans in Britain and 'perhaps the largest and most remarkable building programme ever undertaken [in the British Isles] at any time' according to Wilson. In AD 105 Agricola's conquests in Scotland were given up and the frontier fixed along the road between Carlisle and Corbridge, known as the Stanegate, where a number of forts had already been established. There appears to have been a major uprising in northern Britain in AD 118 and as a result of a personal visit of the Emperor, Hadrian, it was decided to build a wall between the Solway Firth and the Tyne. Hadrian's Wall in fact runs a little to the north of the Stanegate where the main garrison was housed. The original plan called for a wall ten Roman feet wide, but the width was later reduced to eight feet. At every Roman mile along the wall there was a fortlet or 'milecastle' and between each pair of milecastles two look-out turrets. North of the wall ran a continuous ditch 8.5 metres wide and three metres deep, except where the wall ran along a ridge or other defensive feature. In about AD 124 it was decided to evacuate most of the Stanegate forts and move the fighting forces up to the wall itself. This required the building of 12 forts, and four more were added later. In connection with these forts was built a military road linking them and just behind the road to the south an elaborate earthwork known as the *vallum* was built to delineate the military zone of the wall.

The forts are shaped like playing cards, with straight sides and rounded angles. On a cliff edge they are parallel to the wall, e.g. Housesteads (fig. 22), but elsewhere lie north and south, sometimes with their northern third projecting through the wall. They are of two sizes, the larger covering about 1.8–2.2 hectares ($4\frac{1}{2}$–$5\frac{1}{2}$ acres), to house 1,000 men, and the smaller covering 1.2 hectares (3 acres) for 500 men. The general layout of a fort, with its principia, commandant's house, granaries, barracks, workshops and hospital has been described in an earlier chapter (p. 45). The best preserved forts on Hadrian's Wall are Chesters and Housesteads. Chesters contains a well-preserved bath house, remains of a bridge and a well-preserved headquarters building with its courtyard, cross-hall with tribunal, the room for the regimental standards and the strong room under its floor. Close to the nearby fort of Brocolitia (Carrawburgh) are the remains of a mithraeum. Housesteads is also well preserved and boasts the most complete Roman latrine in Britain.

Hadrian's Wall comes at an intermediate stage in the development of fortifications in Britain. The early forts built soon after the conquest were designed as bases for highly mobile troops who left the fort to fight in the open. By the time of Hadrian forts were becoming part of a static defence system and were equipped with ditches and ramparts and later on ballista platforms. Finally in the third and fourth centuries Saxon sea-raiders had begun to harry the coasts of England, the Low Countries and northern France, and as a defence against them a series of coastal forts were built in these areas. These forts of the Saxon shore have much more massive fortifications and took on more the appearance of mediaeval castles. There were 10 or 11 of them along the coast of south-east England. Mostly they had masonry walls about ten metres high with bastions and look-out towers. Communications between them seem to have been by sea because they usually do not lie near Roman roads. Richborough, Pevensey and Porchester are perhaps the finest of these forts. By the early fifth century the defence of Britain was no longer practicable and the island was abandoned by the Romans.

Germany

The northern frontier remained the most difficult to defend throughout the Roman Empire. In his conquest of Gaul Julius Caesar had penetrated as far as the Rhine. After Actium Augustus pushed his armies to the Danube and in a campaign of 12–9 BC the Roman armies crossed the Rhine and reached the Elbe. The Elbe/Danube line provided an excellent natural frontier along a short river boundary, but in AD 6, while Tiberius was actually operating against the Marcomanni beyond the Elbe/Danube line, a revolt in the Balkans caused him to recall his troops. In AD 9 the troops of P. Quinctilius Varus were ambushed between the Rhine and the Elbe and three legions were lost. Thereafter the Roman forces were recalled to the Rhine/Danube line to consolidate their position before advancing again, but no major advance ever took place. In Flavian times the triangle of land between the Neckar and the Rhine/Danube was annexed and the frontier pushed a little beyond the Rhine in the region of Mainz, but these gains were lost in the third century AD.

As early as Claudian times legionary forts began to be built on a more permanent basis in stone, and fortresses became more numerous as more men were posted to the Rhine/Danube frontier.

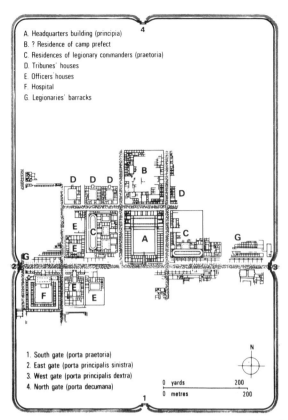

A. Headquarters building (principia)
B. ? Residence of camp prefect
C. Residences of legionary commanders (praetoria)
D. Tribunes' houses
E. Officers' houses
F. Hospital
G. Legionaries' barracks

1. South gate (porta praetoria)
2. East gate (porta principalis sinistra)
3. West gate (porta principalis dextra)
4. North gate (porta decumana)

0 yards 200
0 metres 200

150 Vetera (Xanten), plan of the two-legion fortress (from M. I. Finley, *op. cit.*)

At the time of Trajan no less than 12 legions were permanently stationed on the frontier. By the third century AD there were close to 150 legionary forts along the line of the *limes*, and 12 major legionary fortresses associated with them, Nijmegen, Xanten, Bonn, Neuss, Mainz, Strasbourg, Vindonissa, Regensburg, Vienna, Carnuntum, Brigetio and Aquincum. Where the frontier did not follow the Rhine/Danube, or either the Main or Neckar, wooden palisades were erected, probably at the time of Hadrian. The palisades had a road and timber watch-towers behind, although the latter were later rebuilt of stone. In the Danube region the palisade itself was replaced by a stone wall.

Augusta Treverorum (Trier), situated on the west bank of the Moselle, was established as a military post by Augustus and soon became a leading economic centre of the region. In the first century AD it became the residence of the procurator in charge of Belgic Gaul, and Upper and Lower Germany. The second century witnessed a burst of building activity with the laying out of a large forum, 400×150 metres, a new bridge, an amphitheatre and a large public bath building. The town attained its greatest importance in the late third century AD when it became the capital of Constantius Chlorus (see p. 265).

At Xanten on the lower Rhine there are substantial remains of a legionary fortress designed to house two legions (fig. 150). An older timber fortress covering 45 hectares (111 acres) was rebuilt in stone by Nero to cover 56 hectares (138 acres). Rectangular in shape, it had the normal four gates and the principia in the middle. To the north were the residences of the two legionary commanders. Smaller houses were built for the tribunes, and smaller ones again for the officers. A hospital and barracks have also been uncovered. In the period 98–105 Colonia Ulpia Traiana was established three kilometres to the north. Covering 83 hectares (205 acres), it had a fairly regular street plan, with an amphitheatre in the south-east corner as well as the usual baths, temples and shops.

Carnuntum, on the Danube east of Vienna, is one of the best preserved legionary fortresses. Rebuilt in stone after AD 73 it measures 500 × 400 metres and has the usual principia in the centre with the praetorium to the south. Workshops, a hospital, tribunes' houses as well as the 60 barracks for the centuriae have all been uncovered. Outside the fortress is a legionary amphitheatre which held 8,000 spectators. Three kilometres to the west of the fortress was the civilian settlement which became a colonia under Septimius Severus. The civilian settlement had its own, larger, amphitheatre which could accommodate 13,000 spectators.

The holy mountain of Magdalensberg had been settled by the Celts as early as the second century BC. During the first century BC, because of its fine position, good soil and plentiful water supply, it became an important town in the kingdom of Noricum; perhaps it was the capital, Noreia. In the period 40–20 BC the town was a prosperous trading centre and individual houses were finely frescoed. Following annexation in 15 BC the town entered its period of greatest prosperity with the building of a large classical-style temple within an enclosure, a basilica, a senate house and a bath. However, the founding of the new town of Virunum at the foot of the mountain brought about its decline and little more is heard of it.

The Balkans

The western Balkans became two provinces under Augustus, Pannonia to the north and Dalmatia to the south, while the eastern Balkans formed the province of Moesia. In the early second century AD Trajan added a fourth Balkan province, Dacia. The area was largely agricultural and pastoral, and despite its proximity to the centres of classical civilization it was comparatively slow to assimilate Roman culture.

Salona, situated on the Dalmatian coast, was settled by Roman traders in 47 BC and soon became a colonia, Martia Julia Salona, and under Augustus the capital of Dalmatia. The old town (*urbs vetus*) was probably walled at the time of Julius Caesar. The town spread rapidly eastward and at the time of Marcus Aurelius this new sector (*urbs nova*) was also walled. In the old city was built a fine

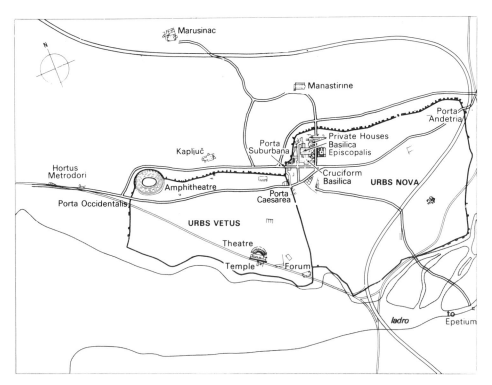

151 Salona (near Split), general plan (from M. I. Finley, op. cit.)

amphitheatre to accommodate 15,000 people as well as a forum, theatre and adjoining temple. The town was still flourishing in the fifth and sixth centuries, as is shown by the series of important Christian churches in the new city and the great Christian burial grounds outside the walls. The Emperor Diocletian was born here in AD 246 and built his famous villa at Split (see p. 263).

Sirmium, on the north bank of the Sara river, became a Roman base during Augustus' conquest of Illyricum and its status was raised to that of colonia in Flavian times. Because of its situation it became important strategically in the third century and Galerius built an imperial residence there. The buildings, which were constructed at great cost in brick included a huge bath building, a public granary and a large and a small palace. Running between these two palaces was a hippodrome.

At Adamclisi near the Black Sea coast of Romania was erected one of the most famous Trajanic monuments, the Tropaeum Traiani to commemorate the conquest of Dacia. Dedicated in AD 109, it consisted of a huge masonry drum 30 metres in diameter raised on nine steps. The drum was decorated with 54 sculpted panels depicting the conflict between the Dacians and Romans. In the valley below the monument a town grew up with the name of Tropaeum Traiani. The town was impressively rebuilt after its destruction by the Goths and most of the monuments, including a large basilica, 60 metres long, are Constantinian.

11 The Eastern Provinces

The Eastern Empire included Greece, Asia Minor, Syria, Arabia as far as the desert, and, under Trajan, large parts of Armenia, Assyria and Mesopotamia. Until the Roman conquest this had been the Hellenistic world, where architectural styles depended upon the use of the columnar Orders which had been developed in Classical Greece. Even under Roman rule this style remained so deep-rooted that the architecture of the Eastern Empire can be viewed as the final development in an unbroken Hellenistic tradition. Such buildings as the Library of Celsus at Ephesus (fig. 160), the Deir at Petra (fig. 168), the Temple of Zeus at Athens (fig. 153) and the Temple of Bel at Palmyra (fig. 165) all owe their effect to a skilful handling of the columnar Orders, with vaulted concrete playing no significant rôle. Clearly, Roman architectural styles were nowhere near so influential here as they were in the west.

Indeed, the East frequently supplied architects to the capital, especially when columnar structures were required. In the Republican period generals took their own Greek or Asiatic architects back to Rome with them (p. 20). Augustus used Greek columnar Orders to rebuild his marble city (p. 49). Trajan's own architect, Apollodorus, was from Syria and Hadrian imported architects from Asia Minor to supervise his building projects (p. 183). It can be argued that Rome's main contribution to architecture lay in the realm of engineering and the development of concrete, while eastern architects continued to develop the Classical Orders. As Lyttelton says:

> ... While the creative energies of the architects of Rome were largely employed in evolving a new architecture of concrete, which depended for its effects on curved and vaulted interiors and the provision of sophisticated and elaborate enclosed spaces, the architects of the eastern provinces devoted their energies for the most part to the development and elaboration of façade designs based on the rectilinear column-and-lintel.

Here a few words should be said about Hellenistic architecture and the Classical Orders on which it is based. The Classical tradition of trabeated columnar architecture was developed in Greece during the period 600 to 400 BC and two highly sophisticated styles of architecture developed, the Doric and the Ionic. Both these systems depended upon a clear and logical relationship between the constituent parts of the building and equal value was given to each part. Thus, in a Classical Greek temple no single side of the building is deemed the 'façade' and temple enclosures were often planned so that the first view of a temple was from a three-quarter viewpoint. The appearance of a temple closely reflected its structure. That is to say, not only did the columns support the horizontal entablature which spanned them, but they had to appear capable of doing so. Therefore they had to be of adequate thickness to take the weight, and sufficiently close together so that the entablature did not appear to be in danger of collapsing. Indeed, structure dictated appearance to the extent that every major element played an essential part in the system.

As early as the fifth century BC, however, some Classical buildings began to include elements superfluous to any structural requirements, but valuable for their effect. For example, in an orthodox Classical temple two rows of columns often ran down the cella. They were to help support the roof, that is to say they were an integral part of the whole structure. However, in the Temple of Apollo at Bassae, which dates to the later fifth century BC, the rows of columns ran so close to the cella walls that they were actually joined to them by a series of spur-walls. In terms of supporting the roof they would have been of very little use, and one could conclude that their purpose was mainly to deceive the eye by giving the impression that they were complete columns and that there were the normal aisles beyond them.

This represents quite a sharp break with previous architectural practice, and soon other architectural elements began to be used in an unorthodox fashion. Columnar screens and façades were often placed in front of a building without regard to structural logic. Half-columns and pilasters were used, both of which appear to act as supports without actually having any independent structural value. Elements which were originally necessary parts of the structure were used decoratively. For example the pediment, which ought to be the triangle produced at the short sides of a building by the slope of its roof, was applied decoratively to façades and over niches or aedicules. Sometimes it became segmental in shape, or it could be hollow at the bottom or broken in the middle.

At this point it may be useful to look more closely at an Eastern building and analyse its component parts. The Deir at Petra (fig. 168) is a rock cut tomb with a columnar façade, designed to impress by its sheer size and position. It is worlds away from the graceful Greek temple designed to be viewed from all sides, with its external columns regular and even. Here the aim is to overwhelm by piling up the Classical Orders to create an dramatic effect, one that relies entirely upon the façade. Here, as in other buildings, the façade is conceived as an independent screen set in front of the building rather than an organic and logical element in the structure as a whole. Note, too, how the central part of the façade is emphasized and the sides build up towards it. The columns are not arranged regularly, reflecting the structures they have to support. Instead they are arranged in terms of rhythms. At the two sides are pilasters, used to articulate rather than to act as supports. The two windows and the doorway on the lower floor have alternately segmental and pedimental heads, a favourite device of the seventeenth-century baroque with which this eastern architecture has so much in common. The two outer columns on each side support a projecting entablature which then breaks off. The third column from the edge supports a short projecting section of entablature, whose only function in projecting is to be supported by the column.

In the upper storey the Orders are used to more dramatic effect. The two pilasters on each end have half columns engaged in them and support a boldly projecting entablature with a triglyph frieze. Once again the only function of these complicated pilasters-cum-half-columns is to support an entablature, whose purpose is to be supported by them. Their real function is, of course, not structural at all, but to give a powerful rhythm to the upper storey by their sheer isolation. Closer to the middle is a pair of columns, straddling the two projecting pieces of entablature on the storey below. Eastern architects were fond of such counter rhythms between the upper and the lower storey, as can be seen in the façade of the library of Celsus at Ephesus (fig. 160).

The pediment of the upper storey is broken and a circular kiosk stands in the middle. Note, however, the sophistication with which this circular element is handled. Its columns are exactly the same height as the flanking ones and even the rhythm of the triglyph frieze is preserved. Also, the acroterion on the top of its conical roof is in exactly the position it would have been if the pediment had been complete.

One must conclude that there is nothing crude about this style. It is a highly sophisticated handling of the Classical Orders by architects who thoroughly understood their true function and were able to break the rules with a deliberate effect in mind. This also presupposes that the clients of such buildings had the taste and understanding to appreciate such subtleties. In order to understand a building which broke the rules, one had to know what the rules were.

Greece

Sulla's sack of Athens in 86 BC was the final blow in the decline of the once great city. Under the Roman Emperors the city became little more than a museum piece, and the influence it had on the course of Roman architecture was largely antiquarian. Additions and repairs to buildings were generally effected piecemeal and conformed strictly to Classical or Hellenistic tradition. The only systematic building programme was under the phil-Hellenic Emperor, Hadrian.

When looking at the Roman architecture of Athens it should be remembered that Athens had enjoyed a splendid architectural past. The architectural achievements of the fifth century BC had established a tradition which even the Athenians found hard to live up to. Hellenistic rulers such as Eumenes and Attalos of Pergamon donated monuments of a largely secular nature, such as the stoas that bear their names, to a city already resplendent with temples such as the Parthenon, Erechtheum and Hephaesteum. By the beginning of the Empire there was, apart from other considerations, very little space left in the centre of the city for large-scale new building projects.

An early Roman addition to the buildings of Athens was the commercial Agora or the Agora of Caesar and Augustus. It is situated in what used to be the eastern Agora until the Stoa of Attalos cut the area off from the main or western Agora. The monumental Doric propylon sets the tone of the building. Utterly conservative, not to say reactionary, in style, its four columns are close copies of fifth-century originals. The entablature, with its heavy triglyph frieze, is completely Classical, although the rest of the building is more Hellenistic in feeling. Beyond the propylon is an open square surrounded on all sides by colonnades of Ionic columns in grey-blue Hymettian marble. Behind are rows of shops, an arrangement common to buildings of the Hellenistic east.

The commercial Agora, dedicated in 10 BC, was the gift of Julius Caesar and later, Augustus. The identity of its donors and its completion date are of some significance because it was one of a number of Classical revival buildings erected towards the end of the first century BC both in Athens and Rome. We know that earlier in the century the Erechtheum, a Classical building of the late fifth century BC, was damaged by fire. In the course of its reconstruction, which was completed in 27 BC, the masons engaged on its repair must have become familiar with the ornate Ionic order employed in the original building to judge by a small circular temple north-east of the Parthenon dedicated to Rome and Augustus in the same year. This small building employs nine Ionic columns closely modelled on those of the Erechtheum.

This short-lived Classical revival in Athens had important repercussions in Rome in the last decades BC when Augustus was promoting the Classical period as a model for the new Imperial art and architecture (see p. 65). Among the products of this Classical revival were the Prima Porta Augustus, based upon the fifth-century

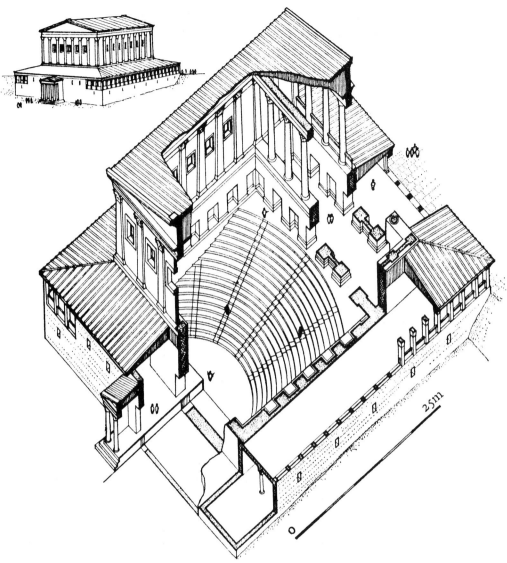

Doryphorus of Polycleitus; the Ara Pacis completed in 9 BC and based upon Classical and Hellenistic prototypes; and the Forum of Augustus replete with its row of caryatids like those of the Erechtheum. In a more general sense the Augustan Classical revival gave purity and discipline to the rash of new architectural forms and styles in vogue in the early years of Augustus' principate (see p. 64). Thus the Classical revival in Athens, although antiquarian in spirit, had more than a passing effect upon the architecture of the Roman Empire.

The old market-place or Agora also underwent considerable rebuilding during the early empire. Most notable was the building of a new odeion by Agrippa, in about 15 BC (fig. 152). Its enormous

152 Athens, Odeion of Agrippa, *c.* 15 BC: elevation and axonometric view (from A. Boethius, *op. cit.*)

235

153 Athens, Temple of Zeus, completed by Hadrian in AD 131–132

bulk must have towered over the elegant stoas all around it and added a startling new dimension to the square. Its ground-plan takes advantage of the site which slopes gently down from south to north. The shallow semicircular banks of seats fit into the slope, so that the orchestra is at the same level as the ground on the north side and the topmost banks of seats at the level of the ground south of the building. The seating is inscribed into a tall square auditorium whose general arrangements are reminiscent of Hellenistic meeting halls, such as the bouleuterion at Miletus, the ecclesiasterion at Priene and the nearby bouleuterion in the Athenian Agora. What is exceptional about the Odeion of Agrippa is its sheer size. The auditorium was roofed with a flat timber ceiling with a maximum span of 25 metres. This daring roof collapsed in the middle of the second century AD. When the building was re-roofed a cross wall was added for support, thus cutting the seating capacity to less than half. Around three sides of the exterior are promenade galleries which must have afforded excellent views over the surrounding Agora.

During Roman times the Agora was the subject of much routine rebuilding and embellishment, but one addition should be singled out for special mention, the Temple of Ares. The building belongs to the later fifth century BC, yet every block bears a Roman mason's mark. The conclusion of the American excavators is that the temple was transported stone by stone in Augustan times, probably from Acharnai at the foot of Mount Parnes, and re-erected in the middle

154 Athens, Arch of Hadrian, *c.* AD 138

of the Agora. Its removal to the Agora may be connected with an inscription honouring Augustus' adopted son, Gaius, as the 'new Ares'. The re-siting of the Temple of Ares is a clear illustration of the Romans' use of temples for purely propaganda purposes, and the changing status of the Agora from commercial to civic centre of Athens.

The most thorough building programme in Athens was that instituted by Hadrian, who first visited Athens in AD 124–125. His greatest project was the completion of the great temple of Olympian Zeus which was originally initiated by the tyrant Peisistratus in the sixth century BC (fig. 153). The huge temple, in the Doric Order, had been left unfinished for hundreds of years, until in 174 BC Antiochus Epiphanes resumed building to the designs of a Roman architect called Cossutius. Cossutius' design was in the Corinthian Order, but was of the same gigantic scale as its predecessor (44 × 110 metres). The outer colonnade was dipteral on the flanks and tripteral at the ends. The columns, 16.89 metres high, are of Pentelic marble. The temple remained half-finished for some time, and the Dictator Sulla even removed some of the columns after the sack of 86 BC and took them to Rome for the rebuilding of the temple of Capitoline Jupiter (see p. 12). Hadrian completed the temple in AD 131–132 and placed in the cella a chryselephantine statue of Zeus.

Near the Olympieion is the Arch of Hadrian (fig. 154). On the side facing the Olympieion is an inscription reading 'This is Athens, the ancient city of Theseus'. On the other side facing the acropolis is the inscription 'This is the city of Hadrian and not of Theseus'. Flanking

155 Athens, Library of Hadrian: part of the façade (AD 117–138)

the very shallow arched passage are two Corinthian columns resting upon plinths. They stand free of the wall and support projecting entablatures. The upper storey consists of an open three-bay columnar screen. The outer pairs of columns support projecting entablatures like the corresponding ones below, while the central ones support a projecting aedicule with a triangular pediment. The aedicule was originally screened and on one side was a statue of Hadrian gazing over his city, and on the other a statue of Theseus. If the arrangement seems an unusual one for a triumphal arch it may be explicable in terms of the kind of rhythmical columnar façades which appeared in contemporary buildings such as the Library of Celsus at Ephesus (see fig. 160).

Similar free-standing columns against a solid wall, supporting a series of projecting entablatures, can be seen on the façade of the Library of Hadrian at Athens (fig. 155). The plain tetrastyle entrance porch of the library is flanked on either side by a finely drafted masonry wall adorned with seven columns each side. Beyond the porch was a large enclosure surrounded, according to Pausanias (I. 18), by a peristyle of 100 columns of Phrygian stone. At the end stood the library proper, with its reading rooms and lecture halls. It is perhaps worth noting that the columns on the façade of the enclosure support two-stepped architraves and that there are consoles and not modillions in the cornice. These features, of Asiatic origin, also appear on Hadrianic monuments in Rome (see p. 183).

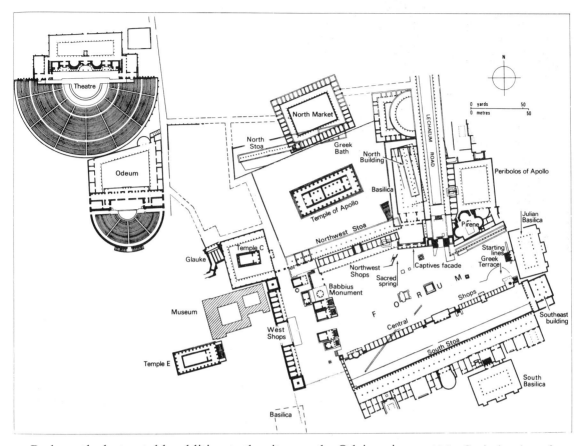

Perhaps the last notable addition to the city was the Odeion given by the wealthy benefactor, Herodes Atticus, in memory of his wife who died about AD 160. It was presumably built because Agrippa's Odeion was now unserviceable owing to the cross-wall. Nestling into the slopes of the acropolis just south of the bastion on which perches the small Temple of Athena Nike, it had a semi-circular auditorium 76 metres wide. The columnar stage buildings and outer façade rose to a height of 28 metres and were richly veneered with marble, as were the seats for the audience. Philostratus (*Vit. Soph.* 551) makes special mention of the fine cedar roof, which is evidenced by a layer of ash discovered by the excavators. Presumably it was burnt in the Herulian sack of AD 267 along with most of the other monuments of the city. The Herulians also set fire to the Agora and devastated the area. A little later the Athenians pulled down their desolated buildings to throw up a new city wall. Apart from a few late buildings which rose among the rubble, little else can be said of the buildings of ancient Athens.

Of the other major towns of Greece, Corinth is worth special note because of its unusual architectural history. Sacked by Mummius in 146 BC it was refounded as a colony by Julius Caesar in 44 BC, and

156 Corinth, plan of the central area (from M. I. Finley, *op. cit.*)

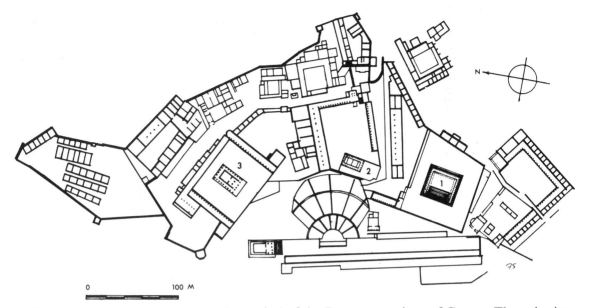

0   100 M

157 Pergamon, general plan

became the capital of the Roman province of Greece. The colonists were Italians and the rebuilding of the city was distinctly Italian in character. The Agora was near the venerable sixth-century Temple of Apollo built upon higher ground to the north (fig. 156). A race track ran across the Agora in an east/west direction and its edges were roughly demarcated by two stoas, one to the north-west and one to the south. The temple and the stoas were rebuilt in their original form, but in general the new town followed distinctly Italian lines. The Agora area was levelled into two terraces separated by a central row of shops with a *bema* or speaker's platform in the middle. Behind the south stoa were buildings that would be more familiar in a Roman context, a curia (or bouleuterion), a basilica and administrative offices for the officials of the Isthmian games. On the east side of the Agora was a second basilica and just to the north a third. Recent excavations have revealed a fourth basilica to the west of the Agora. As Corinth was the capital of Greece these basilicas would have been necessary for conducting the extensive legal business of the province. During the first and second centuries AD six small temples were built along the west side of the Agora. Significantly, they are all podium temples with lofty staircases on the entrance side, a type of temple that has its origins in Italy. A larger temple of the same type was built over the remains of a Hellenistic temple within a large enclosure to the west.

The fountain of Peirene in the north-west corner of the Agora was also rehabilitated in Roman times. In its original Greek form four sunken reservoirs supplied a row of water basins on the south side. In the first century BC the fountain was extended northwards by the addition of a masonry courtyard with a basin in the middle. In the second century AD the fountain was entirely remodelled, probably

240

by Herodes Atticus. Massive half-domed apses were added to three sides, the floor level raised and the walls were revetted in marble. Now totally isolated from the Agora, the fountain must have taken on a rather chilly, theatrical appearance.

The Lechaion road leads out of the north side of the Agora through a marble triumphal arch. It was a very broad road paved in limestone and lined by marble colonnades. As Caskey says:

> When Pausanias visited Corinth in the second century of our era, he saw the arch surmounted by two gilded bronze four-horse chariots bearing the sun-god Helios and his son Phaethon; and the view of the stately street with its marble porticoes leading up to the great marble arch with its gleaming chariots, backed by the sheer gray cliffs of Acrocorinth, must have been memorable.

Asia Minor

When Alexander the Great's death brought about the break-up of his empire, the western coastlands of Asia Minor became one of the most important centres of Hellenistic civilization. Towns like Miletus, Priene, Ephesus and Pergamon were leading centres of Hellenistic culture, but only Pergamon was newly created after Alexander's death and it is instructive to compare it with the older towns. Both Priene and Miletus had the rigid grid-plan supposedly invented by Hippodamos. This is particularly surprising in the case of Priene, which is on a steep slope. In Pergamon there is no attempt to impose such rigid planning. At the top of a hill the Temple of Trajan (3 on fig. 157), the Temple of Athena (2 on fig. 157) and the Great Altar (1 on fig. 157) dominate the curving terrain and face out over the plain below. Beneath them the theatre sits against the slope of the hill like a great fan. Under the theatre a long stoa with the Temple of Dionysus at one end gives stability to the whole scheme. In typically Hellenistic fashion it is the overall grouping which dominates, and individual buildings are subordinated to the effect of the arrangement as a whole. The plan of Pergamon is a masterly exploitation of a difficult site. As Lyttelton says: 'The terraces of Priene might be said to overcome the difficulties of the terrain, whereas those of Pergamon exploit them.' Of the individual buildings of Pergamon the Traianeum is of interest because its architectural details are so close to those of Hadrian's Temple of Venus and Rome (fig. 110), whose two-fascia architrave, consoles supporting the cornice and sima with alternately open and closed palmettes, suggest that it was built by architects trained in the Asiatic tradition (see p. 183).

Miletus was laid out in 479 BC according to a rigid grid system (fig. 158), and the commercial centre was added to in Hellenistic and Roman times. Facing the harbour is a long stoa (9 in fig. 158) behind which is the north agora (13 in fig. 158). Nearby is the circular

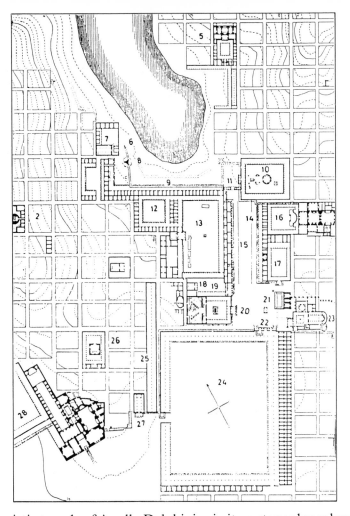

158 Miletus, plan of the city centre

Hellenistic temple of Apollo Delphinius in its rectangular columnar enclosure (10 in fig. 158), and further to the south the gymnasium (17 in fig. 158) and the bouleuterion (20 in fig. 158). South of the bouleuterion is the south agora, which consists of three separate stoas enclosing a vast open space. Hellenistic Miletus therefore had a well developed city centre, but its buildings were only loosely related to each other. The developments of the Roman period forged them into an organically related entity. Fig. 158 shows how three or four elements of town planning achieved this. A gate (11 in fig. 158) was inserted between the harbour stoa and the Delphinion, thus uniting the two and masking the vista in order to accentuate the sense of surprise when one passed through the gate. Beyond the gate colonnades were built along the west and east sides of the area between the north agora and gymnasium, thus turning an open space into a broad street whose vista of columns gives a strong sense of direction southwards. By now most gaps between buildings had been filled unless there was a particular reason for leaving an opening. At the end of the colonnaded street attention was focussed on the dramatic new gateway (22 in fig. 158) to the south stoa with its rather theatrical broken pediment. Nearer the gate an open space appeared on the left dominated by the impressive nymphaeum

with its staggered columns on three storeys (21 in fig. 158).

Another type of terrain presents itself at Ephesus. To the east of the ancient harbour is a flattish area bounded on the south by Mount Koressos and the east by Mount Pion. The theatre is magnificently sited at the foot of Mount Pion and faces the harbour (fig. 159). An 11-metre-broad colonnaded street links it with the harbour 600 metres away. To the north of the street is the vast Harbour Baths complex finished in the later second century AD. The baths are strikingly different in their layout from the conventional Roman Imperial type such as the Baths of Caracalla p. 257). The Greek insistence upon columnar structure is particularly evident. More than half the ground plan (202×238 metres) is devoted to the gymnasium, which is surrounded by multiple porticoes of columns used as covered running tracks. The main bulk of the bath building itself centres around a peristyle courtyard and on each side is a richly decorated room with elaborate columnar screens and niches around three sides. This type of room (often called a 'Marmorsaal') is a recurrent feature of bath buildings in the east. The main bathing rooms to the west are vaulted with stone arches supported by masonry spur walls with an infill of rubble.

A road leads south from the theatre and then begins the steep ascent up the valley between Mount Koressos and Mount Pion. Along this road can be seen a number of monuments designed to attract the eye and divert attention from the many bends in the sloping street. Firstly on the right is the second-century AD Library of Celsus in its colonnaded enclosure. Its façade (fig. 160) is of interest because of the staggered columns of the upper storey, a feature we have already encountered in the nymphaeum at Miletus. Higher up the hill on the left is the Temple of Hadrian, most of

159 Ephesus, colonnaded street leading from the harbour to the theatre

160 Ephesus, library of Celsus, reconstruction of the façade (from W. Wilberg, *Jahreshefte des österreichischen archäologischen Instituts*, XI, 1908

161 Ephesus, Temple of Hadrian

whose ground area is devoted to the arresting façade and porch (fig. 161). The temple is tetrastyle and the middle intercolumniation is wider than the outer pair so as to support a large arch which breaks into the pediment. This so-called 'Syrian pediment' where the entire entablature is carried up over the arch is a favourite eastern device whose origins may be Syrian and which was certainly widely used there.

Asia Minor is so rich in Hellenistic and Roman remains that it is impossible to mention more than a selection here. However, a word should be said about two monuments in Aspendos on the south coast of Turkey: the theatre and the aqueduct. The theatre has a very well preserved *scaenae frons* with a straight back wall and five doors leading on to the stage. Each door is flanked by a pair of Ionic columns which support a projecting section of entablature. The scheme is continued on the storey above with Corinthian columns, each pair of which supports alternately segmental and triangular pediments. The pair of columns in the centre support a massively broken pediment spanning the central doorway. The resultant façade is strongly rhythmic and balanced and yet has exceptional unity.

The aqueduct at Aspendos also deserves mention because instead of being of the free-flow type, the water is carried in enclosed pipes. Thus the water is allowed to run downhill for an interval and then up to a pressure tank from which it again runs down until it is raised up to the next tank.

Syria

The Levantine coastline, the fertile areas around the Euphrates and the arid areas east of the river Jordan, could boast civilizations older than that of Greece. The ports of Byblos, Tyre and Sidon were Phoenician and the storm god, Ba'al, had been worshipped from time immemorial at Baalbek in the Bekaa valley. Further south was Judaea, which was under the enlightened rule of King Herod when it passed under Roman protection. To the east of the Jordan was Nabataean territory, which lay astride the caravan routes from the Arabian ports to Syria and had Petra as its capital. Towns like Jerash and Palmyra also derived their wealth from the caravan trade. Finally, on the eastern fringe of the Empire the town of Dura-Europos was intermittently under Roman rule.

The sanctuary of Jupiter Heliopolitanus at Baalbek is one of the grandest building complexes in the Roman Empire (fig. 162). There had been a sanctuary on this site since the sixth century BC and after the foundation of the Roman colony Julia Augusta Felix Heliopolitana in 16 BC a great rebuilding was begun. The complex consists of a monumental propylon, a hexagonal forecourt, and a huge (96 × 86 metre) colonnaded courtyard dominated by the impressive bulk of the Temple of Jupiter (fig. 163). Standing next to the Temple of

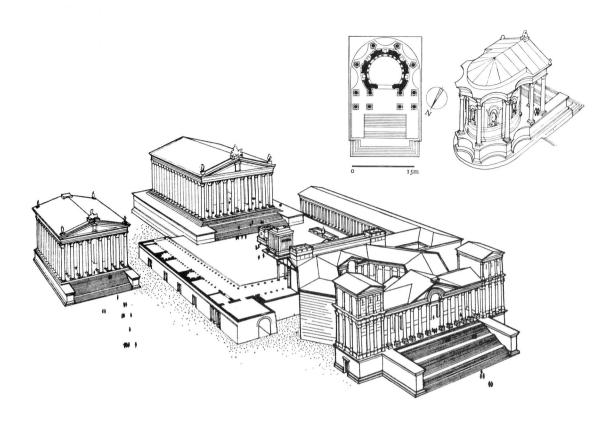

Jupiter but outside the enclosure is the smaller Temple of Bacchus, and a little way to the south-east is the circular Temple of Venus. The oldest building in the complex is the Temple of Jupiter, which must have been standing to capital height in AD 60 to judge by an inscription on one of the columns. The temple, although smaller than some giants like the Temple of Zeus at Athens (it measured 88×48 metres) was most impressively sited. Standing on a high podium it measured nearly 44 metres from the floor of the courtyard to the apex of the pediment. The court of 10×19 columns produced an almost exact double-square ground-plan. The columns themselves, with their unfluted shafts and Corinthian capitals based on those of Augustan Rome, rose to a height of 19.90 metres. The entablature followed traditional lines except for the bull and lion protomes which projected from the frieze, presumably as an allusion to Baal and Astarte.

Parallel to the Temple of Jupiter but outside its enclosure is the Temple of Bacchus, which was begun in the late first century AD and largely built in the second. Smaller than the Temple of Jupiter, it is nonetheless as big as the Parthenon at Athens (35×66 metres). Its exceptional state of preservation allows us to form a clear impression of its scale and grandeur. It has 8×15 unfluted Corinthian columns, closely spaced and very tall (19 metres high), on a high podium approached by a tall triple flight of steps. In terms of detail the order is similar to that of its gigantic neighbour, the Temple of Jupiter, but the treatment of the coffers of the peristyle is much richer. The interior is notable for its fine proportions and sensitive architecture. The cella has a double-square ground-plan and its height is equal to its width. A row of fluted Corinthian half-columns on plinths line the side walls. Between each pair of columns is an arched niche below and a pedimented one above. At the far end of the cella is a flight of steps at the top of which two piers faced with Corinthian half-columns stand out from the wall and frame the *adyton*. The scale of the half-columns is identical with those lining the side walls and their distance from the wall the same as the distance between the columns along the wall. Also their bases are at exactly the same level as the bases of the wall columns. As Fyfe points out, the retention of scale for the free-standing and engaged order is a master touch.

The rectangular courtyard around the Temple of Jupiter appears to date from the same period as the Temple of Bacchus and there are some similarities in design between the two. The courtyard is surrounded on three sides by porticoes of Egyptian granite columns framing the façade of the temple which fills the fourth side. Behind the granite columns are alternate round and square exedrae. The round exedrae are flanked by square Corinthian piers between which stand two granite Corinthian columns, an arrangement reminiscent of the interior of the Pantheon at Rome, although here

162 Baalbek, sanctuary, begun early first century AD and completed AD 250. Axonometric view. Inset, Temple of Venus, third century AD. Plan and axonometric view (from A. Boethius, *op. cit.*)

163 Baalbek, view of Temple of Jupiter, first century AD with the Temple of Bacchus, second century AD, in the foreground. (*By courtesy of Fototeca Unione, Rome*)

the spacing between columns and piers is kept exactly even so that they correspond precisely to the granite columns of the façade of the portico. Preceding the rectangular court is a hexagonal court with closely similar details. As Lyttelton points out, the use of a hexagonal court gives a strong forward impetus as the visitor moves towards the court of the Temple of Jupiter.

The propylaea which gives access to the whole sanctuary was the last part of the complex to be finished, perhaps by Caracalla or Philip the Arab. A lofty staircase leads up to a row of ten Corinthian columns between a pair of two-storeyed towers. The central intercolumniation was wider than the rest, presumably to accommodate an arcuated lintel. The small third-century temple of Venus (fig. 162) has a circular cella surrounded by Corinthian columns, and a tetrastyle porch with a double row of columns. The columns rest upon a podium and steps lead up to the porch. Between each pair of columns both podium and entablature recede towards the cella wall in a series of gentle concavities. As a result the capitals and bases of the columns are five-sided. This fanciful design seems to have had no exact parallel in antiquity, although a remarkably similar scheme is used by Borromini in the seventeenth-century lantern of S Ivo in Rome.

Palmyra is an oasis town mid-way between the Mediterranean ports of Sidon, Tyre and Byblos, and the Euphrates. Caravans bringing products from India, China and Arabia and merchants with goods from Greece, Rome and other Mediterranean countries found the town a convenient place of exchange and trans-shipment. The arrangement saved the merchants ferrying goods the whole length of the caravan route. When in AD 137 duties were levied on imported goods the town entered a period of great prosperity. In the middle of the second century AD a series of public buildings was begun, starting with the great colonnaded street which ran from the Grove temple in the west to the Temple of Bel, a distance of 1,000 metres (fig. 164). The columns, mostly Corinthian and unfluted, are 9.5 metres high, some with projecting brackets for statues. The road changes direction at two points. One of these changes is marked by a monumental Tetrakionia with four huge pedestals each supporting four columns with a statue in the middle. Further to the east the road changes direction more sharply to turn towards the Temple of Bel. Here the change of direction is masked by an ornate triple arch.

The Temple of Bel itself (fig. 165) is known from an inscription to have been dedicated in AD 32, and Lyttelton argues that it belongs mainly to the first century AD. In ground-plan it is pseudodipteral with a column count of 8×15, an arrangement strongly reminiscent of Hermogenes' celebrated Temple of Artemis Leucophryene at Magnesia. The plinths provide the module as in the Temple of Artemis, the spacings and plinths being of the same dimensions. The central intercolumniation on each short side is wider than the rest.

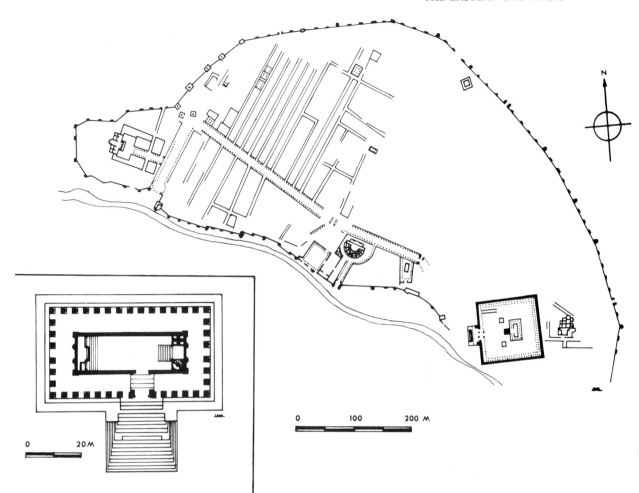

Yet despite its thoroughly Hellenistic layout the cella is not entered from the pronaos, but by an elaborate doorway engaged into the columns in the middle of the west side. Inside are two cult chambers or *thalamoi* at either end of the cella, the result of an adaptation of a Hellenistic type of temple to a Semitic cult. The eastern influence is emphasized on the exterior by the acanthus-clad crowstep merlons which cap the cornice.

Dura-Europos is a Hellenistic foundation dating to about 300 BC, sited on a plateau on the west bank of the Euphrates. On the east side of the city sheer cliffs run down to the river and watercourses have cut out natural defences to north and south. The city was ringed with walls from its inception and these were particularly strong on the exposed desert side to the west. The streets were laid out on strictly Hippodamian lines, with an open agora in the middle. The ruling Seleucids seem to have regarded it as a key defensive site in their struggles with the Parthians, but finally at the end of the second century BC the city fell. In the Parthian period that

164 Palmyra, general plan. Inset, Temple of Bel: plan

165 Palmyra, Temple of Bel, dedicated in AD 32. (*By courtesy of the German Archaeological Institute, Rome*)

followed changes were most evident in the Agora area, which gradually became transformed into an oriental bazaar with narrow lanes and crowded shops. A number of new temples appeared, like those of Atargatis, Bel, Adonis and Azzarathkona. The most common plan for such temples was a walled temenos lined with small rooms and chapels. The main sanctuary, usually located at the end of the temenos, was approximately square with the entrance in the centre, leading into a pronaos and a chamber behind. This rear chamber usually had two smaller rooms, one each side. The origins of this type of temple are to be found in Mesopotamia and perhaps came to Dura from Assur or similar cities.

Dura came briefly under Roman domination at the time of Trajan, but was not permanently part of the Empire until it was recaptured by Lucius Verus in AD 165. At first changes were few. A mithraeum was built, probably for the Roman troops, and some military buildings appeared in the northern part of the city. However, the garrison was increased in AD 210 and larger quarters were built for the military, including a praetorium, a bath, an amphitheatre and new temples. A palace, the largest building in Dura, was built for the *dux ripae* who commanded the troops on the Euphrates frontier. It was entered through an imposing peristyle courtyard with another similar courtyard beyond. Around this second courtyard were public rooms, a dining-room, an audience

166 Gerasa (Jerash), general plan

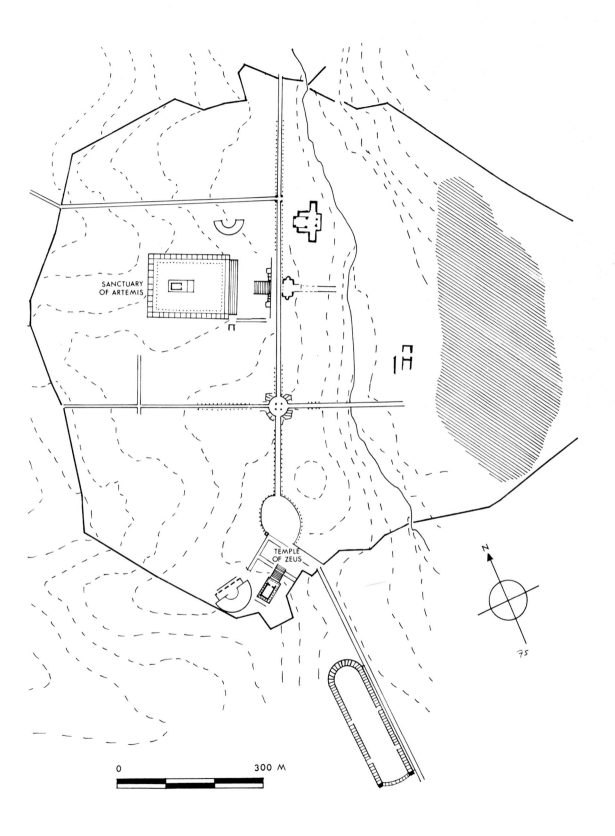

SANCTUARY
OF ARTEMIS

TEMPLE
OF ZEUS

N

75

0   300 M

hall and servants' rooms. At the back, overlooking the river, was an imposing suite of rooms which served as the private quarters of the dux. Although the materials used for this palace were local, the type of building was of Roman origin. Even the unit of measurement reflects its alien nature, the Roman foot instead of the Semitic cubit.

Gerasa (Jerash) became prosperous as a result of the caravan trade. The city is sited in the valley of the river Arysorhoas and the river flows through the town. The flattish eastern bank of the river probably contained the residential quarter and the westernmost of the public monuments (fig. 166). The long straight cardo, lined with Corinthian colonnades along its full length, runs almost parallel to the river along a north/south axis. On rising ground to the west is situated the imposing Temple of Artemis. In the depressions to the north and south of the temple run two decumani which are carried over the river by means of bridges. The intersections between the decumani and the cardo are marked by tetrapylons. The southern one is set in the middle of a circular piazza of 43 metres diameter. The southern part of the decumanus terminates in an obliquely aligned oval piazza dominated from the south-west by the Temple of Zeus.

The sanctuary of Artemis is a masterpiece of planning (fig. 167). The actual temple would have been invisible from the colonnaded street as it is masked by a seven-metre-high retaining wall against which is built a row of shops. In front of the shops is a colonnade which continues the porticoes of the main street, but in the middle are four tall columns framing the propylaea behind. Beyond the

167 Gerasa (Jerash), Sanctuary of Artemis: plan

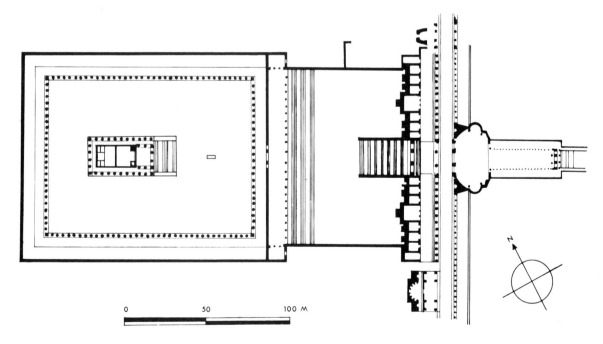

0   50   100 M

propylaea seven flights of steps lead up to a large forecourt. At the end of the forecourt and running its entire width are four further flights of steps which lead into the massive (121 × 161 metres) colonnaded temenos. The temple itself, with twice as much space in front of it as behind, is raised on a 4.32-metre-high podium. Three flights of steps lead up to it. The building has a count of 6 × 11 Corinthian columns and its layout reflects Hellenistic building practice.

Petra nestles deep within the mountains of Edom in the desert south of Jordan. It was not rediscovered by Europeans until the nineteenth century. The Nabataeans, formerly a nomadic people, began to settle in the area during the fourth century BC, and Petra became a centre of the flourishing spice and perfume trade conducted with southern Arabia and India. It reached the height of its prosperity in the first century AD and declined thereafter. Strabo, writing at the period of its greatest prosperity, describes Petra as peaceful and well-governed (16. 4. 21). It was only annexed by Rome in AD 106, and most of the great monuments of Petra used to be dated to the second and third centuries AD, the period of Roman domination. However, recent studies suggest that many of the important monuments of the city date much earlier, and are, to quote Lyttelton, 'a product of the Hellenistic, rather than the Roman, baroque style'.

The town is situated in the Siq gorge which winds its way through the towering mountains either side and provides a perfect natural

168 Petra, the Deir, mid-first century AD. (*By courtesy of the German Archaeological Institute, Rome*)

backdrop to the spectacular monuments which line it. As one approaches the town from the east the rock-cut Khasne or 'Treasury' is the first monument to be glimpsed through a slit in the rock. The upper storey has a circular kiosk in the middle of a massively broken pediment like the Deir (fig. 168), but the lower storey has a more conventional arrangement of columns and pediment. The gorge widens to reveal a rock-cut theatre, and further on a colonnaded street terminating in a triple gate runs through the centre of the town. Beyond the gate is a tall, square Nabataean temple known as the Qasr al bint. Internally the building is divided into three almost equal areas, porch, cella and triple shrine at the back. The outside of the rear wall has an arrangement of half, segmental and triangular pediments, supported on pairs of pilasters. It is perhaps no coincidence that a very similar decorative scheme appears on the hemicycle of Trajan's markets in Rome. The architect of the markets was Apollodorus of Damascus, a man of Syrian origin and perhaps familiar with monuments like the Qasr al bint.

12 The Late Empire

In the reign of Hadrian's successor, Antoninus Pius, the Empire temporarily settled into a period of quiet efficiency, controlled by a scrupulous man whose virtues were summarized by the title 'pius' bestowed upon him by a grateful senate in AD 138. Like Hadrian, he wore a beard, but that was his only concession to Greek taste. Otherwise he lived plainly, often visiting his country seat at Lanuvium, and never left Italy. One can perhaps see the man in the only project he initiated in the capital, the Temple of Antoninus and Faustina. It was dedicated to his wife, Faustina, on whom he doted and who died young in AD 141. As a building it is unexceptional and would pass unnoticed except for its excellent state of preservation, incorporated as it was into the church of S Lorenzo in Miranda. A tall flight of steps leads up to a hexastyle porch of six cipollino columns with Corinthian capitals. The entablature is of Proconnesian marble, and the architrave has the two fasciae reminiscent of late Hadrianic work, but the frieze seems to have been borrowed from the Forum of Trajan. In general the temple has the same lifeless Classicism of Antonine sculptural works, such as the base of the column which Antoninus erected in the Campus Martius.

Although traditional buildings like the Temple of Antoninus and Faustina continued to be built, the Classical repertory of architectural forms was becoming exhausted. However much Antoninus may have wanted to stem the tide, art was moving away from Classicism, especially of the pompous kind current in the mid-second century AD. The movement was toward direct, simple representation in sculpture, in effect a return to the old Roman tradition. The column of Antoninus' successor, Marcus Aurelius, is superficially reminiscent of Trajan's Column, but its sculptures tell another story. The scenes are peopled by dumpy, unpretentious little soldiers, full of the bitterness and harshness of the campaigns they are fighting. The Emperor himself is shown as a brooding, melancholy figure. A philosopher by disposition, he had lofty principles, but the hard facts of empire overtook him. He found himself constantly at war, while the economy at home stagnated. Despite the seeming prosperity of the Antonine age, it was a period of economic decline and lost opportunity. The faces of these Emperors, their smooth velvety skin contrasting with their elaborate coiffure and luxuriant beards, reflects the superficial veneer of later second-century Rome.

The last Emperor of the Antonine line, Commodus, the effete and vain son of Marcus Aurelius, best sums up all the contradictions of the age. His portraits have luxuriant gilded curls and velvet skin, and his head is covered with the lion skin of Hercules. The style is one of overblown Classicism alien to the new realities. He has an aura of wealth and limitless power in an age when both were beginning to slip away. Commodus was murdered in AD 193 and a lengthy civil war ensued (193–197) as a result of which Septimus Severus emerged as the new Emperor.

Septimius Severus was born in the provincial town of Lepcis Magna in North Africa, and his wife was the daughter of the Priest of Baal in Syria. It is no coincidence that many of Severus' building projects reflect his North-African origin; he lavishly endowed his native city with the new form/basilica complex (see p. 197), and on the Palatine made extensive additions to the south-east corner of the palace. Here he built out from the bathing suite beyond the hippodrome a huge artificial terrace supported by two storeys of brick-faced concrete piers. The hillside sloped away steeply at this point and the undercrofting was necessary to preserve the level of the Domitianic structures around the hippodrome. The actual suites on top of the terrace have now disappeared, but they would have enjoyed some of the finest vistas in Rome, across the valley to the Aventine, and down the beginning of the Appian Way. Visitors arriving by ship from Pozzuoli and Brindisi would have travelled to Rome along the Appian Way and this corner of the Palatine would have been their first glimpse of the Imperial Palace. With an eye to these visitors, who would have included his own countrymen from Libya, Severus built a huge and imposing structure to stand at the edge of this new wing, the Septizodium. The structure was essentially a rich columnar screen on three storeys, with three great recesses, similar in effect to the stage of a Roman theatre. It was, essentially, a grand piece of urban scenery of the type common in Hellenistic cities (see p. 198), and may be compared for effect with the nymphaeum he himself built at Lepcis Magna. As at Lepcis, its urban function may also have been to distract attention from a sudden bend in the road, in this case where the Via Appia diverges to the right to become the Via Triumphalis.

Severus' other principal monument in Rome was the great arch he built over the Via Sacra near the slopes of the Capitoline hill (fig. 169). In scale it is gigantic – 20.88 metres high and 23.27 metres wide. It has three passages flanked on each side by lofty Composite columns on high plinths. The inscription in the attic dates it to AD 203. Above the attic was a bronze quadriga containing the Emperor

and his sons. The position of the arch on steeply sloping ground adds to its imposing effect.

Severus was succeeded by his sons Geta and Caracalla. Caracalla was a cruel and dangerous man who lived a life of austere simplicity. He murdered his brother in AD 211 and erased his name from all public monuments, including his father's arch. His greatest building project in the capital was the baths that bear his name (fig. 170). In many respects they represent the highest achievement in Roman bath building. The bathing rooms are set inside a huge enclosure which measures 328 metres by over 400 metres. Around the outer walls were the water cisterns, running tracks, gardens, libraries and other rooms. The main block, itself immense (200 × 114 metres), is entirely detached from the outer enclosure unlike that of the Baths of Trajan. Its planning shows exceptional clarity and within the almost regular outer wall square, rectangular, circular and elliptical rooms, open courtyards, rooms on two storeys, rooms with clerestory lighting, and rooms with inward-facing and outward-facing windows are fitted together with consummate skill. Moving through the baths one passes from dimness to light, from intimate graceful rooms to huge halls with soaring vaults.

Only four doorways pierced the plain, rather austere north-east façade; the outer pair lead into rooms opening directly onto the two palaestras and the inner into rooms flanking the great natatio or open-air swimming pool. Beyond each of the latter rooms was an apodyterion or changing-room, which led to the palaestra. Each palaestra was surrounded on three sides by a concrete barrel-vault, supported by columns of giallo antico, and the walls were lined with white marble pilasters supporting a continuous entablature. The floor was of softly toned mosaic. To the south of the palaestra, with

169 Rome, Forum Romanum showing from left to right, Temple of Saturn, Column of Phocas, two columns of the Temple of Deified Vespasian and the Arch of Septimius Severus. In the background is the Tabularium

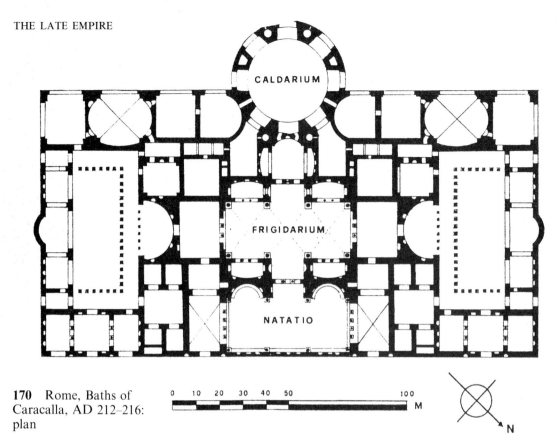

CALDARIUM

FRIGIDARIUM

NATATIO

170 Rome, Baths of Caracalla, AD 212–216: plan

0 10 20 30 40 50   100
M

N

huge windows to take advantage of the midday sun were a series of hot rooms containing steam baths. The climax of the series was the great circular caldarium which projected beyond the line of the block to take fullest advantage of the sun in its afternoon course. Thus, the caldarium was conceived as a gigantic heliocaminus, its drum daringly pierced with large windows, which can have done little to assure the stability of the dome above. The dome spanned 35 metres, not much less than the Pantheon, and it was far higher. Below each of the eight windows was a bay containing a hot plunge bath. The next room was the comparatively small tepidarium with warm plunge baths either side. Entry was through two small doorways designed to keep the heat from penetrating into the cold rooms beyond and vice versa. Two small courtyards either side provided indirect lighting. The frigidarium was the largest room in the complex and commanded vistas along the two main axes of the block. It was covered with three cross-vaults which soared above the level of the surrounding rooms and allowed the area to be lit by the resultant eight lunettes. Three transverse barrel-vaults each side buttressed the main vault, as well as covering the four plunge baths and the thoroughfare between the natatio and the tepidarium. (In general the frigidarium would have resembled the Basilica of Maxentius shown reconstructed in figure 181.) At either end of the central space were large rooms which led into the palaestras. These

rooms were covered with a lower vault than the central space, and because they had no clerestory lighting, must have provided a dim prelude to the bright open-air palaestra beyond.

171 Rome, Baths of Caracalla, AD 212–216: the frigidarium

The natatio or swimming pool was open to the sky. Four huge granite columns divided the south-west wall into three parts, two ending in apses and the central one open to the frigidarium. Columnar screens divided off the two vaulted spaces either side. The towering bulk of the frigidarium would have greatly assisted in keeping the rays of the sun away from the cool swimming area. The pool was walled off by a great concrete screen to the north too. This wall was decorated by two tiers of niches elaborately adorned with projecting marble columns.

Another project of Caracalla's reign was the huge Temple of Serapis, built at the edge of the Quirinal hill and approached by a 21-metre-high staircase. Its size can be gauged by the column fragments which survive. They are nearly two metres in diameter and 21.17 metres high. According to Palladio's drawings the pronaos column arrangement was similar to that of the Pantheon. Columns divided the area into three sections, the two outer of which terminated in apses. However, in this vast edifice there was a further pair of columns either side, bringing the façade column count to 12. It should be noted that the exterior columns support a two-step architrave; the cornice is supported by consoles and the sima has palmettes and lions' heads. The entablature suggests a similar Pergamine influence to that of the temple of Venus and Rome. The temple, according to Palladio, was also richly adorned with statuary. All in all one cannot doubt Palladio's assessment that 'this must have been the greatest and most adorned temple that was in *Rome*'.

259

To finance his extravagances Caracalla extended Roman citizenship to all free-born men within the Empire (AD 212) and thus gained extra taxation. He also introduced a new coin, the Antoninianus, which nominally was worth two denarii although it in fact only weighed one-and-a-half. This debasement of the coinage was to contribute to the inflation which gathered pace in the course of the third century AD.

Caracalla was murdered by his soldiers in AD 218, while marching into Parthia in an attempt to revive Trajan's plans for an eastern Empire. He was succeeded by Heliogabalus, the grand nephew of Julia Domna, the wife of Septimius Severus. He was only 14 at the time of his accession and the main achievement of his reign was to encourage the worship of the sun-god, with whom he identified himself, and hence spread the oriental cult of the living sovereign. He built a temple to Sol Invictus on the edge of the Palatine hill opposite Hadrian's Temple of Venus and Rome. Although smaller than the latter it was a good-sized peripteral building measuring about 60×40 metres. In it Heliogabalus assembled many of the most sacred pagan relics of Rome, the aniconic statue of Cybele, the fire of Vesta, the Palladium and the shields of Mars – a syncretistic attempt to assimilate all of these aspects of paganism into the worship of the sun. The Emperor's caprices led to his murder by the Praetorian guard after he had reigned barely three years.

His successor Alexander Severus built little of note, although he did restore the Temple of Isis in the Campus Martius. The emphasis on eastern cults is noteworthy in this period, such as Caracalla's great Temple of Serapis and Heliogabalus' Temple of the Sun. The only other major Roman monument to date from this period is the small amphitheatre near St John Lateran, the *Amphitheatrum Castrense*, built between AD 225 and 235. Measuring only 88×75.80 metres, it has a façade decorated with Corinthian half-columns of brick flanking round-headed openings; Corinthian pilasters on the next storey and plain windows on the top. The lowest order and parts of the middle survive because the building was incorporated into the Aurelianic wall (see p. 261).

The death of Alexander Severus was followed by a half-century of turmoil and disorder. Emperor succeeded Emperor with bewildering frequency and often generals left key strategic positions undefended in their bid for the highest office. Barbarians waiting on the north-east and eastern frontiers were quick to take advantage of the situation and in the 250s and 260s large parts of the eastern Empire were overrun and some invaders penetrated as far as Ravenna. The Emperor Valerian was actually captured by the Parthians in AD 259 and ended his days in captivity – he was the only Roman Emperor to meet this fate. The situation in the north-east was saved by the campaign of the little known Emperor Claudius II, who earned the title 'Gothicus' as a result. His successor, Aurelian, restored the north-eastern and eastern frontiers, and began repairing the shattered morale of the capital. His greatest building project was the massive circuit of walls which still bear his name. In scale they are as huge as some of the building projects of his predecessors. They were built in some haste and incorporated into their circuit a number of large monuments such as the Pyramid of Cestius, the Porta Maggiore, the Praetorian camp and the Amphitheatrum Castrense. The wall itself was of brick and was about six metres high and 3.58 metres wide. Every hundred Roman feet was a square tower with a ballista platform on top. The most important gateways had two arched entrances flanked by a pair of semicircular towers. In all the circuit was 19 kilometres long and along its course were 383 towers.

The reign of Diocletian, who became Emperor in AD 286, marked a decisive move away from Rome as the capital of the Empire. He instituted a wholesale revision of the Imperial administrative system in order to improve its efficiency. He divided the Empire into four areas, controlled by himself, a co-emperor and two 'Caesars' who were groomed to succeed the two Emperors. The system was known as the Tetrarchy. Diocletian controlled the East; Maximian took Italy and Africa; and the two subordinate Emperors, Galerius and Constantius, the Danube provinces and the Western provinces respectively. These changes were a logical outcome of the movement away from Rome as the centre of the Roman Empire.

Diocletian also sought to stabilize the economy and rescue Rome from the galloping inflation which had bedevilled the Roman monetary system as a result of 50 years of instability. For a fleeting moment it appeared that a new Golden Age had come, a mood perhaps reflected in a return to the Classical manner in contemporary sculpture. The bases of a triumphal arch erected by Diocletian in AD 294 survive in the Boboli gardens at Florence and contain relief Victories whose fussy drapery is unmistakably Classical in origin. The architecture of the Tetrarchy was both conservative and introspective. The baths built by Diocletian in Rome are not so much set within a walled enclosure, as a fortified wall punctuated at intervals by tower-like exedrae (fig. 172). In appearance the outer circuit of the Baths of Diocletian resembles the Aurelianic walls around Rome itself. A similar introspection governs Diocletian's palace at Split in Yugoslavia (fig. 173). Set out on the lines of a Roman camp, it contains all the luxuries of a Roman palace deep inside its forbidding walls. Diocletian's rebuilding of the Roman Forum following the fire under Carinus (AD 283) was on thoroughly conventional lines. Both the Basilica Julia and the Curia were rebuilt in the coldly regular brick-faced concrete of the period, and that is the form in which they survive to this day (fig. 28).

Diocletian's major architectural achievement in Rome was the baths which bear his name (fig. 172). They were begun by Maximian

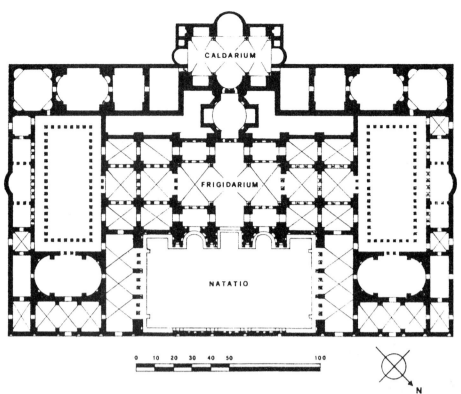

CALDARIUM

FRIGIDARIUM

NATATIO

0 10 20 30 40 50   100

N

172 Rome, Baths of Diocletian, AD 298–306: plan

in AD 298 and dedicated in AD 306 shortly after the two Emperors went into retirement. In scale and layout the building is reminiscent of the Baths of Caracalla. However, a closer look at its plan reveals that there are few of the sweeping curves and bold room shapes that animate the earlier baths. The frigidarium area is a network of rather stereotyped rectangular rooms, and this somewhat monotonous rectangular effect is repeated in the two palaestras and even the caldarium. In scale, however, the Baths of Diocletian are actually a little larger than those of Caracalla. The natatio covers over three times the area of that in the Baths of Caracalla, and the three-bayed frigidarium and adjacent rooms represent a larger area than the equivalent complex in the earlier baths. However, the later baths lack the delicately curving exedras off the natatio and at the sides of the palaestrae. The soaring circular caldarium with its interlocking curved room is replaced by a static rectangular room fitting somewhat solidly against rectangular hot rooms. The small circular tepidarium sits uneasily in the middle of these rectangular shapes and no attempt is made to absorb the space around it. An irregularly shaped service passage results.

Despite the somewhat rigid planning, the Baths of Diocletian are of special interest to modern visitors to Rome because, like the Baths of Caracalla, they are remarkably well preserved. However, whereas the Baths of Caracalla are somewhat removed from the modern centre of Rome, the Baths of Diocletian lie in the heart of the city. To take advantage of the towering mass of masonry, Pope Pius IV in 1563 decided to convert part of the ruins into the church of Santa

Maria degli Angeli. Michelangelo was the architect, and he used the three bays of the frigidarium and two flanking bays as his nave, and the circular tepidarium as an entrance vestibule. The scheme was a clear and logical one and the spaces he selected lent themselves admirably to the purposes of a church. It is worth noting here that he chose one of the two cross axes which dominated the plans of most big Imperial baths after the Baths of Trajan (see p. 157). In 1749 Vanvitelli was commissioned to enlarge the church and added a choir on the site of the natatio, thus transforming Michelangelo's nave into a transept. Vanvitelli's church therefore follows the line of the other axis of the baths. The original church and its eighteenth-century modification thus illustrate the dual axiality inherent in the fully developed Imperial bath building.

A walk through Michelangelo's nave gives one an excellent impression of the huge scale of the original frigidarium. The eight gigantic red granite columns still survive in their original positions, and from their entablatures spring the three soaring cross-vaults. The room is still lit by the eight massive lunette windows under the vault. One or two points should be borne in mind when looking at the present interior. Firstly, the original area of the frigidarium would have been much greater, because the four plunges and the other surrounding rooms were not incorporated into Michelangelo's church. This means that some of the more subtle lighting effects and vistas have been cut off. Also, the vaulting in Roman times was not covered with plain white plaster, but a glittering array of polychrome glass mosaic. Thus the interior would have had more of the jewel-box character of a Ravennate church than the chilly Mannerist appearance it has today.

The same rigid planning can be seen in the great palace that Diocletian built for his retirement on the Yugoslavian coast at Split (fig. 173). More like a permanent fortified camp than a palace, it reflected the uncertainties of the times and the need to enclose the comfortable Roman world within stout walls. Built between AD 300 and 306, it lay on the sea coast and was enclosed in a rectangular circuit of walls measuring approximately 180×216 metres. At each corner is a square bastion, and there are gates in the centres of the three landward sides, flanked by octagonal towers. There are a further six square bastions in the three landward walls, while the façade towards the sea is unbroken. Two intersecting colonnaded streets divide the complex into four rectangular segments. The northern two were probably barracks, and the southern two were the residential part of the palace. The southern arm of the north-south street is replaced by three features: the 'peristyle', a short stretch of street flanked by arcades which give access to a small temple to the west, and an octagonal mausoleum to the east; the domed vestibule of the palace; and a rectangular hall which opens into a long corridor running the length of the south side of the

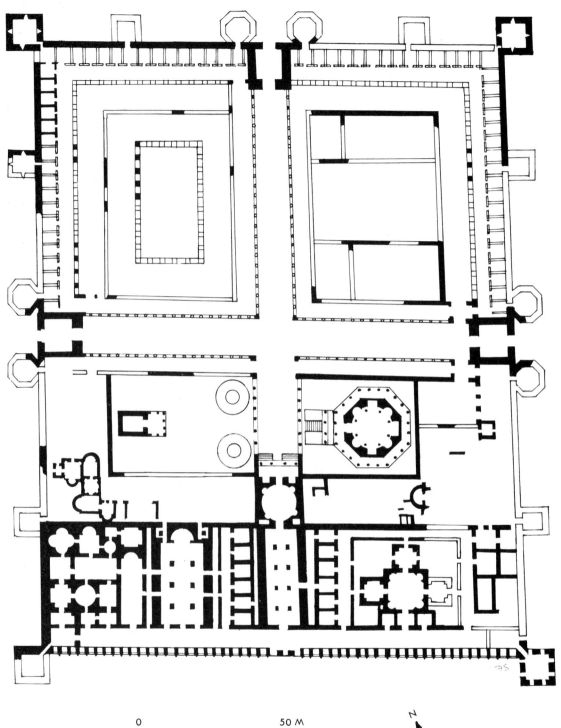

0   50 M

173 Spalato (Split),
Palace of Diocletian,
AD 300–306: plan

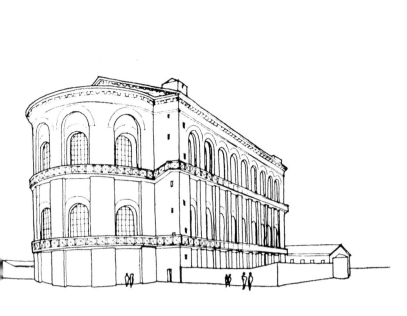

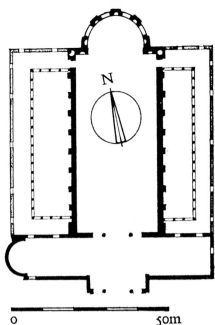

174 Trier, basilica, early fourth century AD: reconstructed view of exterior (left) and plan (right). (From A. Boethius, *op. cit.*)

complex. To the west is an apsed basilical hall, perhaps a throne room with what may be a bedroom and bathing suite beyond, and to the east a set of three smaller rooms opening from a larger central one, perhaps a triclinium. The whole southern section of the complex is taken up with this private suite. The shapes of the rooms and their arrangement has much of the regularity we have already seen in the Baths of Diocletian at Rome. The long transverse corridor which gives access to all these rooms is reminiscent of the Corridor of the Great Hunt in the Villa at Piazza Armerina in Sicily. Ward Perkins points out that the layout of the palace is derived from military camp architecture, and the residential part of the palace occupies the same position as the headquarters building in a camp. He also sees some Syrian features in the palace and suggests that it may be connected with Diocletian's palace at Antioch.

At this point we should turn for a moment to the capitals of the other Tetrarchs. Constantius Chlorus chose Trier (Augusta Trevirorum) as the capital of his Empire, which included Spain, Gaul, and Britain. Trier was an old-established city on the banks of the Moselle and already possessed a number of imposing monuments, including the St Barbara baths and the amphitheatre (see p. 228). However, its greatest period of prosperity dates from the time it became Constantius' capital. His son Constantine resided there for a time and completed the palace and basilica begun by his predecessor and built the cathedral as well as the Imperial baths. He also built a number of warehouses in the harbour district and the famous gate, the Porta Nigra. For a hundred years Trier remained the most important city in the west apart from Rome itself.

Many of these buildings have survived practically intact and take their place among the most conspicuous remnants of Roman architecture in the provinces. The basilica is particularly well preserved (figs. 174, 175). It stands on the site of a smaller basilical hall which probably formed part of the residence of the regional procurator. It is a large hall with a double-square ground-plan measuring 100×200 Roman feet with an apse at one end. The building is lit by two rows of round-headed windows which continue around the apse. The upper windows of the apse are just over a metre lower than the corresponding ones of the nave and they are shorter. Also the central pair of windows of the apse are narrower than the outer ones. These subtle optical devices give the impression that the apse is higher and wider than it in fact is. The optical refinements and unusual construction of the building (it is built entirely of brick, not brick-faced concrete) give rise to the hypothesis that it was built by architects from Asia Minor or Syria.

Externally the building has a strongly vertical accent because of the blind arcading framing the windows. However, nails and impressions in the brick show that originally continuous wooden galleries ran beneath each row of windows, adding a compensating horizontality. There was a colonnaded courtyard either side of the basilica and the building itself had underfloor heating. Externally the building was stuccoed and the window frames were decorated by painted *putti* and vine scrolls in yellow on a red field. The floor was in

175 Trier, the basilica, early fourth century AD. (*By courtesy of Fototeca Unione, Rome*)

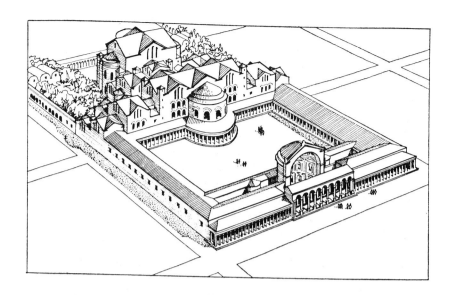

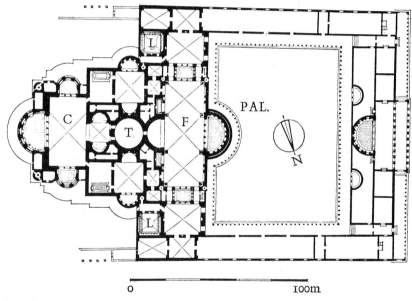

black and white opus sectile and one of the niches contains traces of blue and green scroll patterns on a gold ground in mosaic tesserae. The building originally had a rich interior, very much in contrast to its rather stark grandeur today. It also formed part of a larger palace complex of which only a transverse narthex survives. The rest of the complex is little known and whether or not the basilica joined up with a palace found a little to the north, under the cathedral, must be resolved by excavation.

The great Imperial baths are among the largest outside Rome, and raise the question of why they should have been built at all when Constantius had only recently finished rebuilding the equally large St Barbara Baths. The answer may be that they were not for public

176 Trier, Imperial Baths, early fourth century AD: restored view (above) and plan (below) (from A. Boethius, *op. cit.*)
L = Lavatory.
C = Caldarium.
T = Tepidarium.
F = Frigidarium.
PAL = Palaestra.

267

use, but were connected with the Imperial palace, which occupied a large portion of the eastern town. They were designed to occupy two city blocks, half as a gymnasium and half as the bath block (fig. 176). The main bathing block is much more compactly planned than that of the second-century St Barbara Baths, and betrays the hand of a court architect, perhaps trained in North Africa to judge by the ground plan. In the event it was never finished according to plan because of Constantine's departure for the east in AD 316, and finally the entire frigidarium area was scrapped.

The Porta Nigra was probably built by Constantine, but never finished, which explains its somewhat crude surface treatment (fig. 177). It owes its preservation to the fact that St Simeon lived in it and later a church was erected over the gate incorporating most of the Roman structure. Pierced by two arched passageways with garrison rooms above and two flanking and projecting towers, it follows a well-established Roman type. The first-century Porta Palatina at Turin has four arched passageways, two for traffic and two for pedestrians, and is flanked by even more imposing 16-sided towers. Other Augustan and early Imperial gates are of the same type, such as those at Aosta, Spello and Milan. A feature of these gates is the courtyard behind the tower inside the wall circuit, where no doubt visitors to the town and their merchandise would be checked. The

177 Trier, Porta Nigra, early fourth century AD. (*By courtesy of Fototeca Unione, Rome*)

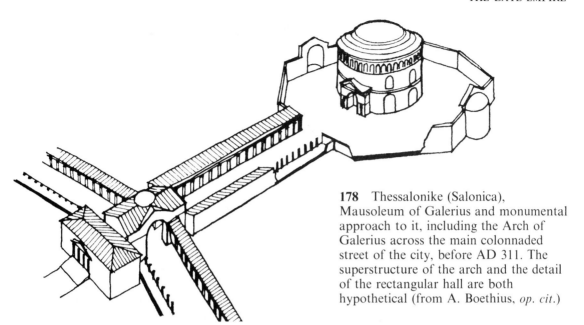

178 Thessalonike (Salonica), Mausoleum of Galerius and monumental approach to it, including the Arch of Galerius across the main colonnaded street of the city, before AD 311. The superstructure of the arch and the detail of the rectangular hall are both hypothetical (from A. Boethius, *op. cit.*)

Aurelianic wall at Rome had a series of such gateways (see p. 261). The Trier gate, like the others, was designed to impress. Towers and guard room are decorated with rows of half columns supporting continuous horizontal entablatures. The effect is clumsy and the work bears signs of haste. Indeed, inscriptions in the masonry show that the third storey went up in three weeks. For whatever reason the gate was never finished.

Diocletian's other Caesar, Galerius, who controlled the Danube provinces, made his capital Thessalonike, in northern Greece. The city was already well established by this date and lay on the strategically important Via Egnatia which linked Asia and Italy. Galerius built his palace to the east of the old town with the palace proper and an adjoining circus to the south of the Via Egnatia and his own mausoleum to the north. The Via Egnatia was colonnaded at this point and another colonnaded street ran north to the mausoleum (fig. 178). At the point where these colonnaded streets intersected a four-sided arch was erected. The sides which faced the Via Egnatia had three openings, one for traffic and two lesser ones for pedestrians. On the other two sides there was a single opening. As the colonnades abutted on the arch it could not be decorated like a free-standing structure. This may partly explain the unusual nature of the reliefs, which consist of a series of long rectangular panels (reminiscent of sarcophagus reliefs) set one on top of the other up the pylons of the arch.

The mausoleum is well preserved mainly because it was converted into the church of St George in the fourth century. It is a domed rotunda with eight barrel-vaulted recesses in the thickness of the drum. Above each recess is a round-headed window. Although the

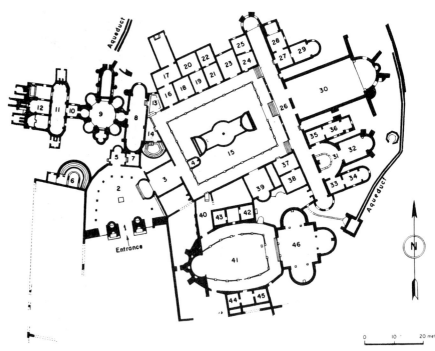

179 Piazza Armerina, Roman villa: plan

walls are massively thick, windows had become the established method of lighting a domed room rather than an oculus, which became rare in the third century. The structure of the vaults is of interest because pitched brick and mortared rubble are used, a technique common in Byzantine times. The dome too is of unusual profile. The lower part of the dome follows the normal curvature of a hemispherical dome, but at a point 2.5 metres from the wall changes to a steeper curvature which adds considerable stability to the structure. The crown of a dome is a point of weakness and it was the shallowness of the crown which caused the dome of Hagia Sophia to collapse shortly after it was completed in AD 537.

Finally mention should be made of the large villa at Piazza Armerina in Sicily. Now dated to the period AD 310–320, it cannot have been built for Maximian as originally thought. It has a loose, rather rambling layout in contrast to the taut planning of Diocletian's Palace at Split. Its polychrome mosaics link it stylistically with North Africa, but its layout is more reminiscent of Hadrian's villa at Tivoli. The main groupings of entrance courtyard (no. 2 on fig. 179), peristyle/audience hall (15 and 30 on fig. 179), baths (8–12 on fig. 179) and triclinium (46 on fig. 179) are loosely related and on differing axes. Like other buildings of the period, the interior dictates the shape of the exterior. The bathing suite, for example, is planned as a series of related interiors and the result is a jumble of irregular spaces outside.

When Diocletian went into voluntary retirement he compelled his fellow-emperor, Maximian, to do so too. The orderly succession he planned did not materialize. A further round of civil war ensued, this time between Maximian's son, Maxentius and the son of Constantius Chlorus, Constantine. For a time Maxentius was Emperor at Rome. As well as ending Diocletian's persecution and restoring church property, he began an ambitious building programme which included rebuilding the Temple of Venus and Rome which had been damaged by fire, beginning a new basilica near the Forum and starting a new complex on the Appian Way with a villa, a mausoleum for his son Romulus and a circus. The circus incorporated many of the refinements one would expect in a building of so late a date. The starting gates are set on a tight curve and strung out between tall towers (*oppida*) which are flush with the banks of seats either side. The spina is angled and, as an extra piece of sophistication, so is the seating between the meta secunda and the carceres. The spina is also short in relation to the arena as a whole. The building is of concrete faced with tufa and brick in alternate bands, a method common to the period and found in most contemporary buildings at Ostia. One constructional device of particular interest is the use of amphorae in the vaults to lighten the structure. Little is known of the villa, which has only partially been excavated. The mausoleum is a domed circular building preceded by a columnar porch in the manner of the Pantheon, and is set inside a colonnaded enclosure.

Constantine emerged as the victor after defeating his rival at the battle of the Milvian bridge just outside Rome (AD 312), a battle depicted on the arch vowed by the Senate to commemorate the victory. Despite the fact that it is the largest surviving triumphal arch, larger than the Arch of Septimius Severus on which it is so clearly modelled, its details reflect the times in which it was built. The Emperor obviously could not find enough monumental sculptors in Rome to decorate the Arch. Panels of sculpture were removed from a variety of Flavian, Trajanic and Antonine monuments for that purpose (fig. 21). Only the victory figures on the plinths and in the spandrels, six narrative reliefs and one or two roundels are Constantinian, all poorly modelled. The soffits of the passageways are left uncoffered. The arch itself is wide in proportion to its height, giving it a rather solid, earth-bound appearance in comparison to the soaring majesty of the Severan arch.

The major project left unfinished by Maxentius was the great basilica, 80 metres long and 25 metres high, the Basilica Nova, on the Velian hill close to the Roman Forum (fig. 180). The building did not follow the columnar plan established by the two earlier basilicas in the Forum and the Basilica Ulpia. Instead it adopted the layout of the frigidarium of a large bath building, such as the Baths of Diocletian completed a few years earlier (fig. 172). Three lateral barrel vaults either side formed the two aisles, and the nave was covered by three huge cross-vaults. Lighting was by the three

180 Rome, Basilica of Maxentius (AD 306–312), completed by Constantine

lunettes on each side and one at each end. The usual eight columns stood against the eight piers of the nave, and from their entablatures sprang the high vaults. The columns were fluted Proconnesian with Corinthian capitals. The only one to survive was transported to the square in front of Santa Maria Maggiore and stands there to this day. Both the lateral barrel-vaults and the cross-vaults were decorated with deeply sunken coffers, once elaborately stuccoed and painted. Today the bulk of the building is impressive even after the collapse of one set of barrel-vaults and all the high vaults. Maxentius built an entrance vestibule on the east end and there was an apse in the middle of the west end. Constantine altered the original arrangement by building a formal entrance of four porphyry columns and a staircase to the south, thus making the shorter axis the main one. He also added an apse opposite his entrance at the far side of the middle bay. In Maxentius' apse he placed a colossal seated statue of himself with the face, arms and legs in marble and the armour in gilt bronze. The marble parts of the statue can still be seen in the Capitoline museum. By changing the axis of the building Constantine was able to put its main entrance on the Sacred Way. That such a project should have been undertaken at all is astonishing at this late date, especially considering the transitory rule of Maxentius, who only reigned for six troubled years (AD 306–312).

Further down the Sacred Way towards the Forum stands a circular temple which has often been thought to be a Temple of Romulus, son of Maxentius. It now seems that the attribution is a false one. The temple is likely to have been dedicated to the Penates who originally had a shrine on the Velia which was swept away when the Basilica Nova was built. Its brickwork fits a Constantinian date

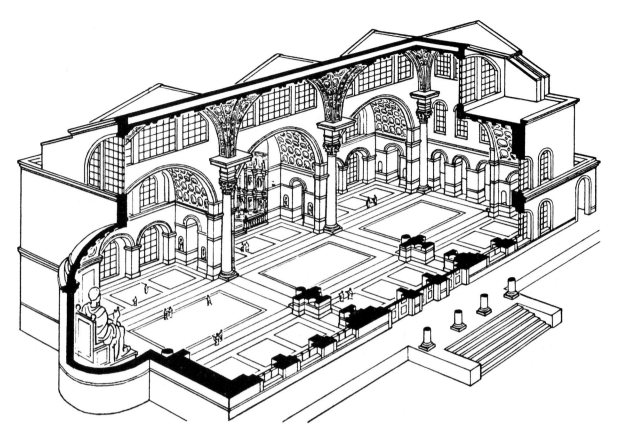

and its position accords with Constantine's interest in monuments fronting onto the Sacred Way. The temple is circular and covered with a dome. The main doorway, flanked by a pair of porphyry columns, has its original bronze doors. In front is a shallow concave forecourt flanked each side by a pair of columns. Each pair of columns also gives access to an apsed room, the two rooms flanking the central rotunda. If the attribution of the temple is correct, cult statues would have been placed in these two rooms.

Another important circular building of the period is the circular pavilion in the Licinian gardens, the so-called 'Temple of Minerva Medica'. It is a decagonal hall, 25 metres in diameter (fig. 182). The lower part of each side wall, apart from the entrance, is pierced by a round-headed niche, and above each niche is a window. The result is an exceptionally light drum which was obviously inadequate to support the weight of the dome. Soon afterwards buttresses were added around the structure to stabilize it. The dome itself was stiffened by the use of brick ribs (fig. 44).

Constantine was the first Christian Emperor of Rome, and, while it is not within the scope of this book to discuss his church building programme, one Christian building should be singled out for mention, the mausoleum of his daughter, St Constantia (fig. 183). It

181 Rome, Basilica of Maxentius (AD 306–312), completed by Constantine. Reconstruction (from H. & R. Leacroft, *The Buildings of Ancient Rome*, Leicester 1969)

273

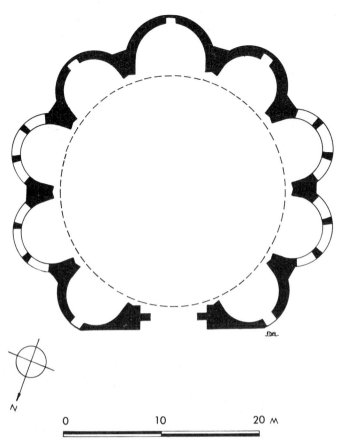

0   10   20 M

182 Rome, 'Temple of Minerva Medica', early fourth century AD: plan

is a circular domed building with arched windows in its drum, like the 'Temple of Minerva Medica', but instead of niches it has an arcade at ground level, supported by pairs of composite columns. Around the drum runs a continuous circular passage covered with a barrel-vault. The mausoleum of St Constantia brings us to the threshold of Byzantine architecture where arcade, circular passage and dome are brought together in a single centralized building. The dome has something of the lightness of that of S Vitale at Ravenna or Hagia Sophia at Istanbul. It is no longer earth-bound like the massive dome of the 'Temple of Mercury' at Baia, with its ponderous concrete drum, or the Pantheon, whose drum, although lightened by the columnar exedrae, has no windows. The circular caldarium of the Baths of Caracalla must have had a much lighter and more airy appearance. However, the 'Temple of Minerva Medica' and St Constantia were the critical links between the late antique and the early Byzantine.

With the accession of Constantine the Emperor had grown into a figure larger than life. The scale of his monuments and of statues like the one in his basilica reflected the new status of the Emperor. He appeared in public rarely and few had the privilege of hearing him

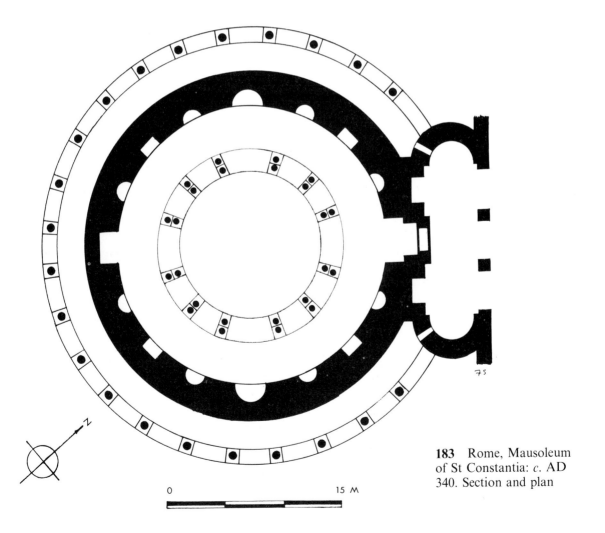

75

183 Rome, Mausoleum of St Constantia: *c*. AD 340. Section and plan

0   15 M

except through a curtain. It was a great honour even to be allowed to kiss his robe. He was addressed and spoke in artificially exalted language, the stone he stepped on was Imperial porphyry and even the ink he used was purple. When he appeared at all he was surrounded by his court officials in strict hierarchy. His portraits show a monarch who has deigned to allow his subjects to gaze upon him in awe.

His conversion to Christianity and his edict of toleration are what he is mainly remembered for. In a world that was increasingly seeking spiritual consolation and tormented by fear of a universal Armageddon his action was a masterstroke. It silenced his most vocal critics and united the Roman world in a powerful new religious force of which he regarded himself as the leader. He was attracted to the riches and spirituality of the East and moved the capital of the Empire to Constantinople in AD 330. This more than any other action spells the end of the Roman Empire in the West and a change towards a new era. The final break with humanism and the Classical tradition makes this an appropriate point to terminate the story of Roman architecture.

Glossary

ADYTON: Inner sanctuary of a temple

AEDICULE: An opening framed by columns or pilasters supporting an entablature and pediment, often used ornamentally

AGGER: Rampart

AGORA: Market place of a Greek town

ALAE: Wings or alcoves opening to left or right of the atrium of a Roman house

ANNULAR VAULT: A vaulted passage running around a circular space

ANTEFIX: Ornament at the eaves of a roof to conceal the end of a tile

APODYTERION: Changing room of a Roman bath

APOPHYGEE: Concave moulding between the shaft and the base of a column

ARCHITRAVE: Horizontal element spanning two columns and forming the lowest part of the entablature. In the Doric Order it is normally plain; in the Ionic and Corinthian it is divided into three horizontal fasciae

ARCUATED LINTEL: A single arched entablature flanked by horizontal entablatures, often in the centre of a façade under the pediment

ASHLAR MASONRY: Regular cut-stone masonry

ASTRAGAL: A small convex semicircular moulding often ornamented with a bead-and-reel ornament

ATRIUM: The main hall of a traditional Roman house. It could be completely roofed (*testudinate*) or have an opening (*compluvium*) in the middle of its roof and a water tank (*impluvium*) in the floor beneath

BELVEDERE: A roofed open-sided building which commands a view

BIPEDALES: Square Roman bricks measuring two Roman feet each side

BEAD-AND-REEL: A moulding consisting of circular or lozenge shaped elements alternating with cylindrical ones (see fig. 34, nos. 27–30)

BUCRANIA: A decorative motif consisting of ox-heads shown frontally

CABLED FLUTING: Fluting filled with a vertical convex moulding, usually confined to the lowest third of the shaft

CALDARIUM: The hot room of a Roman bath

CARCERES: The starting gates for the chariots of a Roman circus

CATENARY: The shape formed by a chain hanging freely from two fixed points

CAULICULUS: The stalk from which spring the volutes and helices of a Corinthian capital

CAVETTO: A concave moulding

CELLA: The central chamber of a temple where the image of the deity was placed

CLERESTORY: Upper part of a wall above the level of adjacent aisles, pierced with windows to light a central room or nave

COFFER: A sunken panel in a ceiling or vault

COMPLUVIUM: See ATRIUM

COMPOSITE CAPITAL: A capital which consists of two rows of acanthus leaves at the bottom and a diagonal Ionic volute above

CONSOLES: Brackets supporting the projecting part of a Corinthian cornice. The term is often used of the two-stepped brackets common in the East, and in Rome from the time of Hadrian onwards, to distinguish them from modillions

CORBEL: A supporting bracket projecting from a wall or sometimes a column shaft

CORINTHIAN ORDER: The richest of the three Greek Orders, recognizable by its acanthus capitals

CORNICE: The top, projecting part of the entablature

CORONA: The vertical face of the projecting part of a cornice, below the sima

CRYPTOPORTICUS: A ground-level or semi-subterranean vaulted corridor, usually lit by openings in the vault. Its primary function is normally to buttress an adjacent structure, and secondarily it is used as a shady place to walk or store goods

CURIA: Meeting-place for the Senate or local Council of a Roman town

CYMA RECTA: A double moulding, concave above, convex below

CYMA REVERSA: A double moulding, convex above, concave below

DECASTYLE: Consisting of ten columns

DENTILS: A series of rectangular blocks under the cornice of an Ionic or Corinthian entablature. In the Corinthian Order they are below the modillions

DIAETA: A summer-house

DIPTERAL: A term applied to a temple with a double row of columns around the cella

DOMUS: A large, single-family house, as distinct from an apartment house

DORIC ORDER: The most austere of the three Greek Orders, distinguished by its plain capital and triglyph frieze

DRAFTING: A plain recessed band around the edges of a block or at the bottom of the riser of a step

ECHINUS: A swelling, cushion-shaped element under the abacus of a Doric or Ionic capital. In the case of the Ionic capital it is ornamented with egg-and-tongue

EGG-AND-DART: An ornament similar to egg-and-tongue, preferred to the latter in Flavian and Severan times (see fig. 34, nos. 23 and 26)

EGG-AND-TONGUE: An ornament consisting of oval elements alternating with downward-pointing tongues, normally applied to an ovolo moulding (see fig. 34, nos. 21, 22, 24 and 25)

ENTABLATURE: A collective term applied to the architrave, frieze and cornice

EXEDRA: A recess, usually semicircular or rectangular in shape

EXTRADOS: The outer curved face of an arch

FASCIA: A plain horizontal band

FAUCES: A passageway in a Roman house, leading from the front door to the atrium

FLUTING: Concave grooves of curved section running vertically up the shaft of a column. In the Doric Order they are broad and shallow and meet in a sharp edge, termed an *arris*. In the Ionic and Corinthian Orders they are deeper and divided by flat fillets or strips

FORNIX: A Republican term for an arch. It is sometimes used of an arch flanked by half-columns which carry an entablature over the top of the arch

FORUM: The market-place or main square of a Roman town

FRIEZE: The middle section of the entablature. In the Doric Order it is divided into triglyphs and metopes; in the Ionic and Corinthian it is continuous and often has either relief sculpture or an inscription

FRIGIDARIUM: The cold room of a Roman bath

GUILLOCHE: A pattern of interlacing bands which form a plait, commonly found on the upper torus of a column base

GUTTAE: Originally the wooden pegs used to secure the beam ends of timber structure and later translated into stone in the Doric Order. There are six under each triglyph and 18 on the underside of each mutule.

HELIOCAMINUS: A room, usually in a bath, oriented to take maximum advantage of the sun's heat

HELIX: A spiral ornament. The term is often used to denote the two inner tendrils which spring from the cauliculus of a Corinthian capital and meet under the abacus

HEREDIUM: The small garden behind a Republican house

HEXASTYLE: Consisting of six columns

HYPOCAUST: A floor raised on small columns to allow the circulation of air underneath

IMPLUVIUM: See ATRIUM

INSULA: A tenement or apartment house

INTERAXIAL: The distance between the centres of two adjacent columns

INTERCOLUMNIATION: The distance between the sides of two adjacent columns

INTRADOS: The inner face or underside of an arch. Also called soffit

IONIC ORDER: One of the three Greek Orders, recognizable by its volute capitals

ISODOMIC: A term applied to masonry with courses of uniform height

LACONICUM: The hot, dry room of a Roman bath

LARARIUM: A shrine to the household gods of a Roman house

LATERES: Roman bricks, either baked (*coctus*) or unbaked (*crudus*)

LUNETTE: A semicircular flat surface or opening

MACELLUM: A meat or provisions market

MEGARON: A rectangular hall in Cretan and Mycenaean architecture

META: The turning point for chariots in a Roman circus. There was one at each end of the spina, the first turn (*meta prima*) being at the curved end of the arena, the second (*meta secunda*) at the *carceres* end

METOPE: The space between two triglyphs, either left plain or filled with relief sculpture

MERLON: The raised portion of battlements

MODILLION: A double scrolled bracket supporting the projecting part of a cornice

MUTULE: Rectangular panels under the soffit of a Doric cornice, adorned with 18 pegs or *guttae*. They represent the projecting rafters in the original timber construction

NARTHEX: An antechamber to the nave of a Christian church

NATATIO: The swimming pool of a Roman bath

NYMPHAEUM: A grotto with a natural water supply dedicated to the nymphs – later an artificial grotto or fountain building

OCTASTYLE: Consisting of eight columns

OCULUS: Circular opening in the apex of a dome

ODEION: A small roofed theatre for musical entertainment

OECUS: The main living room of a Greek house, introduced to Roman architecture along with the peristyle. Often used for dining

ORCHESTRA: The circular dancing area of a Greek theatre, which developed into the semicircular area in front of the stage of a Roman theatre

ORTHOSTAT: A slab of stone laid vertically

OVOLO: A convex moulding

PALAESTRA: An open area surrounded by covered porticoes used for wrestling and exercise, often forming part of a Roman bath complex

PALMETTE: A fan-shaped ornament consisting of lobed or pointed leaves, often found in Roman architecture on the sima of a cornice

PERIPTERAL: A term applied to a cella surrounded by a single row of columns

PERISTYLE: An open courtyard or garden surrounded by columnar porticoes

PILASTER: A rectangular column projecting only slightly from a wall, used to suggest structure. It can be plain or fluted, and have the base and capital of any Order

PLINTH: The projecting base of a wall, or a column pedestal

PODIUM: The raised platform on which the columns and cella of a Roman temple stand

POMERIUM: The area left free of buildings immediately inside and outside the walls of a Roman town

POZZOLANA: A reddish volcanic ash found in central Italy, especially around Pozzuoli, which gave Roman concrete its strength

PRAETORIUM: The official residence of a legionary commander or provincial governor

PRINCIPIA: The headquarters building of a Roman fort where the legionary standards were kept, speeches were made and councils were held

PRONAOS: Porch in front of the cella of a temple

PROPYLAEUM: Monumental entrance gateway to a sanctuary

PROPYLON: A simpler version of a propylaeum

PROSTYLE: A term used of a temple with free-standing columns at the entrance side only

PSEUDODIPTERAL: A dipteral arrangement of columns with the inner row omitted

PSEUDOPERIPTERAL: A term applied to a temple with some of the columns engaged into the cella wall

PULVINATED: Convex in profile. A term usually applied to a frieze

QUADRIGA: A four-horsed chariot

QUOINS: Dressed stones at the corner of a building

ROTUNDA: A building circular in plan, often domed

SCHOLA LABRI: The place where the cold water basin stood in the hot room of a Roman bath

SCIAGRAPHY: The art of projecting shadows onto a drawing of a building

SCOTIA: A concave moulding, usually between the two torus mouldings of a column base

SIMA: The crowning moulding of a cornice, originally the gutter

SOCLE: The lower part of a wall

SOFFIT: The underside of an architectural member

SPANDREL: The triangular space described by the side of an arch, the horizontal line drawn from its apex and the vertical line from its springing

SPINA: The dividing strip running down the arena of a Roman circus

STYLOBATE: The three-stepped platform on which the columns and cella of a Greek temple stand

SUDATORIUM: The sweating-room of a Roman bath

TABERNA: A small shop or workshop

TABLINUM: The central room at the end of the atrium of a Roman house, originally the master bedroom, later used for storing records

TEMENOS: Sacred area around a shrine or temple

TEPIDARIUM: The warm room of a Roman bath

TETRAKIONIA: Monument consisting of four columns or groups of columns placed at the intersection of two major streets

TETRAPYLON: A monument consisting of four pylons, often erected at the intersection of two main streets. It can also refer to a four-sided arch

TETRASTYLE: Consisting of four columns

TORUS: A convex moulding, usually on a column base

TRIBUNAL: The raised platform from which a general or emperor addressed the troops

TRICLINIUM: The dining-room of a Roman house, so-called because of the three banqueting couches (*klinai*) arranged around the walls

TRIGLYPHS: Upright rectangular panels with vertical grooves alternating with the metopes of a Doric frieze. They represent the ends of the ceiling beams in the original timber construction

TRIPTERAL: Columns three deep

VOLUTES: The spiral scrolls at the corner of an Ionic or Corinthian capital

VOUSSOIRS: The wedge-shaped stones which compose a masonry arch

Notes

These are a selection of more important works on individual buildings or periods from which readers can find a fuller bibliography. Where no note exists on a particular topic, see the general bibliography on p. 7.

Chapter 1

p. 14   For the development of the Forum see P. Zanker, *Forum Romanum*, Tübingen 1972.

p. 16   For Cosa see F. E. Brown, *Cosa 1 and 2 in MAAR* vol. xx, 1951, and xxvi, 1960.

p. 16   Lugli discusses these types of walling in *La tecnica edilizia*, Rome 1957, pp. 55ff.

p. 20   The circular temple in the Forum Boarium is the subject of a monograph by F. Rakob and W. D. Heilmeyer, *Der Rundtempel an Tiber in Rom*, Mainz 1973.

p. 20   For the temple at Cori and other late Republican buildings, see R. Delbrueck, *Hellenistische Bauten in Latium*, Strasbourg 1907–12.

p. 22   For a recent discussion on the origins of the basilica see J. J. Coulton, *The Architectural development of the Greek Stoa*, Oxford 1976, pp. 180–83.

p. 23   For the excavations of the Stabian Baths at Pompeii, H. Eschebach, *Die Stabianer Thermen in Pompeji*, Berlin 1979.

p. 26   For a detailed description of the Sanctuary of Fortuna at Palestrina see F. Fasolo, and G. Gallini, *Il Santuario della Fortuna Primigenia a Palestrina*, Rome 1953, who date it to the mid-second century BC. Lugli, in *La tecnica*, dates it to the Sullan period.

Chapter 2

p. 33   Maiuri's excavations in the atria of a number of Pompeian houses are published in *Notizie degli Scavi*, 1930, pp. 381–95; 1942, pp. 404–15; and 1944–45, pp. 130–59. For Patroni see *Rend. Linc.*, 1902, pp. 467–507.

p. 33   See Graham, in *Phoenix*, 1966, p. 7.

p. 33   Packer discusses Pompeian domestic buildings in *The Insulae of Imperial Ostia*, MAAR, 1971.

p. 36   For the architecture of theatres see M. Bieber, *The History of the Greek and Roman Theatre*, Princeton 1961.

p. 38   For Roman circuses see J. H. Humphrey, F. B. Sear and M. Vickers, 'Aspects of the Circus at Lepcis Magna', in *Libya Antiqua*, 9–10, 1972–73, pp. 25–97.

p. 39   The best general work on Roman baths remains D. Krencker and E. Krüger, *Die Trierer Kaiserthermen*, Augsburg 1929.

p. 42   For aqueducts see T. Ashby, *The Aqueducts of Ancient Rome*, Oxford 1935.

Chapter 3

p. 54   For the Augustan remodelling of the Forum see P. Zanker, *Forum Romanum*, Tübingen 1972.

p. 60   For the Forum of Augustus, see P. Zanker, *Forum Augustum*, Tübingen 1958.

p. 64   Strong discusses Augustan Corinthian in 'The Temple of Castor in the Forum Romanum', in *PBSR*, 30, 1962, pp. 1–30, and 'Some observations on early Roman Corinthian' in *JRS*, vol. 53, 1963, pp. 73–84.

Chapter 4

p. 73   For the development of concrete in Pompeii see R. C. Carrington in *JRS*, vol. 23, 1933, p. 125–38.

p. 74   See Delbrueck, *Hellenistische Bauten*, etc.

p. 74   Gatti's identification of the Porticus Aemilia is in *Bull. Comm*, 62, pp. 123–41.

p. 75   Coarelli, in *PBSR*, vol. 45, 1977, pp. 1–23.

p. 77   For brickstamps see Lugli, *La tecnica*.

p. 84   For marbles see R. Gnoli, *Marmora Romana*, Rome 1971.

Chapter 5

p. 92   The Caligulan galleys are described by G. Uccelli, *Le Navi di Nemi*, Rome 1950.

Chapter 6

p. 104   Recent general books on Pompeii and Herculaneum include M. Grant, *Cities of Vesuvius*, London 1974; T. Kraus, *Pompeii and Herculaneum*, New York 1975; E. La Rocca, M. & A. de Vos, *Guida archeologica di Pompei*, Verona 1976.

p. 112   For Maiuri's excavations in the Basilica, see *Notizie degli Scavi*, 1951, pp. 225–60.

p. 112   Ohr's reconstruction is in *Die Basilika in Pompeji*, Karlsruhe 1973.

p. 118   For the last phase of Pompeian architecture see A. Maiuri, *L'ultima fase edilizia di Pompei*, Rome 1942.

p. 118   The basic work on Ostia is R. Meiggs, *Roman Ostia*, Oxford 1973.

Chapter 7

p. 146　For the origins of the Composite Order, see D. E. Strong, 'Some early examples of the Composite capital' in *JRS*, 1960, 119–28.

Chapter 8

p. 157　For the Forum of Trajan, see 'Das Trajansforum in Rom', in *Archäologischer Anzeiger*, 1970.

p. 166　Recent studies of the Pantheon include K. de Fine Licht, *The Rotunda in Rome*, Jutland 1966; W. MacDonald, *The Pantheon*, London 1976.

p. 172　For Hadrian's Villa see H. Kuhler, *Hadrian und seine Villa bei Tivoli*, Berlin 1950; S. Aurigemma, *Villa Adriana*, Rome 1962.

p. 183　For late Hadrianic buildings see 'Late Hadrianic architectural ornament in Rome', in *PBSR*, 21, 1953, pp. 118–51.

Chapter 9

p. 187　For the buildings of Cyrenaica in general see S. Stucchi, *Architettura Cirenaica*, Rome 1975.

p. 187　For Cyrene and Apollonia see R. Goodchild, *Kyrene und Apollonia*, Zurich 1971.

p. 191　G. H. R. Wright discusses the architecture of Ptolemais in C. Kraeling, *Ptolemais* (Oriental Institute Publications, vol. 90), Chicago 1962.

p. 194　For the architecture of Berenice, see F. B. Sear 'Architectural decoration' in *Excavations at Sidi Khrebish Benghazi* (*Berenice*), vol. I (supplements to Libya Antiqua – V), 1977.

p. 194　The best general work on Tripolitania is D. E. L. Haynes, *The Antiquities of Tripolitania*, Tripoli 1965.

p. 202　For Tunisian architecture see A. Lézine, *Architecture romaine d'Afrique*, Tunis.

p. 203　For Dougga see C. Poinssot, *Les Ruines de Dougga*, Tunis 1958.

p. 205　For Timgad see C. Courtois, *Timgad: antique Thamugadi*, Algiers 1951.

p. 208　For Djemila see L. Leschi, *Djémila: antique Cuicul*, Algiers 1953.

p. 209　For Volubilis see R. Thouverst, *Volubilis*, Paris 1949.

Chapter 10

p. 210　For Roman Spain see F. J. Wiseman, *Roman Spain: an introduction to the Roman antiquities of Spain and Portugal*, London 1956.

p. 213　Two general works on Gaul are O. Brogan, *Roman Gaul*, London 1953 and P. MacKendrick, *Roman France*, London 1972.

p. 216　On the dating of the amphitheatres at Arles and Nîmes, see G. Lugli, 'La Datazione degli anfiteatri di Arles e di Nîmes in Provenza', *Rivista dell' Institute Nazionale d'Archaeologia e Storia dell'Arte*, XIII–XIV, 1964–5, pp. 145–99.

p. 216　On the arch at Orange see R. Amy, *L'Arc d'Orange* (XV Suppl. à *Gallia*), Paris 1962.

p. 218　See J. Sautel, *Vaison dans l'antiquité*, 3 vols. Avignon 1941–42 and Lyon 1942.

p. 219　A recent general guide to the Roman sites of Britain is R. J. Wilson, *A Guide to the Roman Remains in Britain*, London 1975. For the towns see J. Wacher, *The Towns of Roman Britain*, London 1975. For the history see S. Frere, *Britannia*, London 1967. For the archaeology see R. G. Collingwood and I. Richmond, *The Archaeology of Roman Britain*, London 1969.

p. 221　For Bath see B. Cunliffe, *Roman Bath Discovered*, London 1971.

p. 224　For Fishbourne see B. Cunliffe, *Fishbourne, a Roman Palace and its Garden*, London 1971.

p. 226　For Hadrian's Wall see J. Collingwood Bruce, *Handbook to the Roman Wall* (12th ed. revised by I. A. Richmond), Newcastle 1965.

p. 227　A recent guide to the Roman sites of Germany is J. von Elbe, *Roman Germany*, Mainz 1977.

p. 228　For the limes, see D. Baatz, *Der Römische Limes*, 2nd ed., Berlin 1975.

p. 229　For the Balkans see J. J. Wilkes, *Dalmatia*, London 1969, A. Mócsy, *Pannonia and Upper Moesia*, London 1974 and P. MacKendrick, *The Dacian stones speak*, Chapel Hill 1975.

Chapter 11

p. 233　For Athens see J. Travlos, *Pictorial Dictionary of Ancient Athens*, London 1971. This includes a detailed bibliography on individual monuments.

p. 239　For Corinth see *Ancient Corinth: a guide to the excavations*, 6th ed. (American School of Classical Studies at Athens), ed. J. L. Caskey

p. 241　General guides to the antiquities of Turkey include E. Akurgal, *Ancient Civilizations and Ruins of Turkey*, Istanbul 1973 and G. E. Bean, *Aegean Turkey*, London 1966.

p. 245　For Baalbek see F. Ragette, *Baalbek*, London 1980.

p. 248　For Palmyra, see K. Michalowski, *Palmyra*, New York 1968.

p. 249　For Dura-Europos see A. Perkins, *The Art of Dura-Europos*, Oxford 1973.

p. 252　For Jerash, see C. H. Kraeling, *Gerasa: City of the Decapolis*, New Haven, 1938.

NOTES

p. 253 For Petra see I. Browning, *Petra*, London 1973.

Chapter 12

p. 261 For the Aurelianic walls see I. A. Richmond, *The City Wall of Imperial Rome*, Oxford 1930.

p. 263 The most recent excavations of the Palace at Split are published in J. and T. Marasović,

S. McNally and J. Wilkes. *Diocletian's Palace* (2 parts), Split 1972 and 1976.

p. 265 For Trier see E. M. Wightman, *Roman Trier and the Treviri*, London 1970.

p. 270 For the dating of the Villa at Piazza Armerina see Ampolo, Carandini and Pucci, in *Mélanges de l'Ecole Française de Rome* (*Antiquité*), 83, 1971, pp. 176–79.

Index

Places

Actium, 53, 58
  Battle of, 227
Adamclisi:
  Tropaeum Traiani, 230
  Basilica, 230
Alatrium, walls, 16, 45
Alban Lake, emissary, 92, 94
Alcantara, bridge, 42, 211; fig. 136
Alexandria, 23, 185 ff.
  Tombs, Shatby, 185; Moustapha Pasha, 185, 187, fig. 113; Anfoushy, 185, 186
Ampurias, *see* Emporion
Anagni, walls, 45
Ancona, Arch of Trajan, 44
Antioch, palace of Diocletian, 265
Antium, 59, 120
Aosta, gate, 268
Apollonia, 191
Aquae Sulis (Bath), 221 ff.
  Baths, 213, 223–24, fig. 147
  Temple of Sulis Minerva, 223, figs. 147, 148
Aquincum, fort, 228
Arausio (Orange), 213, 216–18
  Arch of Tiberius, 213, 216–18
  Theatre, 38, 143, 213, 218, fig. 142
Ardea, walls, 16, 45
Arelate (Arles), 213
  Amphitheatre, 213, 216
Arpinum, walls, 16, 17, fig. 5
Aspendos:
  Aqueduct, 245
  Theatre, 245
Athens, 233–39
  Academy, 175
  Agora, 235–37, 239
  Agora of Caesar and Augustus, 234
  Altar of the Twelve Gods, 65
  Arch of Hadrian, 237–38, fig. 154
  Bouleuterion, 236
  Erechtheum, 61, 64, 65, 173, 181, 234
  Hephaesteum, 234
  Library of Hadrian, 238, fig. 155
  Lyceum, 175
  Odeion of Agrippa, 235–36, fig. 152
  Odeion of Herodes Atticus, 239
  Parthenon, 64, 84, 234, 247
  Stoa of Attalos, 112, 234
  Stoa Poikile, 175–76
  Temple, of Ares, 236–37; of Athena Nike, 239; of Olympian Zeus, 12, 84, 183, 231, 237, 247, fig. 153; of Rome and Augustus, 65, 234
Augusta Raurica (Augst), 213, 219

Capitolium, 219
  Forum/basilica, 159, 219, fig. 144
Augusta Treverorum (Trier), 228, 265–69
  Amphitheatre, 228, 265
  Basilica, 265–67, figs. 174, 175
  Bridge, 228
  Forum, 228
  Imperial Baths, 267–68, fig. 176
  Palace, 267
  Porta Nigra, 265, 268–69, fig. 177
  St Barbara baths, 228, 265, 267

Baiae, Temple of Mercury, 81, 274
Bassae, Temple of Apollo, 232
Bath, *see* Aquae Sulis
Beneventum, Arch of Trajan, 44, 145, 164, fig. 95
Benghazi (Berenice), 194
  Doors, 186, fig. 119
  Mud-brick, 76
Bonn, fort, 228
Borcovicium (Housesteads), 45–47, 226–27, fig. 46
Boscoreale, villa, 34–35
Brigetio, fort, 228
Brocolitia (Carrawburgh), 227
Brundisium (Brindisi), 164, 256
Bulla Regia, 203, 204–205
  Houses, 204–205, fig. 129

Calleva Atrebatum (Silchester), 221, fig. 146
Camulodunum (Colchester), 219, 221
  Temple of Claudius, 221
Canterbury, 219
Capri, Villa Jovis, 88–91, figs. 46–48
Capua:
  Amphitheatre, 37
  Tombs, 47
Carlisle, 226
Carnuntum, colonia, 229
  Fort, 228, 229
Carrawburgh, *see* Brocolitia
Carthage, 195, 202
  Antonine Baths, 202
  Aqueduct, 202–203
Carthago Nova (Cartagena), 210
Cerveteri (Caere), tombs, 47
Chesters, 227
Circelli, walls, 16, 45
Cirencester, *see* Corinium
Colchester, *see* Camulodunum
Constantinople, walls, 47
  Hagia Sophia, 274
Cori, Temple of Hercules, 20–21, fig. 11

Corinium (Cirencester), Chedworth villa, 226
Corinth, 239–41, fig. 156
   Agora, 240–41
   Basilicas, 240
   Bema, 240
   Fountain of Peirene, 240–41
   Lechaion road, 241
   Sack of, 19, 239
   Stoas, 240
   Temples, 240
Cosa, 16–17, 18, 32, fig. 6
   Capitolium, 16–17
   Curia, 17
   Gateway, 18
   Walls, 16
Cuicul (Djemila), 208, figs. 133, 134
   Arch of Caracalla, 208, fig. 134
   Forum, 208
   Macellum, 208
   Severan Temple, 208, fig. 134
Cyrene, 186, 187–91, 194, fig. 114
   Basilica, 190, fig. 115
   Doorways, 186
   Sanctuary of Apollo, 187, 190–91
   Stoa of Hercules and Hermes, 175
   Temple of Zeus, 191
   Theatre, 190–91

Delos, 21, 90, 135
Djemila, see Cuicul
Dougga, see Thugga
Dura Europos, 245, 249–50
   Agora, 249–50
   Palace, 250–52
   Synagogue, 31
   Temples, 250

Eburacum (York), 221
   Principia, 221
El-Djem, see Thysdrus
Emerita Augusta (Merida), 211
Emporion (Ampurias), 210
Ephesus, 241, 243–45
   Harbour Baths, 243
   Library of Celsus, 231, 233, 238, 243, fig. 160
   Temple of Artemis, 182
   Temple of Hadrian, 194, 243–45, fig. 161
   Theatre, 243, fig. 159

Falerii Novi:
   Gate, voussoir arch, 18
   Walls, 16
Ferentinum:
   Shopping arcade, 36, 163
   Walls, 16
Fidenae, quarries, 84
Fishbourne, 220, 224–26, fig. 149
Formiae, Villa of Cicero, 24
Forum Julii (Fréjus), 213
Fucine Lake, 92

Gabii, quarry, 83
Gades (Cadiz), 210
Gela, brick walls, 76
Gerasa (Jerash), 245, 252–53, fig. 166
   Sanctuary of Artemis, 252–53, fig. 167
   Temple of Zeus, 252

Glanum (St Rémy), 213, 218
   Arch of Julii, 218
   Baths, 213, 218
   Houses, 218
   Mausoleum, 47, 218
Gloucester, 219

Hadrian's Wall, 45, 47, 226–27
Herculaneum:
   House of the Mosaic Atrium, 35, 117
   House of the Stags, 35, 117, 134, 210
   Samnite House, 112
   Shops, 36
Housesteads, see Borcovicium

Italica, 154, 210–11, fig. 135

Jerash, see Gerasa

Lambaesis, 206–208, fig. 132
Lanuvium, 255
Lepcis Magna, 187, 195–200, 256, fig. 120
   Arch of Septimius Severus, 199
   Arch of Trajan, 195–97
   Chalcidicum, 195
   Forum and basilica, 32, 159, 197–99, 219, 256, figs. 121–23
   Hadrianic Baths, 40, 197
   Hunting Baths, 40, 199–200, fig. 124
   Macellum, 36, 109, 195
   Nymphaeum, 197–98, 256
   Temple of Rome and Augustus, 195
Lincoln, 219
Londinium (London), 220
Lugdunum (Lyon), 213, 219

Magdalensberg, 229
Magnesia, Temple of Artemis Leuco-phryene, 248
Mainz, fort, 227, 228
Marzabotto, 32
Massilia (Marseilles), 210, 213
Merida, see Emerita Augusta
Milan, gate, 268
Miletus, 241–43, fig. 158
   Bouleuterion, 192, 236, 242
   Grid plan, 241
   Gymnasium, 242
   Nymphaeum, 242–43
   Stoas, 241–42
   Temple of Apollo Delphinios, 241–42
Minturnae, walls, 16
Misurata, 194

Nemausus (Nîmes), 213–16
   Amphitheatre, 38, 143, 215–16, figs. 140, 141
   Maison Carrée, 30, 213, 214–15, 223, fig. 139
   Pont du Gard, 43, 214, fig. 138; water supply, 43, 214; castellum aquae, 43, 214
   Tour Magne, 213–14
   Walls, 213; Gate of Augustus, 214
Nemi, Lake, 86, 92
Neuss, fort, 228
Nijmegen, fort, 228
Nîmes, see Nemausus
Norba, walls, 16

Oea (Tripoli), 187, 200–201
  Arch of Marcus Aurelius, 44, 200–201, fig. 126
Oplontis, 24, 103
Orange, *see* Arausio
Ostia, 118–33, 148, 154, 271, fig. 67
  Baths: Forum, 127, 202, figs. 71, 75, of Neptune, 127
  Barracks of the vigiles, 127
  Castrum, 45, 120–21, 123
  Cults of Cybele and of Isis, 132
  Forum, 120, 123, 125, 132
  Harbour, Claudian, 86, 92–93, 123–24, fig. 68; Trajanic, 93, 124–25
  Horrea, 130, fig. 74, by Trajanic harbour, 124; Epagathiana, 127; great granary, 127
  Houses and insulae, 33, 35, 102, 121, 125, 127–30, fig. 72–73; of Amor and Psyche, 132; fig. 76, of Diana, 128, fig. 73: Garden Houses, 130, fig. 73
  Piazzale delle Corporazioni, 130–31; della Vittoria, 132
  Porta Laurentina, 121; Marina, 121; Romana, 121, 132
  Portus Ostiae, *see* Portus
  School of Trajan, 127
  Shops, 35, 130
  Streets, cardo and decumanus, 120, 121, 123, 125; Via della Foce, 120, 125; Via Laurentina, 120–21; Via dei Molini, 121
  Temples: Republican, 121, 125, 127; Capitolium, 125, fig. 70; of Hercules, 121; of Rome and Augustus, 123; Round Temple, 132; mithraea, 132; synagogue, 132

Paestum, 17
Palestrina, *see* Praeneste
Palmyra, 187, 245, 248–49, fig. 164
  Temple of Bel, 231, 248–49, fig. 165
  Tetrakionia, 248
Pergamon, 21, 241
  Great Altar, 241
  Sanctuary of Athena, 51, 241
  Temple of Dionysus, 70, 241
  Traianeum, 183, 241
Perugia, Arch of Augustus, 18, fig. 7
  Tomb of the Volumnii, 12–14, 32–33, fig. 2
Petra, 245, 253–54
  Deir, 231, 232–33, 254, fig. 168
  Khasne, 192, 254
  Qasr al bint, 254
Pevensey, 227
Piazza Armerina, villa, 265, 270, fig. 179
Pompeii, 103–118
  Amphitheatre, 23, 114, 115, 118, 143, fig. 66
  Basilica, 23, 31–32, 76, 109–12, figs. 62, 63
  Baths: Central, 117; Forum, 23, 39, 114, 116, 213, fig. 65; Stabian, 23, 38–39, 112–13, 114, 145, 213, fig. 19
  Forum, 31, 108–109, 116, fig. 61; Triangular Forum, 104, 112
  Houses, 33, 105–108, 128; of the Faun, 24, 107–108, fig. 59; of Loreius Tiburtinus, 117; of Lucretius Fronto, 100; of the Surgeon, 12, 105–106, fig. 2; of the Vettii, 116–17

Shops, 35, 114; macellum, 36, 108–109, 135
Temples: Doric, 104–105; of Apollo, 108; of Fortuna Augusta, 116; of Isis, 116, 118; of Jupiter, 108; of Vespasian, 116, 117
Villa of the Mysteries, 24, 34, 108, 117, 118, fig. 60
Porchester, 227
Portus, 132–33
  Constantinian wall, 125
  Harbour, 92–93, 123–25, 154
  Imperial Palace, 124–25
  Temples: of Bacchus, 125; of Portunus, 83, 125
Pozzuoli, *see* Puteoli
Praeneste (Palestrina):
  Sanctuary of Fortuna Primigenia, 25–26, figs. 12–13
  Vaulting, 62
Priene, 241
  Ecclesiasterion, 236
  Grid plan, 241
Ptolemais, 191–94
  Palazzo delle Colonne, 187, 191–92, figs. 117–18
  Square of the Cisterns, 90
Puteoli (Pozzuoli), 123, 256
  Harbour, 123
  Macellum, 36, 109, 134, 135, 195
Pyrgi, 16

Ravenna, 260
  S. Vitale, 274
Regensburg, fort, 228
Richborough, 227
Rimini, Arch of Augustus, 43
Rome:
  Aequimalium, 75
  Amphitheatre of Augustus, 37; of Caligula, 37; Castrense, 260
  Aqueduct, 42–43; Anio Novus, 93; Aqua Claudia, 93; Julia, 54; Virgo, 54
  Ara Pacis, 49, 64, 215, 235
  Arch, of the Argentarii, 45; of Augustus, 43, 59, 64, 216, fig. 30; of Constantine, 44, 271, fig. 21; of Domitian, 149; of Drusus, 43; of Fabianus, 43; of Gaius and Lucius, 60; of Janus, 44, 45, 82; of Septimius Severus, 44, 256–57, 271, fig. 169; of Titus, 44, 145–46, 149, 164, 218, fig. 85
  Aventine Hill, 10, 84, 256
  Basilica, Aemilia, 22, 56, 58, 60, 64, fig. 29; Argentaria, 51; Julia, 54, 55–56, 58, 261; of Maxentius, 29, 32, 258, 271–72, figs. 180, 181; of Neptune, 54; Porcia, 22; Sempronia, 23, 55; Ulpia, 32, 158, 159, 177, 199, 271; underground, by Porta Maggiore, 31
  Baths, of Agrippa, 54; of Caracalla, 39–40, 79, 80, 145, 157, 202, 243, 257–59, 262, 274, figs. 170, 171; of Diocletian, 40, 82, 157, 261–63, 271, fig. 172; of Titus, 39, 145, 154, 157, fig. 90; of Trajan, 39, 71, 98, 102, 154, 155–57, 158, 197, 202, 257, 263
  Bridge, Pons Sublicius, 10; Pons Aelius, 84, 184, fig. 112
  Caelian Hill, 10, 98, 135, 164

Rome – *continued*

Campus Martius, Agrippa's programme for, 54; amphitheatre in, 37; masons' and stonecutters' workshops in, 84; Mausoleum of Augustus, 62; Stadium of Domitian, 147; theatre of Marcellus, 53; Temple of Jupiter Stator, 30; Temple of Isis, 260

Capitoline Hill, 10, 51, 60, 71, 75, 92, 135, 147, 256; drains, 18

Circus, of Caligula, 92; Flaminius, 53; Maximus, 37, 53, 153, 211; of Maxentius, 38, 271

Colosseum, 23, 27, 37–38, 71, 78, 83, 134, 135–45, 148, 183, 216, figs. 77–84

Column, of Antoninus Pius, 255; Maenian, 15; of M. Aurelius, 43, 154, 255; of Trajan, 43, 71, 154, 158–59, 255

Comitium, of Caesar, 51, 58; Republican, 15, 51, 58, fig. 3

Curia, Hostilia, 14, 15, 56, fig. 3; Julia, 51, 53, 56–58, 261

Esquiline Hill, 10, 71, 96, 98, 135, 157; Servian wall and agger, 15–16

Fortifications, agger, 15–16; Castra Praetoria, 77, 87, 261

Forum, Boarium, 20, 21, 30, 37, 54, 127; Romanum, 10, 14, 31, 37, 51, 54, 56, 58–59, 60, 75, 92, 98, 135, 149, 164, 261, 271, figs. 26–28; Imperial, 30, 36, 51, 164, fig. 23; of Augustus, 49, 54, 60–61, 64, 65, 83, 85, 147, 154, 157, 158, 235, figs. 31, 32; of Julius Caesar, 51, 54, 58, 60, 83, 135, 157, fig. 24; of Nerva, 147, 154, fig. 89; of Trajan, 36, 61, 71, 147–48, 154, 157–60, 161, 162, 166, 175, 177, 199, 219, 255, figs. 23, 91; of Vespasian, *see* Temple of Peace

Gates, Porta Maggiore, 43, 86, 93, fig. 49; Porta Tiburtina, 43; Porta Trigemina, 120

Graecostasis, 15

Horrea Galbana, 75–76

House, of Augustus, 148; of the Griffins, 75, 149; of the Vestals, 14; Gardens of Sallust, 148; Villa of the Gordians, 82; of Maecenas, 96; of Maxentius, 271

Lacus Iuturnae, 75

Macellum Magnum of Nero, 36, 135, 164

Markets of Trajan, 36, 157–58, 160–64, 166, 254, figs. 92–94

Naumachia, of Augustus, 141

Oppian Hill, 10, 96

Palace, of Domitian (Domus Flavia), 71, 72–73, 96, 145, 148–53, 178, figs. 86–88; of Tiberius (Domus Tiberiana), 77, 86, 87, 96, 148; Domus Transitoria, 96–97, figs. 51–52; Domus Aurea (Nero's Golden House), 39, 71, 79, 80, 86–87, 95, 97–102, 135, 145, 148, 151, 153, 157, 162, 164, 178, figs. 53–55; Severan, 256

Palatine Hill, 10, 61, 71, 73, 92, 96, 98, 135, 148, 260; Germalus, 148; House of the Griffins, 75; hut of Romulus, 148; iron-age huts, 10; Severan structures, 82, 256; Temple of Apollo, 49

Pomerium, 10, 159

Porticus, Aemilia, 19, 27, 74–75, fig. 8; Metelli, 75

Quirinal Hill, 10, 51, 71, 135, 147, 259

Regia, 14

Rostra, of Caesar, 51, 58–59; Republican, 15; on Temple of Julius Caesar, 58–59

Saepta Julia, 37, 54

Septizodium, 256

Sewers, 54, 83; Cloaca Maxima, 18

Shops, 14, 35–36, 51, 163–64

Streets, Via Biberatica, 162–63; Labicana, 93; Praenestina, 93; Sacra, 98, 145, 256, 273; Triumphalis, 256

Subura, 60

Tabularium, 27, 79, 147, fig. 15

Temple, of Antoninus and Faustina, 85, 255; of Augustus, 92, wrongly identified, 149; of Apollo Palatinus, 49, 84; of Apollo Sosianus (in Circo), 54, 64, 84; of Castor, 30, 60, 64, 67, 84, 92, fig. 36; of Claudius, 94, 98, 134, fig. 50; of Concord, 14, 60, 64, 67, 86, 147; of Hadrian, 30, 184, fig. 111; of Hercules Victor, 20, 30, 84, fig. 9; of Isis, 260; of Juno Regina, 75; of Julius Caesar, 53, 58, 60, 84, 123, 195; of Jupiter Capitolinus, 12, 84, 134, 237; of Jupiter Stator, 20, 30, 75, 84; of Magna Mater, 18, 75; of Mars Ultor, 54, 60–61, 67, 147, 167, 199, 215, figs. 31–32; of Minerva, 147; called 'of Minerva Medica', 82–83, 273–74, figs. 44, 182; Pantheon, of Agrippa, 54, 166–67; of Hadrian, 29, 31, 71, 81, 132, 159, 166–172, 258, 271, 274, figs. 96–99; of Peace (Templum Pacis, also called 'Forum of Vespasian'), 100, 134–35, 147, 164, 182; of Portunus, 21–22, 30, 223; of Romulus, or of the Penates, 272–73; of Saturn, 14, 30, 75, fig. 26; of Serapis, 259, 260; of Sol Invictus, 260; of Trajan, 159; of Venus Genetrix, 51, 60, 157, fig. 24; of Venus and Rome, 30, 96, 182–84, 241, 259, 260, 271, figs. 109–10; of Vespasian, 147; of Vesta, 14, 30

Theatre, of Marcellus, 27, 37, 53, 54, 62, 77; of Pompey, 23, 53, 76, 92

Tomb, of Annia Regilla, 48; of Caecilia Metella, 47; of Trebius Justus, 72; of the Pancratii, 48; Mausoleum of Augustus, 47, 62; of Hadrian, 47, 184, fig. 112; of Romulus, son of Maxentius, 271; of St Constantia, 83, 273–74, fig. 183; of the Valerii, 48; pyramid of Cestius, 261

Velian Hill, 10, 135, 271, 272

Viminal Hill, 10

Walls, Aurelianic, 47, 87, 260, 261, 269; of Servius Tullius, 10; 'Servian', 15–16, fig. 4

Russellae (Rosella), 32

Sabratha, 187, 194, 200, 202
Forum, 200
Shop in Ostia, 131
Theatre, 37, 200, 218, fig. 125
St Albans, *see* Verulamium
Salona (Martia Julia Salona), 229–30
Samos, Heraeum, 182
San Giovenale, tombs, 32
San Rocco, Villa, 34
Segovia, aqueduct, 42, 211–13, fig. 137

Side, 64
Signia (Segni), walls, 45
Sirmium, 230
Spello, gate, 268
Sperlonga, Villa of Tiberius, 87–88, fig. 45
Split, Diocletian's palace, 230, 261, 263–65, fig. 173
Stabiae, 103
Strasbourg, fort, 228
Syracuse:
    fall of, 19
    Temple of Apollo, 105

Tarragona, aqueduct, 213
Terracina:
    Republican insula, 36
    Temple of Jupiter Anxur, 27
Thamugadi (Timgad), 205–206, figs. 130–31
    Arch of Trajan, 206
    Capitolium, 206
    Forum, 31, 205
    North Baths, 40
Thessalonike, 269–70
    Arch of Galerius, 269, fig. 178
    Circus, 269
    Mausoleum, 269–70, fig. 178
    Palace, 269
Thuburbo Maius, Temple of Cereres, 208
Thugga (Dougga), 203–204
    Capitolium, 204, 208, fig. 128
    Licinian Baths, 204
Thysdrus (El-Djem), amphitheatre, 203, fig. 127
Tiber:
    Bridges over, 10
    Island in, 10
Tivoli:
    Sanctuary of Hercules, 27, fig. 14
    Temple of Vesta, 22, 62, fig. 10
    Travertine quarries, 83, 139
    Villas, 34, 172
Tivoli, Hadrian's villa, 172–82, fig. 100
    Academy, 181
    Canopus, 173, 175, 180–81, 194, fig. 107
    Hippodrome and triclinium, 177–79

Island villa, 176, fig. 101–102
Large Baths, 179–80, fig. 105
Piazza d'Oro, 176–77, fig. 103
Poikile, 173, 175–76
Republican Villa, 174; Serapeum, 79, 180–81, fig. 106
Small Baths, 40, 179, fig. 104
Temple of Venus, 182, fig. 108
Vale of Tempe, 173
Trier, *see* Augusta Treverorum
Tripoli, *see* Oea
Turin, Porta Palatina, 268

Vasio (Vaison-la-Romaine), 213, 218, fig. 143
Veii, 15
    Grotta Oscura quarries, 84
    Portonaccio Temple, 12
Velia, gateway, 18
Verulamium (St Albans), 219, 220–21, fig 145
Vetera, 228–29, fig. 150
Vetulonia, 32
Vienna (Vienne), 213, 219
Vindonissa, fort, 228
Via:
    Aemilia, 164
    Amerina, 18
    Appia, 164, 256, 271
    Cassia, 164
    Clodia, 164
    Egnatia, 269
    Latina, 164
    Puteolana, 164
    Salaria, 164
    Sublacensis, 164
    Traiana, 164
    see also Rome, streets
Volterra, gateway, 18
Volubilis, 209
Vulci, 18

Xanten, *see* Vetera

York, *see* Eburacum

Architectural terms

These references indicate the main general discussion on a particular building type or architectural feature.

Amphitheatre, 23, 37–38
Aqueduct, 42–43
Arch:
    Triumphal, 43–45
    Voussoir, 17–18, 78–79

Basilica, 22–23, 31–32
    Christian, 31
Baths, 23, 39–41
    Heating systems, 41
Bricks:
    Baked, 76–78
    Bessales, 77, 80
    Bipedales, 72, 77, 81
    Brickstamps, 77–78
    Pentedoron, 76
    Sesquipedales, 77
    Tetradoron, 76
    Tile, 76–77
    Unbaked, 76

Bridge, 42

Castellum aquae, 43
Circus, 38
Column, honorific, 43, 158–59, 255
Composite Order, 62, 146
Concrete, 18–19, 72–76, 79–83, 86–87, 101–102
    Lime mortar, 73
    Pozzolana, 73–74
Concrete facings: opus incertum, 18–19, 74–75; opus reticulatum, 75–76; opus quasi-reticulatum, 75–76; opus testaceum, 74, 76–78
Corinthian Order, 20, 22, 62–68

Forum, 14–15, 31, 36
Fortifications, 15–16, 45–47

Gymnasium, 38

House:
  Etruscan, 12–14
  Roman: domus, 12–14, 23–24, 32–35;
    insula, 35, 127–30

Macellum, 31, 36

Palaestra, 38–39

Sewer, 54, 83
Shop, 35–36
Stoa, 22–23

Temple:
  Etruscan, 12, 17, 19, 20, 30
  Roman, 20–22, 30–31; Mithraeum, 31
Theatre, 36–37

Tomb:
  Etruscan, 12–13, 47
  Roman, 47–48

Vaulting:
  Barrel, 18–19, 79, 80–83
  Cloister (pavilion), 79
  Cross, 79
  Dome, 79
  Domical vault, 79
  Umbrella dome, 79
  Velarium, 37–38, 143–44
  Villa, 24, 34–35

Walling:
  Opus quadratum, 83
  Polygonal, 16

Authors and Passages Cited

Augustus
  Res Gestae: 19–21, 53–54; 20, 56
Aurelius Victor
  de Caesaribus 13.5, 157

Cicero
  Ad Att. IV.16, 51
  de lege agraria II.96, 102
  de Rep. II, 10

Dio Cassius
  Bk 59.28.2, 92
  Bk 60.11.3, 123
  Epit. 66.25.3, 141
  Epit. 69.4.1–5, 176, 182
Dionysius of Halicarnassus
  Ant. Rom. I, 79, 11, 10

Frontinus
  De Aquis: 1.7, 2.72, 75, 43; 2.96, 99, 100,
    117, 71; 2.123, 140

Historia Augusta
  Hadrian 19.10, 167
Horace
  Odes 3.1.33–37, 34

Macrobius
  Saturnalia 2.4.9, 60
Martial
  Epigrams: 8.44, 61; 7.56, 148; 8.36, 10.20
    in Oxford Classical Text, 151

Pausanias
  1.18, 238
Philostratus
  Vit. Soph. 551, 239

Pliny
  Nat. Hist.: 7.212, 15; 9.168, 39; 16.202,
    123; 36.101–102, 53, 56; 37.20, 95
Pliny the Younger
  Ep.: 6.16, 103; 6.33, 56; 10.40, 69

Seneca
  Epist. 44.5, 33
  Ep. 86, 34, 39
Statius
  Silvae 4.2, 151
Strabo
  5.3.8, 22; 16.4.21, 253
Suetonius (The Twelve Caesars)
  Aug. 29, 37
  Julius, 51
  Aug. 28–30, 54
  Aug. 56, 60
  Tib. 1.2, 87
  Tib. 74, 91
  Cal. 38, 92
  Nero 31, 97
  Nero 39.2, 98
  Titus 7, 3, 141
  Domitian 14.4, 149

Tacitus
  Ann.: 12.24, 10; 15.18.3, 123; 15.40, 97;
    15.42, 99; 15.43, 83

Valerius Maximus
  2.4.7, 37
Varro
  De Ling. Lat.: 5, 143, 10; 5, 162, 24
Vitruvius
  De Arch.: 1.1.4, 69; 1.5.8, 76; 2.5.1, 73;
    2.6.1, 74; 2.8.17, 19, 77; 3.5.12, 168;
    4.1.2, 62; 4.3.4, 21; 4.7.2, 12; 5.1.1, 23;
    5.3.1, 57; 5.10.2, 41; 5.10.5, 39; 5.11.1,
    39; 6.3.9, 23; 6.5.3, 108